MEDIUM ÆVUM MONOGRAPHS
NEW SERIES

MEDIUM ÆVUM MONOGRAPHS
NEW SERIES XVII

DE QUATUORDECIM PARTIBUS BEATITUDINIS
(The Fourteen Parts of Blessedness)

Chapter 5 of *Dicta Anselmi* by Alexander of Canterbury, with Anselmian interpolations:

The Latin, Middle English ("The Joys of Paradise") and Anglo-Norman Versions

in

Lichfield Cathedral Library MS. 16, ff. 190r–247v

AVRIL HENRY and D. A. TROTTER

The Society for the Study of
Mediæval Languages and Literature
Oxford
1994

THE SOCIETY FOR THE STUDY OF
MEDIEVAL LANGUAGES AND LITERATURE
http://mediumaevum.modhist.ox.ac.uk

ISBN-13: 978-0-907570-10-3 (pb)

British Library Cataloguing in Publication Data

A catalogue record for this book
is available from the British Library

First published 1994
Reprinted 2016

CONTENTS

ACKNOWLEDGEMENTS

We are grateful first of all to those who made it possible for us to consult the manuscript. The Dean and Chapter of Lichfield Cathedral kindly gave permission for us to edit and reproduce the relevant portions of the manuscript in their custody. The late Prebendary Dr Hill, Honorary Librarian of Lichfield Cathedral Library, and his successor Mrs Pat Bancroft, welcomed us there, and Dr Benedikt S. Benedikz, Sub-Librarian (Special Collections), University of Birmingham Library, allowed the manuscript to be deposited at the University for microfilming and for photography of the three opening pages of our texts by their photographic unit.

Many scholars gave generously of their time and expertise. We are indebted to Dr Kathleen Scott, who shared with us her unequalled knowledge of fifteenth-century English manuscripts' decorated borders; to Dr Jeremy J. Smith, who localized the dialect of the Middle English; to Dr Ian Doyle and Dr Malcolm Parkes for palaeographical advice; and to Miss Elizabeth Westlake, who shared with us her knowledge of *Scire mori*, in advance of submission of her edition of it as a thesis at Birmingham. Through the electronic-mail discussion list MedTextL we received information from Professor George H. Brown, Professor James Marchand, Professor Charles Wright and Professor Paul Schaffner. In Exeter, Dr Sue Braund helped us with more than one Latin crux.

We are grateful for the labours of the editors of *Medium Ævum* Monographs: Dr Helen Cooper, Dr Elspeth Kennedy, Dr Nigel Palmer and Dr David Pattison, as well as to the 'anonymous' reader Dr Tony Hunt for his early encouragement and subsequent advice.

The University of Exeter Research Fund supported the publication with a grant of £500.

LIST OF ABBREVIATIONS

ALDQ	Archetype of all three versions of *De quatuordecim partibus beatitudinis* in Lichfield MS 16 (LL, ME, AN).
AN	The Anglo-Norman version of *De quatuordecim partibus beatitudinis* in Lichfield MS 16.
AND	*Anglo-Norman Dictionary*, ed. W. Rothwell *et al.*, 7 fascs. (London: MHRA, 1977–1992).
ANTS	Anglo-Norman Text Society.
DA	*Dicta Anselmi*, R. W. Southern & F. S. Schmitt, *Memorials of St. Anselm*, Auctores Britannici Medii Aevi, 1 (London: Oxford UP, 1969) 105–95.
DMLBS	R. E. Latham *et al.*, *Dictionary of Medieval Latin from British Sources* (London: Oxford UP for the British Academy, 1975–).
FEW	W. von Wartburg, *Französisches Etymologisches Wörterbuch*, 25 vols (Bonn: Schroeder [fasc. 1]; Basel: Helbing-Lichtenhahn; Basel: Zbinden), 1922–).
Gdf	F. Godefroy, *Dictionnaire de l'ancienne langue française* (Paris: Vieweg, 1880–1902).
GRLMA	*Grundriss der romanischen Literaturen des Mittelalters*, ed. E. Köhler and J. Frappier (Heidelberg: C. Winter, 1968–).
JWCI	*Journal of the Warburg and Courtauld Institutes.*
LL	The Latin version of *De quatuordecim partibus beatitudinis* in Lichfield MS 16.
Manual(1)	*A Manual of the Writings in Middle English 1050-1400.* Gen. ed. John Edwin Wells (with 9 supplements). (New Haven, Conn.: Yale University Press, 1916–1951).
Manual(2)	*A Manual of the Writings in Middle English 1050–1500.* Gen. ed. A. E. Hartung. Vol. 7. (New Haven, Conn.: Connecticut Academy of Arts and Sciences, 1986). 8 vols to date.
ME	The Middle English version of *De quatuordecim partibus beatitudinis* in Lichfield MS 16.
MED	*Middle English Dictionary*, ed. Hans Kurath, Sherman M. Kuhn and John Reidy (Ann Arbor: Michigan UP, 1952–). Fascs A–S to date.
MLR	*Modern Language Review.*

MS	*Mediaeval Studies.*
OED	(*Oxford English Dictionary*). *A New English Dictionary on Historical Principles*, 24 vols, ed. James A. H. Murray (Oxford: Clarendon Press, 1888–1933).
RES	*Review of English Studies.*
RMLWL	R. E. Latham, *Revised Medieval Latin Word-List from British and Irish Sources* (London: Oxford UP for the British Academy, 1965).
SN	*Studia Neophilologica.*
s.v.	*sub voce.*
TL	A. Tobler and E. Lommatzsch, *Altfranzösisches Wörterbuch*, 10 vols. (Berlin: Weidmann, 1925–1936; Wiesbaden: Steiner, 1954–).

LIST OF ILLUSTRATIONS

INTRODUCTION

1. LICHFIELD MS 16

The late fourteenth- or early fifteenth-century Lichfield Cathedral Library MS 16 consists, in effect, of only three texts: (i) *Scire mori*,[1] Book 2 chapter 2 of *Horologium divine sapientiae* by Heinrich Suso, the mid-fourteenth-century German Dominican, in Latin and then the Middle English Version A, ff.1^{r}–34;[2] (ii) *The Prick of Conscience* (Version B, Southern Recension), ff.35^{r}–189^{v};[3] (iii) *De quatuordecim partibus beatitudinis* in Latin, then in Middle English, then in Anglo-Norman, ff.190^{r}–247^{v}. The nature of the three texts is outlined in section 5 below.

The last part of the manuscript, three versions of *De quatuordecim partibus beatitudinis* (ff.190^{r}–247^{v}), is here edited for the first time. The Latin text known under this title is chapter 5 of the early twelfth-century *Dicta Anselmi* (hereafter *DA*).[4] *De quatuordecim partibus beatitudinis* as it appears in our manuscript is hereafter referred to as LL, for 'Lichfield Latin', to distinguish it from other versions, while ALDQ (archetype of Lichfield *De quatuordecim partibus beatitudinis*) will be reserved for the lost Latin manuscript version from which all three of our texts ultimately derive (see section 7). This lost archetype contained not only the most substantial interpolation, found in all three texts, which comes from chapters 24–26 of Anselm's *Proslogion*,[5] but also the small interpolations: (1) at f.193^{r}, beginning (§16) '<Gaudium perfectum solus ille potest habere ...>'; (2) the rubrics, *passim*; (3) the expansions within the Recapitulation (§22). The late fourteenth- or early fifteenth-century translation of *De quatuordecim partibus beatitudinis* into Middle English (hereafter ME) is usually known as *The Joys of Paradise*; the similarly dated Anglo-Norman (hereafter AN) has no popular name. Descriptions of LL, ME and AN are in sections 7.B, 7.C, 7.D below.

The manuscript's six booklets seem to have been originally in an order exactly the reverse of the present one, with AN beginning the book.[6] This Introduction treats the texts in the order in which they currently appear in the manuscript, so making coherent use of the current foliation, and allowing the text which was *composed* first, LL, to be discussed before its later vernacular derivatives. However, our three edited texts themselves, and their illuminated first pages, are presented in the reading-order intended by their compiler: AN, ME, LL.

2. The Ancestor of LL, ME, AN (ALDQ): Inconsistencies in the Fourteen Joys

De quatuordecim partibus beatitudinis resembles works of Anselm which also treat the Joys of the Spirit and Body, though in different contexts, and in different orders: chapter 25 of the much earlier *Proslogion* (from which comes the main interpolation in our text); *De humanis moribus per similitudines* (*De moribus*), perhaps written 'by the hand of an amanuensis';[7] and Eadmer of Canterbury's *De beatitudine perennis vitae sumptum de verbis Beati Anselmi* (*De beatitudine*).[8] This repetition is evidence of the theme's interest to Anselm. It also needs mentioning because differences in the Joys' order in *De quatuordecim partibus beatitudinis* and *Proslogion* produce inconsistencies within all three of our texts, via their common ancestor, ALDQ. To clarify the origin of these inconsistencies, it is necessary to summarize briefly the other texts in which the Joys are described.

Proslogion chapters 24–26

This part of the *Proslogion* (incorporated verbatim in LL §§18–21) consists of an exhortation to the faithful to contemplate God's goodness. It thus forms a perfectly logical part of LL, a treatise which describes the corporal and spiritual joys available to the blessed; and this part of the *Proslogion* uses the same list of joys as occurs in LL. The spirit of the argument follows that of the Ontological Argument for the existence of God: the goodness of the good things created by God is a compelling reason to suppose that their creator must himself be the repository of even greater goodness (chapter 24). Chapter 25, one of the longest in the *Proslogion* (= LL §19), runs through the joys available to the good, both body and soul, thus leading onward, inward and upward to eventual consideration of the ultimate Good, God. It is followed by chapter 26 (= LL §§20–21), explaining that this is indeed the complete joy promised by God to the faithful (= LL §20), and by a short prayer (= LL §21) that such joy might be granted.

De moribus

The first half of Anselm's *De humanis moribus per similitudines* consists of two analytical parts. The first part is devoted to the three forms of self-will. The second part (chapters 48–71) treats the fourteen rewards and punishments of the obedient and disobedient will, and has been called 'the first attempt at a systematic study of the psychology of the religious life'. The second half of *De moribus* presents allegories illustrating the first half.[9]

De beatitudine

The preface to *De beatitudine* explains that Eadmer, Anselm's contemporary biographer, sent this version of a speech by Anselm at Cluny to his friend William, as requested.[10] After an introduction, the work describes seven Joys of the Body (*pulchritudo*, *velocitas*, *fortitudo*, *libertas*, *impassibilitas*, *voluptas*, *diuturnitas*), the Joys of the Soul and then the miseries of the damned. The sermon closes with an exhortation to use this information in the pursuit of virtue, followed by a reference to Anselm's having checked the transcription.

De quatuordecim partibus beatitudinis: ALDQ

The first inconsistency in our texts is that, as the Table below shows, the order of Joys of the Body in LL §§3–9 inclusive is not echoed in the list of Joys of the Body in §19, '*Que et quanta sint bona fruentibus deo*' (f.223v). This is because the order of the Joys of the Body in the early *Proslogion* (from which §19 is interpolated) was improved in the three later works mentioned above, *De quatuordecim partibus beatitudinis* included; 'the differences between the *Proslogion* and the other sources are ... evident and the superiority of the later arrangement could easily be demonstrated'.[11] In the Table below, the column on the left is, of course, the 'later arrangement'.[12]

The alterations from the *Proslogion* are as follows. First, Joys which in the *Proslogion* are grouped together (*velocitas aut fortitudo aut libertas corporis*), and so are placed under one number by Southern and Schmitt – though not actually given numbers in either Latin text – are treated individually in LL §§3–9. Second, *Proslogion*'s *longa et salubris vita* becomes in the later version *diuturnitas*, which is placed last. Third, *sacietas* and *ebrietas* are subsumed into *sanitas*. Fourth, *melodia* is cut out.[13]

The second inconsistency is found in LL's treatment of the Joys of the Soul, which are also present in all four sources mentioned above.

TABLE

LL §§3–99	LL §19 AND *PROSLOGION*
1 *Pulchritudo*	1 *pulchritudo*
2 *velocitas*	*velocitas aut*]
3 *fortitudo*	2 *fortitudo aut*]
4 *libertas*	*libertas corporis*]
5 *sanitas*	3 *longa et salubris vita*[14]
6 *voluptas*	4 *sacietas*
7 *diuturnitas*	5 *ebrietas*[15]
	6 *melodia*
	7 *voluptas*

Proslogion and *De beatitudine* give *sapientia*, *amicitia*, *concordia*, *potestas*, *honor*, *securitas*, *gaudium*. In *De moribus* and DA_1, and hence in LL, *potestas* and *honor* are reversed in the paragraphs treating each joy. Southern and Schmitt point out that 'Alexander corrected *DA* on the basis of *De beatitudine* and adopted the other order'.[16] It is thus only the second recension of *DA* that follows the *Proslogion* order at this point.

3. *DICTA ANSELMI*: SOME OTHER MANUSCRIPTS

The nature of our edition of LL inevitably differs from that of the two other texts offered here: it is by way of an 'interim' edition. The reasons for this will become clear when an account is given of other manuscripts known to contain chapter 5 of *DA* as a separate item (i.e. not in the context of the whole of *DA*). Southern and Schmitt identify (pp.15, 27–28) a number of such manuscripts:

British Library, Harley 232 ff.14^{v}–16
British Library, Royal 5 A xii ff.140ra–147ra
British Library, Royal 5 F ix ff.45^{v}–52^{v}
British Library, Royal 6 D viii ff.112^{v}–115
British Library, Royal 8 D viii ff.79–81^{v}
Cambridge University Library, Ff.4.45 ff.22^{r}–25^{r}

Recensions vary: Harley 232, Royal 5 F ix and Royal 8 D viii are first-recension texts, Royal 6 D viii is second-recension. The incipits to all four manuscripts are the same, *Queritur inter homines* .... All four manuscripts have rubricated short paragraph titles (Royal 5 F ix, Royal 8 D viii), unrubricated titles (Harley 232), or spaces for titles which were evidently never added (Royal 6 D viii). These titles take such forms as *De pulchritudine*, *De velocitate*, etc. In the Cambridge manuscript, the text of *DA* chapter 5 is incorporated in an acephalous text identified in the catalogue as Eadmer, *De similibus*, which begins *in medias res* on f.22^{r}, after a half-blank verso.[17] The fifth London manuscript, Royal 5 A xii f.140ra–147ra, is the most interesting. A fifteenth-century copy, formerly in the possession of the vicar of Blokely (Worcestershire), it begins (as does LL) *Nunc investigare iuvat* ...; it belongs to the first recension. There are rubricated chapter headings which are virtually identical with those in LL. Above all, the major Anselmian interpolations found in LL are also found in this copy (starting at f.144vb). This raises a number of important questions. First, and most obviously, are Royal 5 A xii and Lichfield MS 16 related? This seemingly straightforward question is not, alas, so easily resolved, for it is apparent that there are, in fact, many more extant copies of *De quatuordecim partibus beatitudinis* than are indicated in Southern and Schmitt (who in fact suggest as much on p.28). Preliminary investigation has revealed the existence of the following manuscripts where the text begins with the more common (apparently second-recension) incipit *Queritur inter homines* ...:

Oxford, Bodleian Library, Laud. Misc. 6
Oxford, Magdalen College, 56
Cambridge, Peterhouse, 246[18]

also

Paris, Bibliothèque Nationale, fonds latin 1925
Rouen,[19] Bibliothèque municipale [?], 26.136

and

Vatican, Codices Reginenses Latini 262
Vatican, Codices Reginenses Latini 285
Vatican, Codices Reginenses Latini 292[20]

There is, in addition, an early printed version, in Henricus Sommalius (ed.), *Paradisus animae, sive De virtutibus libellus ... In fine vero adjectus est D. Anselmi ... tractatus perelegans de XIIII animae ac corporis dotibus sive beatitudinibus* (Antwerp, 1602); there is a copy in Paris, Bibliothèque Nationale, shelfmark D.16044, but none in the British Library. We are under no illusions that this list is anywhere near complete. Moreover, it seems (to judge by the incipits) that all these manuscripts are likely to contain second-recension texts. Only by a systematic and time-consuming investigation of all these versions, and any others not so far unearthed, could all the problems of LL's status be resolved, and a fully critical edition be offered.

The second question, which could again only be answered by lengthy enquiry, is of course whether the LL and Royal 5 A xii version of *De quatuordecim partibus beatitudinis* exists in other manuscripts. Is it, in fact, a separate reworking of the first recension of this part of *DA*? Finally, are there second-recension texts with the interpolations? These questions must be left to inheritors of the mantle of Southern and Schmitt.

4. The Purpose of this Edition

The texts edited from Lichfield MS 16 are important for a number of reasons. Although our edition of LL must be an interim one, when presented against ME and AN it is evidence of the three texts' derivation from a common source. LL is a copy of a hitherto unnoticed recension of *De quatuordecim partibus beatitudinis*, with substantial interpolations, chiefly from Anselm's *Proslogion*, not found in the copies used by Southern and Schmitt in their edition. ME and AN are also unique, offering additional evidence of late medieval practice in Anglo-Norman and Middle English literal translation from Latin. Vernacular translation, that central medieval literary activity, is the subject of several recent studies,[21] but there is still room for research into the incidence and purpose of so-called 'inexpert' translation, which is, after all, the norm. The contrast between the literalism of the AN and the expansion in ME, albeit slight, may be of interest in this context.

As the only known individual English translation of this part of *DA*, ME joins the surviving body of Middle English Anselmian material (see section 6.c).[22] There is no other known Anselmian material at all in Anglo-Norman; in continental French there is only a fifteenth-century translation of the *Cur Deus homo*, by Pierre Crapillet.[23] ME and AN also join a group of works which exist in both Middle English and Anglo-Norman, for example writings of Richard Rolle,

Ancren Riwle and its Anglo-Norman versions, and the Anglo-Norman translations of Edmund of Abingdon's *Speculum ecclesie.*[24]

Furthermore, this edition is a step towards the fuller understanding of Lichfield MS 16. Our three texts constitute one element in what seems to have been a planned medieval miscellany of contemplative and devotional material existing in Latin and a vernacular either within the manuscript or outside it. (That the two vernacular texts were apparently designed to be bound alongside the Latin is an occurrence sufficiently rare to be noteworthy in the history of late medieval translation.) The existence, in the late fourteenth or early fifteenth century, of texts of this type comes as no surprise: the later Middle Ages were the high point of production of vernacular treatises (often translations from Latin) destined for either a lay public or, frequently, for religious communities (men as well as women) whose level of Latin prevented their reading such texts in the original.[25]

In spite of the fact that any purpose-made miscellany is important to the study of late medieval English religion and literature, Lichfield MS 16's texts have until now received scant scholarly attention. Their neglect is all the more surprising when one recalls that the survival of one of them – *The Prick of Conscience* – in four versions and some 130 copies suggests that it was the most popular Middle English poem.[26] (The length of *The Prick of Conscience* may explain why Lichfield MS 16 does not include a Latin version of it, which would have made the manuscript a set of three Latin texts with vernacular translations.) Attention is now beginning to focus on Lichfield MS 16's texts.[27] The complex manuscript tradition of *The Prick of Conscience* is under study,[28] and one may hope at last for critical editions of the various versions, so that we do not have to rely solely on Morris's elderly book.[29]

Finally, both ME and AN are worthy of linguistic attention; as our notes to the text endeavour to show, AN is particularly rich in lexical and syntactic coinages not otherwise attested in Anglo-Norman, and ME shows a number of latinizing neologisms.

5. The Nature of the Lichfield MS 16 Texts

Our three texts need to be seen in the context of the other works in the manuscript. Lichfield MS 16 begins with a copy of *Scire mori*, from book 2 of Heinrich Suso's *Horologium sapientiae*, followed by 'the Lichfield translation of *Scire mori*' in Middle English.[30] There follows the long *Prick of Conscience* (the Middle English only, not including the

Latin version). Our three versions of *De quatuordecim partibus beatitudinis* end the manuscript as at present bound.

There are copies of *The Prick of Conscience* that include 'an *ad hoc* manual to enhance the usefulness of the volume',[31] and it is tempting at first to regard the manuscript as *The Prick of Conscience* (occupying some 154 folios) with supplementary texts. However, though it is the longest text in the manuscript, the presentation of the poem does not give it special emphasis,[32] and the other texts, particularly *De quatuordecim partibus beatitudinis*, are more spiritually and theologically sophisticated than is common in supplementary material. Perhaps the manuscript is part of the increased demand for *ars moriendi* material that accompanied the spiritual emancipation of the laity.

Little has been said about the manuscript as a whole beyond the observation that a high proportion of its content is concerned with preparation for death and the life hereafter. All three texts in some sense treat ways of recovering the image of God in man's soul. They present the goal of human life (AN, ME, LL, all derived from *De quatuordecim partibus beatitudinis* via ALDQ); advice on the living of life to obtain that goal, with an account of the latter and its alternative (*The Prick of Conscience*); and advice on how to die (the two versions of *Scire mori*). Indeed, as already pointed out, this was apparently the original order of material (see section 7.A.b).

It is perhaps just worth noting that works by all three of the authors represented in Lichfield MS 16 – Suso, Anselm and the anonymous author of the *Prick of Conscience* (though not, as far as we are aware, the actual works by Anselm and Suso which are found in Lichfield MS 16) – were once attributed to the English mystic Richard Rolle. Part of the First Meditation of St Anselm is falsely attributed to Rolle in one manuscript,[33] while the 'Prayer to the Name of Jesus' once attributed to him is actually the latter part of the Second Meditation;[34] the 'Hours of the Name of Jesus' are really Suso's *Cursus de aeterna sapientia*, which is referred to in *Horologium sapientiae*, and like the latter personifies Wisdom.[35] The possibility of a mystical emphasis in the manuscript is discussed below, in section 6.c.

Scire mori, which begins our manuscript as it is at present made up, belongs to the large corpus of works offering advice on how to die, although *Horologium divine sapientiae* (of which it is book 2) is essentially an allegorical dialogue between Love and Wisdom, listed by Doyle under books of contemplative doctrine and no doubt used, like many similar treatises on death, in 'ordinary piety, not merely *in extremis*'.[36] The *Horologium* itself 'must have come to England about the beginning of the fifteenth century and seems to have been copied first in the Charterhouses, so that it may have been introduced by the same order'.[37] The Latin copies written by English scribes, and all the English translations (*Tretyse of Þe Sevene Poyntes of Trewe Love and Everlastynge Wisdom*)[38] go back to a common ancestor made early in the century for Witham Charterhouse.[39] The Lichfield Translation of *Scire Mori* was thus written early in the English history of Suso.

The Latin *Scire mori* (here summarized from Künzle's edition, to which the parenthesized page numbers refer), is a homiletic disquisition on death, preparation for it, and the need to mend one's ways during life. It is written in the form of a dialogue between Wisdom (who subsequently becomes *Similitudo mortis*, reverting to *Sapientia* at the end) and a young man called the *discipulus*. Wisdom, now dead (hence *Similitudo mortis*, *Imago mortis*) laments his misspent youth, advising the *discipulus* to repent. Substantial parts of the work are devoted to *Imago mortis*'s vision of his future sufferings and to vivid evocations of the torments of the damned (pp.536–7). The *discipulus* is duly convinced and repents forthwith (p.538).

No Anselmian connections are currently postulated for *Scire mori*, but so many texts in the same specific genre derive from Anselm that one wonders if *Scire mori* might, by association, have been mistakenly linked with Anselm by the compiler of the miscellany, and so selected for inclusion with other wholly or partially Anselmian texts. (The Hereford/Gloucester area with which Lichfield MS 16's copies of *Scire mori*[40] and ME are scribally connected – see section 7.C.d – has been associated with interest in Anselm.)[41] The *Boke of Craft of Dying*, from the popular *Ars moriendi*, derives its chapter 3 from Anselm's *Admonitio morienti*, and presents the saint himself addressing the dying man.[42] From *Admonitio morienti* are derived the West Midland verse *Instructions for Parish Priests*, composed *c.* 1400,[43] four of the five Middle English versions of the early fifteenth-century prose treatise *De visitacione infirmorum*, version D being a close translation of *Admonitio* chapters 6 and 7,[44] and parts of John Audelay's similarly named 31-stanza poem *De visitacione infirmorum et consolacione miserorum*, from the first half of the fifteenth century.[45] Moreover, the Anselmian treatment of the seven Dowers of the Body and seven Dowers of the Soul that forms *De quatuordecim partibus beatitudinis* is also found in Part 7 of *The Prick of Conscience*.[46]

The Prick of Conscience, an anonymous eschatological poem, exists in four versions. Originally Northern, it has a Second Recension thought to have originated in the Thames Valley. There is also a Latin translation. Over 9,600 lines in rhyming couplets form a prologue and seven parts, treating the nature of man and the Four Last Things: death, judgement, heaven and hell. The Prologue describes man as God's creation and image, and explains how he must attain self-knowledge in order to reach heaven. The parts are as follows: (1) the corruption of man's nature; (2) the dangers of the world; (3) the horror of, and preparation for, death; (4) the nature of Purgatory, the sins leading to it and the reduction of its pains; (5) the signs of Doomsday, and judgement; (6) the pains of hell; (7) the joys of heaven including the Dowers of the Body and Soul and the New Jerusalem, and the contrasting fates of the blessed and damned. (The Dowers of the Body and Soul derive, like LL, ME and AN, from *De quatuordecim partibus beatitudinis*, one of its many sources.) The poem was itself an important influence on Middle English writers.[47]

De quatuordecim partibus beatitudinis is ostensibly devoted to straightforward religious instruction in the nature of the body and soul after death. However, in its repeated opposition of the qualities of good and evil souls it has been seen as a form of theological *Psychomachia*.[48] It is a discussion of the joys of, first, the body and, second, the soul of those who attain blessedness. The text presents all Fourteen Joys consecutively, with rubrics indicating which pertain to the body and which to the soul. The former are *pulchritudo* (§3 in our text), *velocitas* (§4), *fortitudo* (§5), *libertas* (§6), *sanitas* (§7), *voluptas* (§8), *diuturnitas* (§9); to the soul belong *sapiencia* (§10), *amicicia* (§11), *concordia* (§12), *honor* (§13), *potestas* (§14), *securitas* (§15), *gaudium* (§16). Each of the joys is briefly discussed. There follows a short interpolation (end of §16, rubric of §17) on the last of them, *gaudium* itself, introducing the long excerpt from Anselm's *Proslogion* (§§18–21) which is a distinguishing feature of all three of our texts. LL's rubric at the beginning of §18, *Excitacio mentis ad contemplandum summum bonum* ..., is the title rubric to chapter 1 of the *Proslogion*, and does not belong to chapter 24, from which this part of Anselm's text in fact comes.[49] The interpolation is followed by a short Recapitulation (§22), in which LL, ME and AN expand considerably on the other known texts of *De quatuordecim partibus beatitudinis*, by means of reiterations of material found in the main body of each text.

Evidence that Lichfield MS 16 originated in the Hereford/Worcester/Gloucester area is accumulating as its texts are studied. As this evidence is drawn not only from the texts edited here, but also from the other two vernacular texts, it is given in full elsewhere.[50] Here it is sufficient to summarize. *The Prick of Conscience*'s Hand A uses a dialect of Somerset/Gloucestershire or east Wiltshire; Lewis and McIntosh's distribution map of the Southern Recension of *The Prick of Conscience*, to which the copy in Lichfield MS 16 belongs, shows a concentration in the Hereford, Worcester, Gloucester area;[51] the dialect of ME has been established as mid-Herefordshire/Southern Worcestershire (see section 7.C.d below). Both versions of *Scire mori* are scribally connected with the Hereford/Gloucester area.[52]

6. Audience and Literary Context of the Edited Texts

6.a. Audience: LL, ME, AN

The original audience of *De quatuordecim partibus beatitudinis* was twelfth-century: LL and its annotator tell us that there was still a public for it in the fifteenth century.[53] Perhaps this is due to what Constable has called an 'affinity of religious temperament' between the two centuries, in terms of 'an inward-looking and affective piety based on the doctrine of contemplation stressing personal will, liberty, and experience'.[54] Self-knowledge was the first step of contemplation: it is easy to see how the desire for self-knowledge, leading to fulfilment of human potential through liberty and experience, would be fed by our text's account of the body and soul liberated to their true nature in heaven.

LL's presentation together with ME and AN may or may not tell us something additional. The difficulty of identifying the texts' audience is exacerbated by the very fact that the texts in three languages are together in the one manuscript, for which they were clearly designed. It looks as if LL, like the other Latin text in the manuscript, is present as *auctoritas*, the two vernacular versions being intended to make the material available to the widest possible range of readers. (A summary of the evidence for AN's taking precedence over all the other texts, and the Middle English texts taking precedence over the Latin versions, is presented below in section 7.A.b).

The question of audiences for each of the individual texts in their original form is quite separate from the question of the audience for the three versions as they form part of the miscellany comprised by Lichfield MS 16, for both vernacular versions appear to have had vernacular exemplars. For example, the evidence, cited below, that ME may originally have been aimed at a female audience may shed no light on its function in the whole of this manuscript.

The fact that both ME and AN contain all the interpolations peculiar to LL (described in section 1) raises an interesting point. The compiler of the Lichfield miscellany might have found vernacular versions of his text to hand, in which case the version of the Latin with interpolations was once more common than the rarity of LL would suggest. Alternatively, vernacular versions were commissioned for this miscellany. The second theory could be supported by the indifferent quality of the translation in AN and ME, which is possibly a result of *ad hoc* local work commissioned in accordance with current trends, for 'the major developments in the productions of religious books in the period 1375–1475 are responses to, and catalysts of, the rapidly developing interest in and market for vernacular guides to godliness'.[55] In this case, the two vernacular exemplars lying behind AN and ME were by the translators, and our scribes were commissioned to execute some standardization in layout.

The two vernacular versions really need to be placed in separate literary contexts, each appropriate to its language.

6.b. LL: The Fifteenth-Century Audience: Anselm and *DA*

On the one hand, Anselm is noted for his innovative contribution to affective devotion: his nineteen prayers and three meditations, written while he was Abbot of Bec, have been described as a 'turning point in the devotional literature of the Western Church ... His writings are characterized by an intense, emotional intimacy that is quite unlike anything known before his time.'[56] On the other hand, it is said that his Meditations and prayers show not an emotional but an underlying ascetic attitude, focussing on the intellectual rather than the emotional approach to God.[57]

Anselm's *Proslogion* is, of course, best known for its Ontological Argument for the existence of God (chapter 24) – an argument which has generated a whole library of secondary philosophical and theological material. However, Benedicta Ward regards the *Proslogion* itself as one of Anselm's prayers and Meditations rather than as an example of the theoretical theology suggested by the emphasis subsequently placed on the Ontological Argument.[58] There is contemporary evidence to support this interpretation. The material in *Proslogion* chapters 24–26, from which the most substantial interpolation in our text derives, is found also in the anonymous twelfth-century pseudo-Anselmian 'Meditation 21' (*PL* CLVIII 817–818 (which Glorieux attributes to an 'unknown compiler' at the end of the twelfth century), where the relevant passage begins in the middle of column 817 at *Excita nunc*).[59]

It is not hard to understand how *De quatuordecim partibus beatitudinis* might be used in meditation, for these closing chapters from the *Proslogion* describe the fulfilment of all human qualities in the glorified body and soul obtaining the vision of God, albeit the aim of these chapters is to stir the reader to attain that end rather than to stir emotion towards God:[60]

> Excita nunc anima mea, et erige totum intellectum tuum, et cogita quantum potes, quantum et quale sit illud bonum, de quo tot ac tantorum manat copia bonorum. (§18)

One reason for the existence of the late medieval LL and its vernacular translations may be that *De quatuordecim partibus beatitudinis* clearly shades from devotional into meditational, even mystical literature, if one allows the latter to include works concerned with the accomplishment of any or all of the three stages of contemplation – purgation, illumination and union.

> Gaudium perfectum solus ille potest habere, qui predictas omnes beatitudinis partes valet optinere. Quod ergo beacius isto, qui tanto replebitur gaudio? Adhuc tamen ad cumulum beatitudinis sue, aliud habebit unde magis possit gaudere. Quia enim quisquis sicut se alterum amabit, patet quia sic de illius felicitate ut de sua gaudebit. Quot ergo et quanta gaudia **quisque** optinebit, qui de tot beatitudine sanctorum iubilabit? Quod si tantum de aliis quos ut se diliget, gaudebit; quantum de Deo quem super se diliget, exultabit? Tantam ergo beatitudinem possidebit, quantam mens humana estimare non sufficit. (§16)

We must not forget that demand for the mystical Christian writers was so compelling in the period 1450–1550 'that it resulted in the publication of practically every work in this class which we now consider to be of importance and value'.[61]

The relevance of the mystical tradition is most readily understood in the context of ME, rather than AN.

6.c. ME: Audience, Genre, Literary Context

It seems that the intended audience of ME will not fit easily into the category of what Norman Blake calls the 'general audience'. Translations for this audience were usually from French, although this audience was composed of unlearned clerics and lower classes of lay society, for whom religious works tended to be translations rather than original compositions – translations, moreover, which like ME show no continuity of style within the development of 'good' Middle English meditational prose.[62] On the other hand, the frequent inaccuracy of ME's translation and the poor quality of its English do not suggest that ME was made for the 'traditional audience', the learned, works for whom do show a developing continuity of English style. Presumably it occupies the postulated (but not illustrated) 'middle position'.[63]

Placing ME within the corpus of Middle English prose may be attempted in the light of M. G. Sargent's chapter on 'Minor Devotional Writings', but is hampered by the fact that 'a proper reference work treating manuscript and printed Middle English prayers and meditations has yet to be written'.[64] It bears comparison, for example, with the two Middle English versions of the thirteenth-century Franciscan David of Augsburg's *De exterioris et interioris hominis compositione*,[65] which describes the reforming of the fallen soul to the image of God, and the destruction of the image of sin. Like ME, which speaks 'to everi man and womon' (f.206^{r}) this was addressed 'not only to religious who have no Latin, but also to all – even secular men and women – who desire to serve God'.[66]

Anselm has long been claimed as an English mystic. Colledge, for example, describes the 'Meditation on the Dread of Judgement' as inspired by 'the purest mystical passion':[67] *Meditatio ad concitandum timorem* was quoted several times by the author of one version of the thirteenth-century Middle English *Ancren Riwle*.[68] Anselm and Ælred popularized in England a form of spiritual exercise which greatly influenced the medieval English mystics.[69] Parts of the composite Middle English prose treatise *A Talkynge of the Loue of God*,[70] a minor, popularized example of mystical writing, derive from and modify Anselm. Its preface is a translation of his instructions on how his prayers are to be used; the second of its three parts is composed of translations of his prayers to John the Baptist and Sts Paul and Mary, and of his Third Meditation; this central part is sandwiched between quasi-mystical texts.[71] Richard Rolle has been seen as a translator of

Anselm's First Meditation.[72] In much devotional literature influenced by Anselm, intellectual asceticism is replaced by an emphasis on pleasure in the loving of God: the derivative texts develop and exaggerate emotion in what Benedicta Ward has called 'the particular kind of betrayal which a partial appreciation of Anselm caused'.[73] The tendency to exaggerate emotional content at the expense of the rational appears also in the work of Julian of Norwich.[74] Her desire for the three wounds of contrition, compassion (co-Passion) and sincere longing for God echoes Anselm's emphasis on sharing the Passion and his expression of delight in God in terms of the senses. (Both saints also refer to Christ as our mother: Anselm's *curre sub alas Iesu matris tuae ... Christe mater*, from his Prayer to St Paul, finds an echo in Julian's 'hevynly moder Jhesu'.)[75] Margery Kempe perhaps shows the best and the worst effects of the Anselmian spiritual exercises.[76]

ME bridges two categories of Middle English prose, not simply instructing (category 1), but also using affective methods designed to stir emotional response (category 3).[77] It is partly in the latter category by virtue of its source. ME needs to be seen against the background of the Middle English tendency to exaggerate the emotional emphasis in Anselmian devotional works, precisely because, although ME slightly expands on ALDQ, the essential literalism of ME (albeit not so rigid as that of AN) prevents the kind of 'betrayal' described above. The translator did not develop the emotional dimension of his original. The emotional dimension is found primarily in our texts' principal *interpolations* – as opposed to minor elaborations from the translators or scribes of the two vernacular versions – and the principal interpolations are of authentic Anselmian material. In other words, the interpolations make this version of *De quatuordecim partibus beatitudinis* (ALDQ) more, not less, genuinely Anselmian, and also more emotional, while the translators' small modifications do nothing to violate that Anselmian quality.

Anselm's effect on later medieval philosophy and theology is well known.[78] However, his literary influence outside the work of the main Middle English mystics is less well documented – indeed, it is a research topic awaiting attention. His treatise *De libero arbitrio* is found in a unique late fifteenth-century Middle English version.[79] At least two texts derive from Anselm's *Liber de similitudinibus*. It has been said that the figure of the unruly wife/will in the allegory of the inner man in *Sawles Warde*[80] recalls chapter 2, 'Similitudo inter mulierem et voluntatem', of *De similitudinibus*. The short *VII Degrees of Humylyte*, surviving in manuscripts of *c.* 1450 and 1450–1500, shows how progress in humility takes the soul from recognition of its sinfulness, through contrition and confession, and on to increasing degrees of patient suffering.[81]

Chapters 48–49 of Anselm's *De moribus* may have been a source for some details in the prose *XIV Maneris of Helle.*[82] Book 3 of Thomas Usk's prose *Testament of Love* (1384–1385), which treats love in the context of free will and predestination, draws on Anselm's *De concordia praescientiae et praedestinationis.*[83] The prose parable *An Bispel*[84] is a retelling of Anselm's *De similiter inter Deum et quemlibet regem suos judi cantem.* The lyric 'Qwhan drighten dere his doom schal dresse (*Lamentatio S. Anselmi*)' is based on Anselm's *Deploratio male amissae virginitatis.*[85] As already mentioned, the saint's influence is present in the longest work in our manuscript, *The Prick of Conscience.*[86]

Various works once attributed to Anselm have also been influential. The alliterative prose *Wohunge of Ure Lauerd* and *On Ureisun of Oure Louerde* have been described as largely influenced by French clerical writers in Latin, including the writer of *DA*, Alexander of Canterbury.[87] The pseudo-Anselmian *Miraculum de conceptione Beatae Mariae*[88] is thought to have influenced several versions of the tale 'The Origin of the Festival of the Conception of Mary' as it appears in works such as *Cursor Mundi,*[89] the fifteenth-century *South English Legendary*, *Mirk's Festial*, *Speculum Sacerdotale* and the *Golden Legend.*[90] ME should add to the growing evidence of Anselm's varied influence on late medieval English literature – evidence which will be ripe for correlation when the long-awaited mystics volume of the revised *Manual*(2) appears.

6.d. AN: Anglo-Norman and Middle French Literature

Perhaps surprisingly, there is no body of mystical literature in Anglo-Norman to compare with that which survives in Middle English. With odd exceptions, such as Henry of Lancaster's *Livre de seyntz medicines*, much of the fairly small amount of Anglo-Norman writing of this type is translated material: from Middle English, like the two versions of *Ancren Riwle*, or from Latin, like the Anglo-Norman version of Edmund of Abingdon's *Speculum ecclesie.* There is a sizeable body of religious lyric poetry,[91] but there appears to be no real tradition of autonomous mystical writing in Anglo-Norman.

Riehle suggests that the development of female religious communities is one of the causes of the expansion of mystical writing in

English.[92] There is some evidence that nuns were more likely to be able to read French than Latin,[93] but it does not seem that a great deal was written expressly for them. We have Robert of Gretham's *Mirur* (or *Evangiles des domnees*: it consists of a series of verse sermons on the Gospels used on Sundays), John Pecham's *Jerarchie* (a discussion of the court of heaven) and John of Howden's *Rossignol* (a poem on the life and Passion of Christ, which he first wrote in Latin as *Philomena*), but these were apparently written for aristocratic ladies, rather than for women in holy orders. An exception is Adgar's *Gracial*, probably written for Maud, Abbess of Barking, in the late twelfth century. The survival of these works, and of isolated sermons in Anglo-Norman, points to the existence of a public for religious literature (in the most general sense) in French, and it is, presumably, to this public that AN itself was addressed.

7.A. Description of the Edited Portion

7.A.a. Hands

Notwithstanding Ker's and Benedikz's descriptions of the manuscript,[94] the hand changes not only between LL and ME (f.206^{r}) but also between ME and AN (f.233^{r}) and possibly within AN at ff.240^{v}/241^{r}. Significant differences between the two vernacular texts – including some important differences in layout – are discussed below. Our tentative suggestion is that the two translations are the work of different authors as well as different scribes, and that neither was translated by the scribe of LL. Though very different, the scribes' hands are contemporary with each other, as is shown not only by their style but also by the melding of the first page of each text with its illuminated border.

7.A.b. Layout and Decoration

The material in this section is selected and summarized from an article on the manuscript as a whole,[95] including the layout and decoration of texts other than those edited here. This summary is intended merely to indicate the importance of illuminated borders and other decoration in Lichfield MS 16, and to point to the fact that our texts once held pride of place in the manuscript. The three borders relating to our texts are illustrated in Plates 1–3.

Each of Lichfield MS 16's six texts forms a booklet. This is clear from the distribution of hands, the blanks at the end of texts, and the absence of any complete signature or catchword system. AN and ME have no catchwords or signatures at all; LL has one catchword, on f.197^{v}; the opening leaves of some quires in AN and LL bear numbers – those relevant to the misbinding of LL being described in section 7.B.a. The only foliation and section numbering running consecutively throughout is post-medieval. However, the manuscript is a planned compilation: not only are all the scribes roughly contemporary;[96] there is also a general similarity of vellum, numbers of lines of text, and ink rulings, details of which will be found in the article.

Each booklet bears on its first (recto) page an illuminated initial that is an integral part of a text-framing border (ff.1^{r}, 17^{r}, 35^{r}, 190^{r}, 206^{r}, 233^{r}). The illumination is dated 'before 1410, and probably c. 1400'.[97] The borders' subtle visual language indicates misbinding of the booklets in reverse order. There is no codicological evidence to contradict this hypothesis, and there is some to support it. If the present booklet order is simply reversed, the succession of borders suddenly makes sense, the most impressive coming first, the least last, as in Plates 1–3. Moreover, the six borders are arranged in a double order of descending importance: an outer sequence with inner sequences contained in it. The borders which adorn the first pages of LL, ME and AN cannot, therefore, be fully understood without reference to the complete sequence, in which the manuscript was intended to begin with AN, followed by ME and LL, then *The Prick of Conscience*, the Lichfield translation of *Scire mori*, and finally *Scire mori* in Latin. In this order, the manuscript begins with the celestial goal to which the rest directs the soul, ending with a *memento mori*.

Indeed, the opening text attempts, in one sense, to present the ultimate spiritual experience – a kind of transposition of the Beatific Vision. As *De quatuordecim partibus beatitudinis* suggests at the end of section 2, the nearest we can at present come to understanding the nature of God is to study the nature of the glorified human body and soul. *De quatuordecim partibus beatitudinis* may be presented here as a kind of mystical exercise – an intellectual approach not only to the nature of man, but also to the nature of God.

Only two aspects of the double sequence formed by the borders need concern us here. First, as already mentioned, the work here edited is given priority. The outer sequence consists of the main version of each of the three texts which essentially comprise the manuscript (*De quatuordecim partibus beatitudinis*, led by AN; *The Prick of Conscience*, the only member of its group; *Scire mori*, led by the Middle English version).

Second, borders in each text group show family resemblances: AN's border differs somewhat from those in ME and LL because of its position, which seems, interestingly, to be due to its being the only text in Anglo-Norman. Both sequences may be indicated by a number of factors: the form of the illuminated frame (bar or band); illuminated initials' size and elaboration; the number of, and relationships between, foliage units springing from the frame; the size and complexity of sprays extending into margins; the degree of imaginative pattern variation, the number and type of details peculiar to a border; incipits; decoration of the text itself.

All the borders are conventional, showing the main design elements defined by Dr Scott as typical of English borders of the period.[98] All are from the same school: AN by one hand, ME and LL by another. However, the three borders vary in highly considered ways. All are bar borders, except for that of AN, which is prioritized by a band border. Not only is AN's border more imposing (though not more subtle) than ME's, but also the latter is more imposing than LL's. A similar descending importance is obvious in the sprays which project into the three borders' right-hand and lower margins. In this manuscript, Latin versions are subordinated to their vernacular equivalents in position, presentation and, presumably, function.

AN, ME and LL are naturally similar in their largely standardized layout of the written text. All have incipits, and illuminated capitals beginning each of the 22 sections;[99] all have rubrics; in section 22, all have red marginalia naming the Blessednesses. However, even here LL shows slightly less elaboration than the first two, except for its running titles in red (see section 7.B.a).

7.B. Description of LL

7.B.a. Content of LL

The present foliation of this part of Lichfield MS 16 is incorrect. LL occupies quires 24 and 25,[100] each containing eight folios:

Quire 24 190–191–192–193–194–195–196–197
Quire 25 198–199–200–201–202–203–204–205

The text runs as follows: 190, 199–204, 197, 198, 191–196, 205. In other words, the outer leaves of each of the two quires are

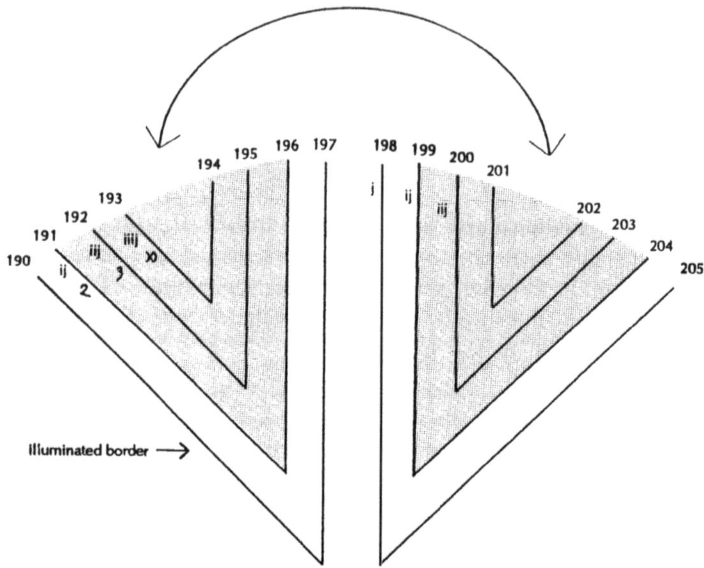

Fig. 1. Quires 24 and 25 (LL): the shaded portions have been transposed.

correctly placed in the manuscript, but the inner portions of the two quires have been transposed (see Fig. 1). Our edition restores the logical order of the text.

Some numbering of leaves suggests that this misplacement is early. The first of these quires as currently bound (quire 24) bears two sets of medieval numbers: one roman (similar to others elsewhere in the manuscript) and one arabic – the latter the significant series. The roman numbers are clear and bold in black ink. On ff.191^{r}, 192^{r} there are *ij*, *iij*, respectively – a *j* is unnecessary on f.190^{r}, the illuminated border of which identifies the first page of the text. There is a slightly cropped *iiij* on the extreme right-hand side of f.193^{r}, but it is smaller and lower than the *ij* and *iij*, and could be a survivor of an earlier *ij*–*iiij* sequence, though if this were so, it would indicate an unlikely medieval cropping. There is a similar sequence – *j*, *ij*, *iij* – on ff.198^{r}, 199^{r}, 200^{r}, but these are in a different ink and hand (the *j* is necessary in this quire, as its first page is not identified by an illuminated border).

The second, arabic series is on ff.191^{r}, 192^{r}, 193^{r}, the second, third and fourth folios of the text as currently bound: large, faint pencil *2*, *3*, *4* in the bottom right-hand corners. This series is at first sight superfluous, for these folios already bear the roman *ij*, *iij* and slightly cropped *iiij*. The most logical explanation of the arabic numbers' presence (and the absence of any echo of them at the start of the second quire of LL), is that someone was numbering what he or she took to be folios 2, 3 and 4 in this whole Latin text. There would be no need then to renumber the inner portion of the second quire. Unfortunately the writer, who presumably did not read Latin, transposed the inner quire portions, perhaps as a result of their having fallen out, being still unbound at this stage. These arabic numbers' form, size and medium are quite out of keeping with any others in the manuscript, but they have medieval forms: long '3', and '4' made like an 'X' without lifting the pen, so that the right-hand extremities are joined. This form of '4' is one not used after the late sixteenth century,[101] so it looks as if this transposition predates the present binding, and indeed the bequest of the manuscript to the Cathedral by the Duchess of Somerset in 1673.[102]

(In Lichfield MS 16 pencil marks or notes – which might conceivably be in the hand that made these arabic numbers – are rare, but on f.188^{r}, the penultimate leaf of the last quire of *The Prick of Conscience*, is a faint marginal pencil note next to a passage which begins at the end of the previous page: 'And to be syker of heuene blysse / ȝyf he hym amende of þat he doþ amys / And to drede ouȝt to do aȝens godeys wille / And al hijs comaundementes euer to fulfylle.' Maddeningly, in the absence of any notes with which to compare it, we can neither date nor decipher the note, though it looks post-medieval, and the last, isolated letter seems to be a capital *A* with lower-case form.)

LL is an important copy of the earlier recension of *De quatuordecim partibus beatitudinis* published by Southern and Schmitt,[103] who list one complete manuscript of this recension of *DA* (Cambridge, Corpus Christi College, 316).[104] LL does not appear to diverge substantially from their critical edition, but LL's particular importance lies in the fact that it contains a number of interpolations (all noted in our edition) which are not found in the published text. The most substantial interpolation comes from chapters 24–26 of Anselm's *Proslogion*;[105] this passage recurs in a pseudo-Anselmian Meditation.[106] Dom A. Wilmart established that this Meditation is not by Anselm;[107] it seems, however, to have been attributed to him during or shortly after his lifetime.[108] LL seems closer to the *Proslogion* than to the Meditation (for example, it has the rubrics found in the former but absent from the latter).

With this one exception, the interpolations absent from the main tradition of *De quatuordecim partibus beatitudinis* are not apparently by Anselm;[109] their origin has proved elusive. The purpose of some of them seems to be a rather heavy-handed clarification (see section 7.C.e.iv for similar tendencies in ME); for example, in the Recapitulation which closes ALDQ, where minor interpolations all constitute expansions of the initial statements of contrast between the states of the blessed and the damned, the expansions serve little purpose beyond the provision of additional images illustrating the points made.

7.B.b. LL: *De quatuordecim partibus beatitudinis* and *DA*

The extraction of *De quatuordecim partibus beatitudinis* from its context as chapter 5 of *DA* is not as curious as it may seem, for *DA* is a collection of discourses spoken by Anselm *in commune* (in chapter or in formal sermons), and arranged by their recorder in no particular order.[110] Moreover, chapter 5 of *DA* survives as an independent text in at least six manuscripts.[111]

Our scant knowledge of *DA*'s composition is based on its preface. The 'sayings' were compiled from notes, some of which had been lost. *DA* is ingeniously attributed to Alexander of Canterbury, who with three other monks (Baldwin, Eustace, Eadmer) accompanied Anselm on his second exile between 1103 and 1106, and then joined his household.[112] It was written when Alexander seems partly to have taken Eadmer's place as secretary,[113] or perhaps after Anselm's death in 1109.[114]

G. R. Evans describes the processes by which such 'sayings' and extracts are pirated and modified, both accident and intent affecting material composed from lecture notes and not subjected to the speaker's scrutiny. *DA* 'is likely to be substantially Anselm's ... the distilled essence of [his] talk, recorded precisely because it is so characteristic. But the text may have undergone reworking in a dozen ways, and we may be some way from the author's words.'[115]

7.B.c. Layout and Decoration of LL

The illuminated borders of the first page are described above in section 7.A.b. The layout of the Recapitulation paragraph presents particular problems, discussed under Editorial Procedure, in sections 8a and 8b. There are 22 decorated capitals, with extensions occupying some 10–12 lines. LL is the only text with running titles, in red; the erasure they have suffered may suggest a scribe acting on his own initiative rather than following an exemplar:

De xiiii partibus / Beatitudinis ff.190^{v}–191^{r}
contem / placio ff.193^{v}–194^{r}, 194^{v}–195^{r} (over section 18 'Excitacio mentis ad contemplandum summum bonum et coniectacio quale et quantum sit hoc bonum')
oracio (with an otiose bar over the r) Recapitulacio / Recapitulacio ff.195^{v}–196^{r}
Recapitulacio / Beatitudinis ff.196^{v}–197^{r}
De xiiij partibus / Beatitudinis ff.197^{v}–198^{r}
/ Beatitudinis f.199^{r}
De xiiij par... [erasure] / Beatitudinis ff.199^{v}–200^{r}
De xiiij partibus / Beatitudinis ff.200^{v}–201^{r}, 201^{v}–202^{r}
De xiiij par... [erasure] / Beatitudinis ff.202^{v}–203^{r}, 203^{v}–204^{r}
De xiiij partibus / f.204^{v}
Recapitulacio f.205^{v}.

7.B.d. Scribes and Annotators of LL

i) Scribal Practice

LL seems to be the work of one careful scribe, whose relatively few, and venial, errors are all of the type widespread in medieval manuscripts: omission of abbreviations (LL n.74); confusion of final 't' and 'd' (LL n.25); dittography (LL n.64); omitted nasals (LL n.55). Those scribal errors which appear to be of some significance in establishing the relationship between the three versions in Lichfield MS 16 are discussed in section 7.E. The text of LL is not heavily abbreviated, and the abbreviations used are entirely conventional.

ii) Other Hands

There is a limited amount of correction, both in the margin and in the form of inserted letters or expuncted errors (e.g. LL nn.4, 5, 12, 39). The marginal comments, and perhaps the insertions and expunctions, are by an early fifteenth-century hand.[116] This annotator's work does not appear on the five other texts. In LL it occurs 19 times. Twice the annotator makes or attempts correction: the marking of a possible dittography by *abcissimus* may suggest that he was making a copy of the text. On 11 occasions, listed below, he marks a passage with a marginal *nota* like a curlicue. Seven times he briefly comments, as when (f.200[v]) he marks 'Velocitatem tantam habebunt hii qui cum Deo erunt, quantam habet radius solis, vel alicuius oculi clare videntis' by 'aciës', or when (f.201[r]) beside 'Omnes quippe s[c]imus Petrum apostolum Dominum negavisse, Mariam Magdalenam peccatricem fuisse, nec eos latet quia nos scimus' he writes 'sub velura nota'. All these occasions are noted in the edition. In general, LL is a careful copy. In this respect, LL differs markedly from the two vernacular texts, and in particular from the heavily corrected ME.

iii) Marginal Marks

LL is adorned with eleven marginal curlicues, apparently by the fifteenth-century annotator, though they are not always associated with comments or corrections; all are indicated in our notes. Their locations in the manuscript (with footnote numbers from our edition of LL) are as follows: 191[r]/11 (n.70); 194[r]/4 (n.79); 197[r]/12–13 (n.60); 197[r]/12–13 (n.61); 199[v]/16 (n.16); 201[r]/13 (n.32); 201[r]/20 (n.34); 203[v]/17 (n.50); 204[v]/20 (n.58); 205[r]/1 (n.129); 205[v]/6 (n.136).

7.C. Description of ME

7.C.a. Content of ME

ME, *The Joys of Paradise*, occupies quires 26–29, ff.206[r]–232[r].

7.C.b. Layout and Decoration of ME

The illuminated borders of the first page are described above in section 7.A.b. The interesting layout of the Recapitulation and its possible purpose are described in section 7.C.e.iv. There are 22 decorated capitals; the maximum number of lines occupied by their extensions is 8: less than in LL. Capital letters, including the first-person pronoun, are commonly touched in red.

7.C.c. Date of ME

It is possible that this is the first formal copy of the translation, made from the translator's autograph, which may be little earlier than this early fifteenth-century copy. This is suggested by the relatively low level of errors derived from the misreading of Middle English, and is perhaps supported by the use of two words first attested at roughly the time of ME's copying: *MED*'s earliest example of 'disparkeled' (f.210r/–8) is 1384, and its earliest example of *president* adj. (1450) is predated by the example on f.208v/5. Elizabeth Westlake comes to similar conclusions about Lichfield 16's Middle English version of *Scire mori*, observing that the 'translator may have been someone preparing the text for the scribe, or the scribe himself working from his exemplar rather than the Latin text in the manuscript ... the small number of differences between the Latin and the English suggest that this translation was produced close to the production of Lichfield 16, possibly even for it. This is supported by the fact that there are no other extant manuscripts containing Latin and Middle English extracts from the *Horologium*.'[117]

7.C.d. Dialect of ME

Using the text and our concordance of it, Dr Jeremy Smith has kindly localized the dialect (which may show traces of translator as well as scribe) to mid-Herefordshire/southern Worcestershire. He observes that relevant forms include *mony*, *eorthe*, *beþ* (pres. pl.), *whare*, *wham* 'whom', *fuyre* 'fire', *throw* 'through', *weche* 'which', occasional 'v' for 'f', -*nis* for '-ness', and *whodir* 'whether'; 'o'-forms for this last item have a very restricted distribution. Preference is given to mid-Herefordshire rather than southern Worcestershire, because *throw* 'through' is rather more common there. Forms in '-y', such as *asky*, *wilny* from OE Class II weak verbs *ascian* and *wilnian*, also suggest the south-west Midlands; in addition, the form *seyth* beside *sith* may be a variant of the *seþe* types common throughout that area.

7.C.e. Translator of ME

i) Misunderstandings

The ME translation forms an interesting contrast to the literal AN, being free to the point of paraphrase and distortion. That the Latin is sometimes imperfectly understood, and biblical quotations are not always recognized, may suggest translation by a lay person, nun, student, or unlearned member of the clergy, but the more bizarre examples of misunderstanding could reflect corruption in the Latin source manuscript. The following selected examples are not documented in footnotes.

f.213r 'Put ȝe ȝowre veniaunce that ȝe wolle have do on myn handys & I wold do hit' loses the possessive force of the 'michi vindictam· et ego retribuam'.

f.214^{r} 'And ȝif he wold drawe out myn other appul with the same turment'; 'transfoderet' is entirely appropriate to destruction of an eye's pupil, which it would be difficult to 'drawe out'.

f.214^{v} 'This temporale delyȝt & lust passynge awey of this world is only yhadde & felyd whilys we lyvyth in eorth in every part of oure body· but thylke delyte & lust that schal be in hevyn· schul be felid in hem that schul be savid· as for as muche joye and gladnys· as was the peyne of fuyre brennyn in here most sorwe'. The sense should be that heavenly joy is not divided but whole, fire being an image of heat, not pain.

f.217^{v} 'And therfore what evere thou be that seist so, that desyrist that al men schul love thy fadir & thy modir, wham thou lovist specially afore al other, as muche as thou lovyst hem· thynke thou how muche thou woldist thy silfe forto be bylovyd in that place': besides the awkward syntax, there is no source for 'thynke ... place'; conceivably the translator's source bore an error like that in LL, where 'que' for 'quem' may be inherited.

f.220^{r} 'how we schul be transfigurid & purid in the siȝt of God' barely relates to 'cuius corporis membra tunc erimus'.

f.222^{r} 'to oure frendys that brouȝt us in to thys world' misrepresents 'amicis et parentibus karissimis'.

f.225^{r} 'heredes quidem Dei, coheredes autem Christi' is rendered by 'And thare as is the sone of God· thare schul they be the ayrys of Crist Jhesus'; again the translator apparently did not recognize, and so confused, the quotation.

ii) Eyeskip in Latin

At least one omission in ME is due to the translator's eyeskip between words in the Latin exemplar. On f.224^{v} (ME n.263), eyeskip was from 'Dei' to 'Dei'. On f.230^{r} (ME n.331), 'But the dampnyd soulys schul be yȝeve drynke of the bittur replecioun of the sorwys of helle· ∞∞∞∞∞', the 'reflection line' (indicated here by '∞∞∞∞∞') is not followed by the usual expansion of the initial statement of contrast: there is no equivalent for 'Illi enim sicut ferrum ignitum quaque sui parte continet ignem sic in se voluptatem, mali vero sencient anxi[e]tatem.' That AN inserts the equivalent of 'sic ... sencient' in its bottom margin may indicate difficulty in a Latin ancestor common at some stage to AN and ME.

Two other examples are more ambiguous – probably eyeskip in ME, but possibly in the source Latin, and so by the translator: f.222^{r} (ME n.215) probably shows eyeskip from 'blisse' to 'blys' rather than from 'gaudio' to 'gaudere'; and f.225^{r} (ME n.271) probably from 'goddys' to 'goddys' rather than from from 'vocabuntur' to 'erunt'.

iii) Language

The style of ME is inelegant at best; examples of its weakness include the following: f.207ᵛ 'þa̲t wondirful wordis þa̲t ys sayd abofe'; f.219ᵛ the referents of the pronouns are unclear in 'Then reverence & worschip schul be of al men do, by cause of his lord, to hym, & they wold plese him· for they wold have hys love· & noȝt hys wrethe'; f.230ᵛ 'The body & soule of every seynt· and also seyntys schul have so gret concordaunce to gadere' is a nonsensical distortion of 'Corpus enim et anima cuiusque sancti immo concordie tante omnes erunt electi.'

iv) The Translator (and/or Scribe) to the Reader

Four elements in ME seem to indicate particular concern for the reader – a concern above and beyond that apparent in LL or AN: a particular care to address women as well as men; frequent quotation of and reference to its Latin source; additions clearly made for clarification or emphasis; unusual layout in the Recapitulation. A fifth element, the high level of correction (to which the notes bear ample witness), indicates a concern for accuracy that may be pedagogic, but perhaps says still more about the shortcomings of the scribe or his exemplar.[118]

Expansion of References to One Gender

ME may have been a translation made for a female readership. The Latin's impersonal or masculine terminology is repeatedly expanded in ME to include women: f.206ʳ 'Hit is spedful to everi man and womon' ('sibimet'); f.206ʳ 'how muche godenes a man or womon may do to hym silf' ('ipse'); f.210ʳ 'whan al eorthely men & wemen schul arise' ('uniuscuiusque hominis'); f.210ʳ 'than schal every partye þat bilongeth to every man & woman be knyȝtte to gedere' (no equivalent in *DA*); f.210ʳ 'or eny membre of eny man or woman' ('alicuius'); f.210ʳ 'the yȝe of a man or woman' ('oculus'); f.211ʳ 'God forbede that eny man or woman' ('aliquis'); f.211ʳ 'men & wemen that dredeth him' ('timencium'); f.216ᵛ 'thou eny man or woman wold atwyte vs' ('qui'); f.217ʳ 'if hit so be· that eny man or woman' ('dicat quis'); f.217ᵛ 'his fadir & hir modir' ('patrem aut parentes'); f.217ᵛ 'al other men & women also' ('omnes alii'); f.223ʳ 'if a man or woman lyve welle' ('beate vivere'); f.227ʳ 'no creature schal love none other man ne woman' ('alium'); f.231ᵛ 'Every ryȝtfulle man & woman' ('bonus'); f.232ʳ 'no man no woman that thynketh to be savyd' ('nullus').[119]

Quotation of, and Reference to, the Latin Source
At the start of each main paragraph, the translator gives the Latin title (found in LL but not in *DA*) and the first few words of the Latin text. The reader is usually told that the 'meaning of this passage in English is ...', before the translation begins. The exception is on f.228^{r}, where no such reminder occurs at the start of the paragraph 'Oratio pro hoc gaudio impetrando'. The Latin heading here is also defective. Perhaps the repetition of 'the meaning of this passage in English is ...' shows careful avoidance of claim to authorship; similarly, when the Bible is quoted, the translator gives the Latin before the translation. At the end of each paragraph, the translator adds a brief reference to the next, as in 'And therfore we have sette to thys another chapitur that is of everelastyngnys' (f.215^{r}).

Additions for Clarification or Emphasis
Within his text, the translator often uses explanatory expansions. On f.207^{r} 'ne renatum mors secunda possideat' becomes 'þat þe secunde deth schuld have no powere on him that is baptisid· & bilevyth on Crist'; f.208^{v} 'de pulchritudine' becomes 'what feyrnys seyntys havyth in hevyn'; f.209^{v} 'qui dicebat' becomes 'The holy man David considerit wel and sawe wel this feire blessidnys and this blessid feyrnys, whan he seid thus'; and 'the weche is the secunde partye of blessidnys that seyntes havyth' has no source in *DA*; f.210^{v} 'qui Danieli prandium porrexit· Quo facto' becomes 'whare on liouns were ordeyned to devoure Danyel· whan Abacuk broȝt mete to hym· ¶ and whan the prophete had fulfillid the comaundement of the angel'; f.211^{r} 'vocatur' becomes 'callid in Holy Wryȝt'; f.213^{v} 'in atriis Ierusalem' becomes 'in the blis of hevyn'; f.215^{v} the translator adds the '·vii·' in 'Whe have schortely overe seye & in fwe wordys comprehendyd thys ·vii· blessidnys[ys]'; f.216^{r} 'negavisse' becomes 'forsoke ... thre tymes'; f.216^{v} 'quod dicis' is clarified to 'that \y/ forsoke God'; f.216^{v} 'for as the apostole seyth' before 'Cum enim essem parvulus' is added; f.218^{v} in 'God that ys here hedde', 'God that ys' has no source in *DA*, and metaphor is again made explicit: 'capud' becomes 'God'; f.219^{r} 'corpore corruptibili hominis corruptibilis' becomes 'the corruptibile body of men that lyveyth here in eorthe'; f.220^{v} a reference to the paragraph dealing with 'fortitudinem' becomes 'in the thred chapitur', while 'superius' becomes 'in the fowrth chapitur'; f.221^{v} 'Take thou, that hopyst to come to thylke place, go\od/ hede now to my wordis' is added, not for clarification but with clear didactic intent; f.223^{r} 'ut

gaudium nostrum sit plenum, nichil desit timentibus Deum' becomes 'For his joye wolle nouȝt be so ful· that he schuld have sufficience ther on if he were unnemyȝty & impotent· And therfore syth no manere thynge schal wanti neythe\r/ lacki to Goddys seyntys here joye here gladnys & here murthe schal evere be fulle to hem withoute ende· amen'; f.223^{v} 'facta' becomes 'whan hit is ordeynned & made in mannys body'; f.224^{v} 'potestate utique non natura' becomes 'by powere of God & noȝt by hys owen kynde'; f.230^{r} 'non possint meditare' becomes 'schul not have myȝt to underestond how muche hit schal be for sorwe'.

Many small expansions show less clear intention, often appearing redundant, though the line between the otiose and the functional is hard to draw from our perspective: f.206^{v} 'equis' becomes 'horse of gret valoure'; f.207^{v} 'consideramus' becomes 'biholde we & considere we'; f.208^{r} 'felicitate' becomes 'blessidnys þat is in hevyn'; f.208^{v} 'et potens et gloriosus super omnia ineffabiliter est' becomes 'þat ys ful of myȝt & ful of joye· al þynge havynge Crist him silf'; f.208^{v} 'Audi' becomes '& if þow wolt knowe how hit is huyre þow & take gode hede'; ff.208^{v}–209^{r} 'et sol septempliciter sicut lux septem dierum· Si ergo corpora nostra "fulgebunt sicut sol", qui multiplicatum lumen septem dierum habebit, magna et incomparabiliter magna illa pulchritudo erit' becomes '& the sonne schal schyne sevynfold cleroure þan he doth nowe· & þoȝ hit myȝ\t/ be þat þe schynnynge of the sonne of vii dayes myȝt be gadered to gadere on a day· ȝut schal þe sonne have at tha\t/ tyme as mucche clernes as have now ·vii· dayys: þoȝ þey myȝ\t/ be had on one day· Therfore seþþe oure bodyes "schul schyne as bryȝt as the sonne" the wycche sonne schal have þe clernys on hym silf of ·vii· daies· þan withowte dowte ful gret & withoute comparison þat feyrnes schal be & overe passynge gret'; f.213^{r} 'suspenderit' becomes '& put his wronge to be avengyd throw him· whytoute dowȝte'; f.213^{v} 'incomparabiliter' becomes 'passyngly & withoute comparison'; f.217^{v} 'sit' becomes 'hit is th[u]s brouȝt to gedere'. The translator sometimes expands as if to hedge his bets: f.219^{r} 'debitorum ... putaret' becomes 'were ... bounde to & in dette'; f.231^{r} 'vestibus preciosis' becomes 'he wold clothe hym with precious stonys & clothys'. Sometimes the elaboration seems merely to add a verbal flourish: in f.220^{v} 'y speke & make mensioun here' the repetition is added. Further expansions include: f.228^{v} 'et promittis accipe[re]' becomes 'that we schul aske as thou bihetist us that we schuld have oure askynge, that is'; f.228^{v} 'Meditetur interim inde mens mea' becomes 'Therfore in the tyme of my life graunte thou to me that.my mynde may thenke ther on'; f.231r 'bonum' becomes 'his gode trewe servant'.

The following have no source in *DA*, and mostly serve to increase the presence of a didactic 'narrator': f.209v 'ȝee schul undirstonde that'; f.210v 'they schul have more ther to. And that is strengthe'; f.211r 'ȝus without dowȝte he schal ȝeve hem muche more strengthe and muche bettur strengthe than the devyl hath' (ME repeats); f.211v 'than withoute dowȝte'; f.211v 'And therfore hit is no dowȝte but thylke blessid multitude of hevyn schul be ful fre & sikere fro al bondage' (ME repeats); f.211v 'And they schul have so gret liberalte'; f.212v 'And ȝe schul understande that'; f.213r 'he aske not veniaunce for his wrongis· but'; f.213r '[W]ithoute dowte'; f.214r 'as is in the hous of God'; f.216v '& so ded y never'; f.216v 'that we dede before tyme'; f.217v 'as thou hast to thy frende'; f.219r 'for as hit ys wrete'; f.219r 'that had so graciusly do to him'; f.219v the adjectival phrase in 'God, fourme of al creaturis'; f.220v 'Haply many man thynkyth thys· & seyth thus in his mynde· Hit were litille joye to eny man to serve God· but if he myȝth have sykyrnis of his joyes & blessidnissis that beth aforsayd'; f.221r 'that nevyr schal have ende'; f.223r 'And therfore syth no manere thynge schal wanti neythe\r/ lacki to Goddys seyntys here joye here gladnys & here murthe schal evere be fulle to hem withoute ende· amen'; f.224r 'that is God'; f.224r 'withoute comparison'; f.228r '& thow I may nouȝt fully fele that joye'; f.228v 'as thou bihetist us'; f.228v 'and most gracious lord'; f.228v 'in the tyme of my life graunte thou to me'; f.229r '& feyroure coloure'; f.232r 'that nevere schal have ende'; f.232r 'for here deservynge that evere schal last'.

(In view of all these expansions, it is surprising to find some omissions and reductions. On f.211r 'Diabolus Dei inimicus' becomes 'the devyl'; f.211v shows no ME equivalent at the end of 'De fortitudine' for 'Aderit itaque, et non modica'; later 'clauso sepulcro' becomes 'sepulcre'; f.215v has no equivalent for 'adiuvante Domino' in 'Whe have schortely overe seye & in fwe wordys comprehendyd thys ·vii· blessidnys[sys]'; f.220v 'filio Dei' becomes 'God'. At the end (f.232r), in a marked change of emphasis, 'Whare fro God defende us' replaces 'cui gloria et imperium hunc et in perpetuum', and the scribe or translator, ignored – if he had it in the exemplar – 'Explicit libellus beati Anselmi Archiepiscopi Cantuarensis xiiii partibus beatitudinum·'.)

The Recapitulation: Attempts to Clarify by Layout

In the concluding recapitulation ME initiates, or preserves, a striking form of syntactic decoration which has no counterpart in the other two versions. As mentioned in the notes to the Recapitulation, either the translator or the scribe attempted to clarify the structure of his material by use, within the text, of decorative lines whose different constructions we have indicated by calling them 'tilde' (≈≈≈) and 'reflection' (∞∞∞) lines (ff.229r–232r). This attempt is not wholly conducive to clarity (see ME nn.321–2, 331, 334, 335, for the confusing effects of an error in the handling of this device).

The fourteen paragraphs treat the Fourteen Joys of the blessed paired with the Fourteen Pains of the damned. In both LL and ME these antithetical pairs are briefly described and are named in the margins (e.g. 'Pulcri· Fedi·'). Each brief description is followed by a short (interpolated) development of the initial statement of opposites. In LL, the introduction of each of the fourteen paragraph subjects within the recapitulation is, with two exceptions discussed below, marked by a paraph. This helpful use of paraphs is confusingly absent (with one possibly accidental exception) from ME. On the other hand, in ME striking red decorative lines (which we have called 'tilde lines') mark the end of each statement of the condition of the blessed, and the end of each statement of the condition of the damned is marked by the different decorative/syntactic elements that we have called 'reflection lines'. Each of the latter is usually followed by a coloured paraph, so perhaps the inventor of 'reflection lines' saw them not as marking the end of the description of the damned, but as marking the beginning of the interpolated 'expansions' which should in every case follow. It is not easy to imagine why in ME these divisions should be emphasized, while the major divisions, those between paragraph subjects, are left so hard to detect. It is hard to believe that the variable formulae used at the start of each section (formulae which contrast with the regularity found in LL and AN) could have served as sufficient indication of 'paragraphing'. They are:

1. 'They that schul be savyd schul'
2. 'And aȝenst the overe passynge strengthe'
3. 'Ryȝtful men schul have'
4. 'Seyntys of God schul evere have'
5. 'Ryȝthful men schul be'
6. '¶ Ryȝtful men schul have' (cited above)
7. 'And ryȝth as ryȝtful men schul have'

8. 'Godes frendys schul have'
9. '¶ ¶ Goddys seyntys schul be' (cited above)
10. 'Goddys seyntys schul be'
11. 'Ryȝtful men schul have'
12. 'Ryȝthful men schul be'
13. 'Every ryȝtfulle man & woman may have & schul have'
14. 'Godes frendys schul have'.

There are two apparent exceptions to the practice of failing to mark the start of paragraph subjects with a paraph. The first is an illusion. On f.230^{r} '¶ Ryȝtful men schul have longe abydynge in here blisse' begins with a paraph ostensibly marking a paragraph. In fact, it follows omission of an 'expansion' (ME n.331): the scribe clearly thought it was an expansion that he was marking with the paraph, as he usually does. On f.230^{v} a new paragraph subject is indeed marked – by two paraphs separated by a line-ending: '¶/¶ Goddys seyntys schul be acordynge to gadere in perpetual pes.' This is difficult to explain, unless the scribe referred back to the start of the previous paragraph, 'Godes frendys schul have ful hyȝe frendeschippe & love bitwene eche other', and finding that statement similar to 'Goddys seyntys schul be acordynge to gadere in perpetual pes' momentarily thought of the latter as a expansion, not as the start of a paragraph subject. Alternatively, this might be a relic of the exemplar's layout.

7.C.f. Scribes and Correctors of ME

i) Scribal Eyeskip in ME

The scribe of ME worked from a Middle English exemplar, for some passages have been omitted as a result of eyeskip between Middle English words, where there is no possibility of it in the Latin. These omissions are therefore scribal, not authorial (though scribe and translator may, of course, have been one person). On f.218^{r} a passage, later inserted, was omitted by eyeskip from 'thedirward' (ME n.171). On f.222^{r}, as already mentioned, one was omitted by eyeskip from 'blisse' (ME n.217). The omission on f.225^{r} has already been explained as more likely to be due to eyeskip in Middle English than in Latin (p.26). On f.230^{r} (ME nn.334, 335), the 'tilde line' required after 'blisse' is misplaced after 'lyve' as a result of eyeskip from 'but'. This evidence suggests that ME was copied for Lichfield MS 16, not translated for it.

The ambiguous evidence for and against there being any common ancestor for ME and AN below the lost Latin archetype is presented in section 7.E below.

ii) The Scribe's Hand and Practice

Differentiation between 'þ' and 'y' is poor: the dot over the latter is frequently absent. The scribe does not use flourishes. However, final 'g', except on one occasion where it ends a line and may be the work of Hand C, described below ('thyng' f.212^{v}/9), is usually written with a separate comma-like suspension mark following it. This may or may not indicate final 'e'. The full form ending in '-ge' appears once (but over erasure – f.217^{r}; ME n.153), so the ambiguous letter is always expanded to 'ge', to be on the safe side. The usual abbreviations are found. Where space is short, there is a suspended 's'. The abbreviation for '-ar/-er/-or' is sometimes the same (e.g f.208^{v} 'corpora' in the rubric). The paraph and *punctus* are common. Double *punctus* occurs once; *punctus elevatus* occurs only in the Recapitulation, where with one exception (explained by error, see ME n.321) it precedes the distinctive decorative lines which are also a form of punctuation. There are no question-marks, though there are many interrogative constructions. Once (f.215^{v}/8, at the end of the line beginning §10, 'Igitur consideratis & breviter insinuatis & cetera') the rubricator makes what is presumably a *nota*, resembling a division-sign with two horizontal strokes. Small gaps at line endings are sometimes filled by a light double stroke, indistinguishable from the scribe's end-of-line hyphen.

iii) Hands B, C and D

Numerous corrections and insertions were made in the margin by Hand B – apparently before rubrication, for on f.223^{v} one was made and then erased before rubrication was carried out. They are in a small, cursive script that now, after systematic erasure, appears pale yellow – occasionally, fragments of this imperfectly erased ink are blackish. Before being erased, the corrections were usually executed in the text in book-hand, by someone whose work appears in the left-hand margin on f.221^{v} and the bottom margin on f.222^{r}.

Hand C is found in three areas: over erasure in the text (e.g. 'þat nothyng þere' f.225^{v}/–3); making small insertions in the text; and correcting larger omissions in the margins. In major insertions or corrections over erasure in the text, this hand uses an ink very similar to the scribe's; in small insertions the ink is greenish, suggesting more than one pass over the text. Hand C, which wrote the insertion at the foot of f.222^{r} and in the right-hand margin of f.224^{r}, is distinguished from that of the scribe in several marked ways: by a more condensed, upright script; by 'g' finished by a short horizontal stroke off the main element, not a flourish; by an 'h' with a smoothly curved final stroke; by the use of a 'sc' ligature; by a 'w' the upright strokes of which are straighter and taller than those made by the scribe; by a 'y' descender swung left then hooked right and so quite different from 'þ'. A fourth hand (Hand D) also appears in some marginal corrections. It is larger and rougher than any of the others.

The level of scribal error is markedly greater after f.223^{r}. The tight binding may conceal further erased corrections.

iv) Marginal Marks

From f.221^{r} to f.228^{v} small pencil X-type crosses occur occasionally in the margins. Their date is difficult to establish. Possibly they are modern and so should receive no mention. Their function is uncertain, but as they mark three lines which contain the words 'joysy' or 'joysynge' on f.227^{v} and f.228^{r}, and 'velyd' and 'velid' on f.223^{r}, they may mark unfamiliar words, and so indicate a hand later than any of the correctors'. (Uniquely, the word 'eyes' appears in the left-hand margin of f.229^{v}, annotating the text's 'yen').

7.D. Description of AN

7.D.a. Content of AN

AN occupies quires 30–31, ff.233^{r}–247^{v}.

7.D.b. Layout and Decoration of AN

The illuminated borders of the first page are described above (section 7.A.b). Rubrics, and the only Latin quotation in the whole of AN, often contain scribal errors (e.g. ff.235^{r}, 235^{v}, 246^{r} and corresponding notes; AN nn.50, 66, 323). The Latin rubrics have initial capitals decorated in blue. Latin words in the margin are in red. The first capitals of paragraphs in the manuscript are almost all decorated with gold leaf. Capitals are rubricated, the more important capitals within paragraphs being preceded by blue or red paraphs.

7.D.c. Date of AN

The dating of Anglo-Norman prose texts is notoriously difficult.

Neither external evidence nor palaeographical information is of much help in the case of AN, the work of fifteenth-century scribes copying a text apparently derived ultimately from an early twelfth-century Latin original. The *termini a quo* and *ad quem* thereby provided are of little use. Certain linguistic features, insofar as they *may* be authorial and not merely scribal, point to the fourteenth or fifteenth century: these include (perhaps) denasalization (cf. AN n.157), raising of post-tonic 'e' to 'i' (cf. AN nn.18, 270); instability of verb conjugations. The lexis of AN is so heavily latinized as to make any conclusion based on this element of the language quite impossible; and, indeed, the degree of contamination of the language as a whole by the Latin of the presumed original vitiates to a considerable extent any attempt to place it within the evolving traditions of Anglo-Norman. It seems hazardous to do more than suggest that the translation represented by AN belongs to the later (post-1300) period of Anglo-Norman.

7.D.d. Translator of AN

The language may be characterized as typical, in its orthographic vagaries, of later Anglo-Norman; any attempt to separate scribal from authorial features would be further complicated by the heavily latinized syntax and lexis of the AN. The translator was evidently an enthusiastic exponent of the literal method of translation.

7.D.e. Scribes and Annotators in AN

The text of AN is a reasonably careful copy, with some added correction, errors which are largely explicable, and only straightforward, conventional abbreviation. There may well be a change of scribe at f.241^{r} (cf. AN n.201), which coincides with a change of quire, but the two hands (if such they be) are in any case not dissimilar. Errors (or apparent errors) in the manuscript include omission of nasals (cf. AN nn.157, 216); repeated words (AN n.164); omission of letters or syllables (AN n.14); and a number of cases of eyeskip and errors in common with LL, perhaps of use in establishing the relationship between LL and AN (dealt with later: see section 7.E below). Most of the main omissions are corrected in the margin by a single hand (or closely similar hands, cf. AN nn.345, 353), and have been incorporated into our text. More serious errors, which may be the fault of AN or may go back to its exemplar, include some garbled passages (cf. AN nn.168, 257 – the latter with a parallel in LL); translation errors (e.g. AN n.278); and a number of misunderstandings which could be imputed to either scribe or author (e.g. AN n.17). An oddity in the manuscript up to f.240^{v} is a consistent use of '-onis' (with a stroke over the 'i') for ind. pr. 4 verbal forms: this we have printed as '-oms' (cf. AN n.18). AN, throughout, displays a carelessness when dealing with the limited amount of Latin contained in the text, which suggests a shaky knowledge of that language by the scribe or scribes and, in addition, reinforces the impression that AN derives from an Anglo-Norman exemplar (see section 7.E below).

7.E. TEXTUAL TRANSMISSION: LL, ME, AN

It is noteworthy, and unfortunate, that neither AN nor ME is complete: the former lacks the concluding three lines or so that would have been on its last (missing) folio, the latter lacks the explicit. The ME text ends half-way down the verso of a folio, and there is more than enough room at the bottom of the last folio of AN to allow a scribe to finish the text. Purely practical considerations of space do not therefore explain the unfinished nature of the two vernacular texts. *De quatuordecim partibus beatitudinis* is frequently encountered as an independent text,[120] and there is no reason to suppose that the scribes intended to append anything (for example, a further chapter) to it. The evidence concerning the relationship between the three texts in Lichfield MS 16, and their supposed transmission from any postulated exemplar or exemplars, is inconclusive and in some respects contradictory. Our principal findings may be summarized as follows.

7.E.a. Rubrics: LL, ME, AN

The rubrics in the three texts (not found in *DA*) differ, albeit in trivial ways (e.g. 'ipsorum' instead of 'eorum'), in the three versions.

7.E.b. AN in relation to LL

The closeness of AN to LL suggests that this vernacular version was made from a text very similar to that represented by LL. In both lexis and syntax, AN is heavily influenced by (and often calqued on) its Latin exemplar. There are certain errors which confirm the impression of a close relationship between LL and AN: 'locis' for 'jocis' (f.190^{r}) corresponding to 'lieus' for 'jeus' (f.233^{r}, AN n.9); 'quantum et male' (read 'quale') (f.193^{v}) translated by 'comme maveis' (f.243^{v},

AN n.257); 'locum leonum' (read 'lacum') (f.201^{r}) translated by 'lieu dez leons' (f.235^{v}, cf. AN n.75, LL n.33). The AN text, however, makes a surprising number of errors in dealing with the LL rubrics, viz. 'primi pars' for 'prima pars' (f.235^{r}); 'De volocitate' for 'De velocitate' (f.235^{v}); two errors in the rubric introducing the Recapitulation (f.246^{r}). In the only biblical quotation preserved in Latin in the AN text (f.241^{r}) 'minus' has been substituted for 'nimis' – a common palaeographical error. On several occasions, the last verb in the well-known quotation from I Cor. 2,9 ('nec oculus vidit, nec auris audivit, nec in cor hominis ascendit') is translated (f.234^{r}, twice on f.245^{v}) by various forms of 'descendre' rather than of the expected 'ascendre' (used in the first quotation of this passage, f.233^{r}). This evidence seems to suggest that the scribe of AN did not know very much Latin.

The error in AN which might most plausibly be explained by eyeskip in copying from an Anglo-Norman exemplar can, equally, be explained as the result of a similar process with a Latin text as the starting-point. The omission (f.246^{r}) of a passage from 'serront \my changez' to 'seront/ glorifier' could also have arisen from the same process occurring with the endings of the corresponding Latin verbs, 'inmutabuntur' – 'glorificabuntur', in a Latin exemplar.

7.E.c. ME in Relation to LL

Some errors in LL have no echo in ME: 'locis' for 'iocis' is not echoed (f.206^{r}, ME n.8); 'quartadicima' for 'quartadecima' is not echoed in ME's rubric (f.221^{r}, ME n.202).

In addition, some small variations between LL and ME suggest that ME's Latin exemplar bore abbreviations at some points where LL does not. On f.215^{r} (ME n.128), the opening words are 'Accedat et' in ME, 'Accedat igitur' in LL; on the other hand, on f.228^{r} (ME n.305), the translator twice read or saw 'et tibi' for 'et ibi', his exemplar no doubt bearing, unlike LL, the full form of 'et'. On f.208^{v} (ME n.49), ME's rubric ends with 'pertinens', LL's with 'pertinentis'; on f.210^{v} (ME n.78), ME's rubric ends with 'eorum', LL with 'ipsorum'; on f.219^{r} (ME n.177), the rubric begins in ME with 'De honore sanctorum que', and in LL with 'De honore sanctorum qui'.

7.E.d. Difficulties Shared by AN and ME

On a striking number of occasions, AN and ME concur in apparently encountering some difficulty in deciphering or perhaps in understanding the Latin. The appearance of corruption in corresponding places in ME and AN, where nothing is amiss in LL, may suggest derivation of the two vernacular texts from a common exemplar which was *not* LL. Difficulty seems to have been experienced by the translator(s) of both ME and AN in the following places, further documented in the notes:

LL (f.196v) 'Illi enim sicut ferrum ignitum quaque sui parte continet ignem sic in se voluptatem, mali vero sencient anxi[e]tatem. In bonis ...'; ME (f·230r, n.331) does not translate the sentence before 'In bonis', just possibly by eyeskip from 'Illi' to 'In', which would be possible if the minims of 'In' were malformed or part of a capital form; AN f.246v (AN n.345) has an omission, following another omission on the recto of the same folio (f.246r), corresponding to 'ignem ... sencient' inclusive. This, and the ME, could both be explained by eyeskip from 'continet' to 'sencient' in the archetype; the AN omission could also, of course, have arisen though copying from an AN exemplar ('contient' – 'sentirent');

LL (f.197r) 'nichil nobis contaret, eo quod tempus et etas illa iam pertransiret'; ME (f.216v) 'Withoute douȝt hit were no schame to us, in so muche that thilke tyme & thilke age had none undirstandynge'; AN (f.239v, AN n.168) has a lacuna;

LL (f.197v) 'Quod si dicat quis patrem aut parentes se amplius ceteris velle diligere, videat apud se quid dicat, et quia non bene sentit veraciter intelligat'; ME (f.217r–v): '& if hit so be. that eny man or woman that lyvyth nowe in eorthe sey that he wolle love his fadir & hir modir more than eny other, be he awhare of that opynyoun & undirstande that he felith not truly in that that he seyd \so/'; AN (f.239v): 'Qe si ascum die, plus outre soi vuille amer soun pere ou sez parentz devant autrez, lez lui regarder a lui mesmez qei il dist.'

LL (f·198r) 'Nam si unus oculus sursum vel deorsum ... conspectione'; ME (f.218r, n.171) has an omission by eyeskip ('thedirward' – 'þudyrward') which is supplied in the right-hand margin; AN (f.240v, n.191) has a confusion here ('et leg[e]res' for 'levaque').

7.E.e. Title-Pages: LL, ME, AN

The relationship between the three texts' title-pages has been described above (section 7.A.b): they appear to have been decorated in the same scriptorium, LL and ME certainly by the same hand.

7.E.f. Conclusion: Relationships between LL, ME AN

In the light of the above considerations, it seems, at this stage, futile to speculate further on the connections between the three versions now preserved in Lichfield MS 16. We have seen that they were meant to be available together (section 7.A.b), that they were meant to belong to the miscellany represented by Lichfield MS 16 (section 7.A.b), and that their textual transmission is indefinable beyond the observation that none is the source for any of the others, that the translators of the two vernacular texts were not the same, and that ME and AN probably had vernacular exemplars, the former, at least, being the original or close to it.

8. Editorial Procedure

The general practice adopted in the edition is described first and followed by any variations in the three individual texts.

8.a. General Editorial Procedure

Paragraph divisions and capitals in the manuscript have not, except in one area, been retained. Retention of them would have involved either printing three differently divided texts (with all the difficulty of cross-reference which that would create), or forcing two texts (ME and AN) to conform to the other (LL), thus creating a semblance of conformity between the three versions which the manuscript does not present. It seemed preferable to dispense with paragraph divisions altogether in the main body of the text. Instead, paragraph numbering has been introduced, with numbered paragraphs corresponding to the sub-divisions of the work, which in LL are marked by introductory illuminated capitals after the rubric. Paraphs in the manuscript are represented by the sign ¶. Capital letters following illuminated letters have been silently transcribed as lower-case, and proper nouns have been capitalized where necessary. Treatment of other changes of case differs in the three texts (see below).

The Recapitulation at the end of the text, has, however, been treated differently (see sections 7.A.b; 7.C.e.iv). Here, the paragraph divisions of LL have, where possible, been retained in all three texts, on the grounds that the archetype appears to have had an arrangement of the text (with corresponding paragraph divisions) which served to emphasize the series of oppositions between the blessed and the damned (*pulchri/fedi*, *liberi/clausi*, etc.). None of the three versions in Lichfield MS 16 preserves this arrangement perfectly, although LL comes close to it. For this part of the text, therefore, the AN and ME texts have been made to conform with LL's paragraphing.

Each of the three texts has been separately punctuated; where possible, however, the sentence division of the manuscript has been respected in each case.

Manuscript 'j' (which does not occur in LL) is transcribed as 'i', and 'v' as 'u' where they are vocalic; 'i' is transcribed 'j' (but not in LL), and 'u' as 'v' where they are consonantal. Expansions of abbreviated forms, indicated by underlining, follow the commonest unabbreviated form in the manuscript.

Interpolations (material not found in *DA*) are identified in our texts by being placed within angle brackets (< >).

Material inserted by a scribe or corrector is contained by oblique strokes (\ /). Contemporary corrections (which may be scribal) have been incorporated whenever they provide an obvious improvement on manuscript readings. All such modifications to the manuscript readings have, of course, also been indicated in the notes.

Biblical quotations are identified in notes only in LL, but are indicated by quotation-marks in all three texts. ME and AN carry cross-references to notes in LL which explain the meaning of LL as well as ME and AN.

Editorial alterations to the manuscript's readings are indicated by notes referring the reader to the rejected manuscript readings. Editorial additions are contained in square brackets ([ ]) and explained in the footnotes.

In all three texts, bold type indicates the main rubrics; in ME it also indicates the rubrication used in certain unusual features of layout in the Recapitulation, described below, in section 7.C.e.iv; in notes it indicates dictionary headwords. The enlargement and decoration of capital letters beginning paragraphs, and minor rubrication, such as paraphs and other capitals, are not indicated.

8.b. Editorial Procedure Specific to LL

In LL's sentence and word division and punctuation (as well as the solving of many minor editorial dilemmas), the edition by Southern and Schmitt has been gratefully followed. Our edition includes page-references to Southern and Schmitt in brackets. Notes warn of changes of case.

8.c. Editorial Procedure Specific to ME

In the Recapitulation, ME's curious ignoring of the main paragraph divisions makes the structure of the material particularly hard to apprehend. Though the main divisions suggested by logic and as indicated in LL are followed for the sake of clarity, it should not be forgotten that this absence of clarity may be among the evidence that ME does not derive from LL. On the other hand, certain marked design elements of ME in this section, which are intended to clarify the series of oppositions just described, are represented in the edition (see section 7.C.e.iv).

The scribe used double *punctus*, *punctus elevatus* and above all *punctus*, the latter correctly marking and controlling the translator's loose but usually lucid syntax. The manuscript sentence structure as indicated by a *punctus* followed by a paraph is followed. However, to interpret as modern sentences those clauses which begin with a capital letter after *punctus* without paraph would result in dozens of sentences beginning with words like 'And', 'For' and 'But'. In these circumstances, no new sentence has been begun, and the manuscript capital letter has been silently altered to lower case. The result is many sentences of inordinate length, which, however, accurately echo the uninterrupted movement which is often part of the meaning of the Middle English (as, for example, the single 'sentence' that forms most of §11, where the unbroken, interactive charity of the blessed is described). Question- and quotation-marks are editorial.

One unusual punctuation element of ME has necessarily been represented in the edition: the use of what we have called 'tilde' and 'reflection' lines as visual clarifications of the structure of the Recapitulation (see section 7.C.e.iv). The colouring of these, as of the names of the Blessednesses where rubrication of them was used to clarify the structure of the text, is indicated by emboldening.

Word division follows modern practice if the scribe offers any precedent for its doing so, even though his usual practice may be otherwise; for example, 'riȝtfulmen' is usually one word but appears as two on f.208^{v}/18: we use 'riȝtful men'; 'withoute' is usually two words but appears as one on f.220^{v}/12: we use 'withoute'; prefixes 'y/I/i' and 'a' are usually separated ('y greuyd' f.207^{r}/–6; 'I armyd' f.211^{r}/12; even 'i·sette' f.208^{r}/13, where in the manuscript the prefix is followed by a *punctus*; 'a whare' f.213^{r}/4; 'a fore' f.209^{r}/13–14, but precedents for joining them are in 'ywryte' f.208^{v}/–8; 'yclosyd' f.211^{v}/–6: we follow the latter practice. Where 'y' is the personal pronoun, it is transcribed 'I'.

It is assumed that nasal bars indicate omission of the nasal, but it is always possible that the nasal was written and the vowel omitted.[121] We have expanded to 'per' or 'par' in accordance with the scribe's practice where he offers precedent, and modern practice where he does not. Ampersand has been silently expanded to 'and' or 'et'.

Insertions within the text itself are so small and distorted that it is often impossible to identify their hand. However, some (e.g. f.228^{v}/2) are clearly made by the main marginal annotator (Hand C). Modifications and insertions made by contemporary correctors which have been incorporated in the text are left unattributed in the notes if their hand is uncertain.

8.d. Editorial Procedure Specific to AN

Punctuation and word division, whilst intended not to do violence to the original, are editorial. The printed text respects manuscript sentence division as far as possible, departures from this being indicated in the notes. Notes warn of changes of case.

Scribal usage with regard to abbreviation is predictably inconsistent, so that (e.g.) 'quant' when written in full has the unvelarized form, but 'taunt' and 'graunt' have the typically Anglo-Norman spelling. Anomalous unabbreviated forms, needless to say, have not been regularized.

The superscript nasal bar has normally been taken to indicate an omitted nasal consonant but, as is common, the bar is often over what may be not '-ou' but '-on', so that technically the expansion should be '-oun'. The nasal bar is also, again as is common, sometimes used to indicate additional omission of 'i' in '-ioun/-ioun'. In the case of '(si)com' with abbreviations (including nasal bar) over the 'o', we have transcribed as '(si)come' rather than '(si)comm'.[122] Manuscript 'q'' has been expanded to 'qe', since unabbreviated 'qe' is more than twice as frequent as unabbreviated 'que'. There is one occurrence of 'Donque' and one of 'Queconque', and none of either word in '-qe', so the forms with '-que' have been adopted for all compounds except 'illoeqe(s)', where the '-qe(s)' form is more frequent. The policy adopted in expanding abbreviations of the 'enyv'ez' type assumes the (at least intermittent) existence of the so-called svarabhaktic 'e'.[122] In unabbreviated forms of the verbs *aver*, *faire* and *saver*, the scribe in fact omits the vocalic glide more often than he indicates it. The policy adopted here can, however, be justified by analogy with his use of the same abbreviation in unambiguous cases such as 'divers', and because unabbreviated future forms ('-era', etc.) of verbs such as *enbeivre* include '-e-'. On the grounds that unabbreviated 'mesme' (5 occurrences) is more common in this text than 'mesmes' (4) with a singular pronoun, 'mesm'' has been expanded to 'mesme' when accompanied by a singular pronoun, and to 'mesmes' with a plural pronoun.

NOTES

1 *Heinrich Seuses Horologium Sapientiae: Erste kritische Ausgabe unter Benützung der Vorarbeiten von Dominikus Planzer OP*, ed. Pius Künzle, Spicilegium Friburgense, 23 (Fribourg, Schweiz: Universitätsverlag, 1977) 526–540.

2 Book 2 chapter 2 of the *Horologium* was popular in England in the fifteenth century, being translated three times into Middle English prose (Versions A, B and C, with MS Lichfield 16 the sole example of A), besides Hoccleve's *Ars Sciendi Mori (Lerne to Die)*. For the Hoccleve see *Manual*(2), Vol. 3, VIII [6]; for the versions A, B and C see *Manual*(2), Vol. 7, XX [221], under the heading 'To Kunne to Diȝe'. Elizabeth Westlake ('Learn to Live and Learn to Die: Heinrich Suso's *Scire mori* in Fifteenth-century England', Diss., Birmingham, UK, 1993) distinguishes between what she terms *To Kunne Deie* and 'the Lichfield translation of *Scire Mori*': her terminology is adopted here. Two of the three versions of the ME translation of *Scire Mori* appear to be related to the Middle English translation known as *Tretyse of Þe Sevene Poyntes of Trewe Love and Everlastynge Wisdom*, derived from the whole *Horologium* (*Manual*(2) Vol. 7, 2365, 2568 and Vol. 9, XXIII [80] 3125–27). There is no satisfactory published edition of any of the Middle English versions of *Scire mori*, but see Westlake 299-323. See also Roger Lovatt, 'Henry Suso and the Medieval Mystical Tradition in England', *The Medieval Mystical Tradition in England: Papers Read at Dartington Hall, July 1982*, ed. Marion Glasscoe (Exeter: Exeter UP, 1982) 47–62.

3 *Manual*(2), Vol. 7, 2268–2270 [18]. See also Stacy A. Waters, 'A History of *Prick of Conscience* Studies', *SN* 55 (1983): 147–51, and her '*The Prick of Conscience*: The Southern Recension, Book V', Diss. U of Edinburgh, 1976, where *The Prick of Conscience* in Lichfield MS 16 is described on pp.36–37 as her MS 3.13. She observes that Hand A is in a strong south-western dialect (Somerset/Gloucestershire or east Wiltshire), and Hand B shows a strong East Anglian underlay; her conjectural stemma is on p.62.

4 A summary of *DA* is in *Memorials of St Anselm*, ed. R. W. Southern and F. S. Schmitt, Auctores Britannici Medii Ævi, 1 (London: Oxford UP, 1969) 108, which offers an edition of the second recension, noting the readings of the first recension in the form of variants.

5 *S. Anselmi Cantuariensis Archiepiscopi opera omnia*, ed. F. S. Schmitt, Vol. 1 (Seckau: [n.p.], 1938; Edinburgh: Nelson, 1946) 117–122.

6 Avril Henry, 'Lichfield Cathedral MS 16: Its Illuminated Borders and Original Order', forthcoming in *Scriptorium* 48.1 (1994). See section 7.A.b below for a summary of the arguments for the proposed order.

7 *Memorials* 8; the text is on *Memorials* 37–104.

8 *Memorials* 31; the text is on *Memorials* 271–291.

9 *Memorials* 4.

10 *Memorials* 273.

11 *Memorials* 9–10.

12 *Memorials* 9–10.

13 The mention of Melodia in the *Proslogion* attracted the attention of Gilbert, who cryptically observes: '*Melodia* est un *hapax* chez Anselme, qui, de musique, ne connaît que *musicum* dans la lettre 146 (293,22). On rappelle que le *De musica* de saint Augustin est un vrai traité de mathématiques' (P. Gilbert, *Le Proslogion de S. Anselm: Silence de Dieu et joie de l'homme*, Analecta Gregoriana, 257 (Rome: Editrice Pontificia Universitate Gregoriana, Ser. Facultatis Philosophiae, A.14, 1990) 227; Gilbert's book carries a large and helpful bibliography). Gilbert seems to mean that this is the only example of the word *melodia* in Anselm's writings. The angelic music is analogous to the 'harmony' of the soul (see *MED s.v.* **melodie** 1(a), the fifth a 1398 quotation).

14 The order of Joys of the Body in *Proslogion* and §19 of LL and AN is the same in ME §19 when one reads the latter's '**diuturnitas** If longe and hole life dely3te the, ther is everelastynge life & helthe' as equivalent to 'longa [et] salubris vita'.

15 *Proslogion*'s separated *sacietas* and *ebrietas* appear only in ME §9 as 'Sacietas, ebrietas', as if synonymous – and they are treated as one: 'Sacietas, ebrietas If thou desirist, or they þat schul be in hevyn desyrith, to have replecion of eny manere thynge ...'.

16 *Memorials* 9 n.1, which refers us to the *DA* text on their pages 137–139.

17 *A Catalogue of the Manuscripts Preserved in the University of Cambridge*, Vol. 2 (Cambridge: Cambridge UP, 1857; repr. Munich: Krause-Thomson, and Hildesheim: Georg Olms, 1980) 476.

18 These three are listed in *Incipits of Latin Works on the Virtues and Vices, 1100–1500 A.D.*, ed. Morton W. Bloomfield, Bertrand-Georges Guyot, Donald R. Howard and Thyra B. Kabealo (Cambridge, Mass.: Medieval Academy of America, 1979).

19 These two are listed in B. Hauréau, *Initia operum scriptorum latinorum* (photographic reproduction of handwritten list in Paris, Bibliothèque Nationale, nouvelles acquisitions françaises 2400), but the reference to the Rouen manuscript appears not to correspond to anything in the catalogue of the Bibliothèque municipale.

20 A. Wilmart, *Bibliothecae Vaticanae Codices Reginenses Latini*, 3 vols (Rome: Vatican, 1945) 2:37.

21 See P. Jolliffe, 'Middle English Translations of *De exterioris et interioris hominis compositione*', *MS* 36 (1974): 259–277; Roger Ellis, 'The Choices of the Translator in the Late Middle English Period', *The Medieval Mystical Tradition in England*, ed. Marion Glasscoe (Exeter: Exeter UP, 1982) 18–46; Phyllis Hodgson, '*A Ladder of Foure Ronges by the Whiche Men Mowe Wele Clyme to Heaven*: A Study of the Prose Style of a Middle English Translation', *MLR* 44 (1949): 465–475; *Medieval Translators and Their Craft*, ed. Jeanette Beer, Studies in Medieval Culture, 25 (Kalamazoo: Western Michigan U, 1989) includes six studies of translations into French; *The Medieval Translator: The Theory and Practice of Translation in the Middle Ages*, ed. Roger Ellis *et al.* (Cambridge: Cambridge UP, 1989); *The Medieval Translator II*, ed. Roger Ellis, Westfield Publications in Medieval Studies, 5 (London: Centre for Medieval Studies, Queen Mary and Westfield College, 1991).

22 See *The Middle English* Weye of Paradys *& the Middle French* Voie de Paradis*: A Parallel-text Edition*, ed. F. N. M. Diekstra (Leiden: E. J. Brill, 1991), p.435, n. to F 247,7, for Middle English translations of Anselm's Second Meditation.

23 See *Le* Cur Deus homo *d'Anselme de Cantorbéry et le* De arrha animae *d'Hugues de Saint Victor traduits pour Philippe le Bon*, ed. R. Bultot and G. Hasenohr, Publications de l'Institut d'études médiévales, 2.vi, (Louvain-la-Neuve: Université de Louvain-la-Neuve, 1984), and G. Hasenohr, 'La littérature religieuse', *GRLMA* 8.i (Heidelberg: C. Winter, 1988) 270.

24 See also Giles Constable, 'The Popularity of Twelfth-Century Spiritual Writers in the Late Middle Ages', *Renaissance Studies in Honor of Hans Baron*, ed. A. Molho and J. A. Tedeschi (Florence, 1971) 3–28.

25 For a general survey, see Wolfgang Riehle, *The Middle English Mystics*, trans. Bernard Standring (London: Routledge & Kegan Paul, 1981, first published 1977 as *Studien zur englischen Mystik des Mittelalters unter besonderer Berücksichtigung ihrer Metaphorik*) chapter I: 'The Public for Mystical Literature in England', pp.13–23.

26 *The Prick of Conscience* heads the Brown–Robbins table of 'Preservation of Texts', where it is closely followed by *The Canterbury Tales* and *Piers Plowman* (Carleton Brown and Rossell Hope Robbins, *Index of Middle English Verse* (New York: Columbia UP for the Index Society, 1943) 737); see also Rossell Hope Robbins and J. L. Cutler, *Supplement to the Index of Middle English Verse* (Lexington: U of Kentucky Press, 1965) 521, where the number of manuscripts is modified to 117. The poem's importance in the fourteenth century is also indicated by the fact that it is also one of the few texts in the Vernon manuscript to be singled out by illumination: a historiated capital thorn holds a 'Throne of Grace' (see the coloured facsimile in *The Vernon Manuscript* p.xv). Part of *The Prick of Conscience* was chosen also for inclusion in the great miscellany which is the Thornton manuscript (Lincoln Cathedral, 91).

27 See n. 2 above for Elizabeth Westlake's thesis on *Scire mori* in fifteenth-century England.

28 R. E. Lewis and A. McIntosh, *A Descriptive Guide to the Manuscripts of the* Prick of Conscience, Medium Ævum Monographs, ns 12 (Oxford: Society for the Study of Mediæval Languages and Literature, 1982).

29 *The Prick of Conscience (Stimulus Conscientiae): A Northumbrian Poem by Richard Rolle de Hampole*, ed. R. Morris (Berlin: Philological Society, 1863). See also Waters.

30 See n.2 above.

31 Gillespie 309, referring to Lewis and McIntosh 42, 43, 56, 62, 81, 85.

32 See n.6 above for an article presenting the evidence for its intended position and function in the manuscript.

33 Emily Hope Allen, *Writings Ascribed to Richard Rolle, Hermit of Hampole*, MLA Monograph ser., 3 (New York: Oxford UP, 1927) 347.

34 Allen 316.

35 Allen 10 and 349.

36 A. I. Doyle, 'A Survey of the Origins and Circulation of Theological Writings in England in the Fourteenth and Fifteenth Centuries', Diss. U of Cambridge 1954: 1.220.

37 Doyle 1.212. Lovatt 51–52 suggests 1375 or earlier, and gives an account of the very varied readership of the *Horologium*.

38 See n.2 above.

39 Doyle 1.217.

40 Elizabeth Westlake, information orally communicated.

41 *Memorials* 11–12.

42 *Manual*(2), Vol. 7, 2361, 2362.

43 *Manual*(2), Vol. 7, 2370.

44 *Manual*(2), Vol. 7, 2360.

45 *Manual*(2), Vol. 7, 2364.

46 *The Prick of Conscience* pp.212–220, the joys of the body and soul beginning at lines 7875 and 8181 respectively.

47 *Manual*(2), Vol. 7, 2268; for texts it directly influenced, see 2309, 2331 2333, 2336.

48 G. R. Evans, 'Sententia ad aedificationem: The *Dicta* of St Anselm and St Bernard', *Revue Bénédictine* 92 (1982): 167.

49 *S. Anselmi Cantuarensis Archiepiscopi opera omnia* 1:140–141.

50 See n.6 above.

51 Lewis and McIntosh 136, and Map 2; see also Waters (1976), cited in n.3 avove.

52 Elizabeth Westlake, information orally communicated. In her thesis (295) Dr Westlake observes: 'one may speculate whether the extensive involvement of Edward Seymour, First Duke of Somerset, in the dissolution of the monasteries may have provided the opportunity for the acquisition of such a manuscript ... He acquired monastic lands in Somerset and Gloucester, including Histon and Glastonbury, as well as a large number of less well-known foundations.' See *Seymour Papers 1532–1686*, ed. Marjorie Blatcher, Historical Manu-

scripts Commission, vol. 4 of *Calendar of the Manuscripts of the Marquis of Bath* [here called *Report of the Manuscripts of the Most Honourable the Marquess of Bath, Preserved at Longleat*], 5 vols (London: HMSO 1904–1980). Dr Westlake also lists religious houses in the area which once owned texts related to those in Lichfield MS 16: for example, Glastonbury; Llantony Priory II, Gloucestershire; Hereford Cathedral; Gloucester Abbey and Hayles Abbey (which, according to T. W. Williams, 'Gloucestershire Medieval Libraries. *Transactions of the Bristol and Gloucester Archaeological Society* 32–32 (1908–1909): 137, possessed early manuscripts of *De quatuordecim partibus beatitudinis*). In addition, Dr Kathleen Scott has written in a private letter that she senses a western flavour in the illuminated borders of Lichfield MS 16 (which bear, incidentally, a very general resemblance to those in Hereford Cathedral O.VII.i – the 'Cider' Bible *c.* 1420, whose provenance, however, has yet to be established).

53 See section 7.B.d below for further details of this annotator.

54 Giles Constable, *Twelfth-Century Spirituality and the Late Middle Ages*, Medieval and Renaissance Studies, 5 (Chapel Hill, NC, 1971) 27–60, reprinted with the original pagination in his *Religious Life and Thought (11th–12th Centuries)* (London: Variorum Reprint, 1979). The audience of the text currently first in the manuscript, *Scire mori*, is known to have been wide, and may give us a sense of the audience for the whole. Doyle has shown that the manuscript tradition of the translation of *Scire mori* known as *Tretyse of Þe Sevene Poyntes of Trewe Love and Everlastynge Wisdom* reveals a readership among both religious and lay persons, although he refers to Lichfield MS 16 and its unique rendering of *Scire mori* as 'presumably also of ecclesiastical ownership'. *Scire mori* was also translated by Hoccleve as a 'tretise of death' and included in a volume made for the Countess of Westmorland, and in a volume later bound with a small collection for a middle-class fifteenth-century family (Doyle 1.219).

55 Vincent Gillespie, 'Vernacular Books of Religion', *Book Production and Publishing in Britain 1375–1475*, ed. Jeremy Griffiths and Derek Pearsall, Cambridge Studies in Publishing and Printing History (Cambridge: Cambridge UP, 1989) 317.

56 T. H. Bestul, 'St Augustine and the *Orationes sive Meditationes* of St. Anselm', *Anselm Studies* 2 (1988): 597.

57 See, for example, Benedicta Ward, 'Inward Feeling and Deep Thinking: The Prayers and Meditations of St Anselm Revisited', *Anselm Studies* 1 (1983): 178–81; Evans 169 refers to Anselm as a 'speculative theologian'.

58 *The Prayers and Meditations of Anselm*, trans. Benedicta Ward (Harmondsworth: Penguin, 1973) 72.

59 Our texts resemble the *Proslogion* more closely than the Meditation, where in the list of Joys of the Body *ebrietas* and *melodia* are transposed.

60 Ward (1983) 181.

61 E. Ph. Goldschmidt, *Medieval Texts and their First Appearance in Print*, Supplement to the Bibliographical Society's Transactions, 16 (London: Oxford UP for the Bibliographical Society, 1943) 51.

62 See, for example, Margery M. Morgan, '*A Talking of the Love of God* and the

Continuity of Stylistic Tradition in Middle English Prose Meditations', *RES* n.s. 3 (1952): 97–116.

63 N. F. Blake, 'Middle English Prose and its Audience', *Anglia* 90 (1972): 437–455.

64 M. G. Sargent, 'Minor Devotional Writings', *Middle English Prose: A Critical Guide to Major Authors and Genres*, ed. A. S. G. Edwards (New Brunswick, NJ: Rutgers UP, 1984) 147–75; the quotation is on p.148.

65 P. Jolliffe, *Check-List of Middle English Prose Writings of Spiritual Guidance* (Toronto: Pontifical Institute of Mediaeval Studies, 1974) H22.

66 Sargent 150.

67 Eric Colledge, *The Medieval Mystics of England* (London: John Murray, 1962) 23.

68 Oxford, Bodleian Library, Eng.poet.a.1 (the Vernon manuscript) f.386v; Mary Baldwin, 'Some Difficult Words in the *Ancrene Riwle*', *MS* 38 (1976): 270 – both cited in *The Book of the Showings to the Anchoress Julian of Norwich*, 2 parts, ed. Edmund Colledge and James Walsh, Studies and Texts, 35, Part II *The Long Text* (Toronto: Pontifical Institute of Mediaeval Studies, 1978) 491.

69 For a survey of work on the English mystics, see V. Lagorio and R. Bradley, *The Fourteenth-Century English Mystics: A Comprehensive Annotated Bibliography* (New York: Garland, 1981).

70 Ed. M. Salvine Westra (The Hague: M. Nijhoff, 1950).

71 Ward (1983) 177. The quasi-mystical texts are a free version of *On Wel Swuthe God Ureisun of God Almihti* and *The Wohunge of Ure Lauerd*, both in *Þe Wohunge of Ure Lauerd*, ed. W. Meredith Thompson, EETS os 241 (London: Oxford UP for EETS, 1958). Like our text, *A Talkynge of the Loue of God* is found in a medieval miscellany – this time in the great Vernon manuscript (q.v.).

72 Ward (1983) 177–178, citing the *Meditation by St Anselm* ('Here is a good meditation which Saint Anselm made') *Yorkshire Writers* 2:443–445; see also Allen 347.

73 Ward (1983) 182: the earlier analysis of *A Talkynge of the Loue of God* is on pp.178–181.

74 *The Book of the Showings* 491; Ward (1983) 177–178. It has been said that 'her theology, in her description of the Son–Servant who is at once Adam the gardener and the Redeemer, is that of Anselm and Hilton' (Colledge (1962) 87).

75 *The Book of the Showings*, 604; see Benedicta Ward 'Faith Seeking Understanding: Anselm of Canterbury and Julian of Norwich', *Julian of Norwich* (Oxford: SLG Press, 1973) 6–38, and C. W. Bynum, *Jesus as Mother: Studies in the Spirituality of the High Middle Ages*, Publications of the Center for Medieval and Renaissance Studies UCLA, 16 (London: U of California Press, 1982, repr. 1984).

76 Colledge (1962) 23, 34, 88.

77 Categories 1 and 3 in Norman Blake, 'Varieties of Middle English Prose',

Chaucer and Middle English Studies, ed. Beryl Rowland (London: Allen & Unwin, 1974) 348–356.

78 For example, Arthur R. Lee, 'Anselm and Thomas of Buckingham: An Examination of the *Quaestiones super sententias*', *Anselm Studies* 1 (1983): 237–249, traces the influence of thirteen Anselm works, including *Proslogion*, on *Quæstiones super sententias*, written between 1335 and 1343 by Thomas of Buckingham, Chancellor of Exeter Cathedral; Vernon J. Bourke, 'A Millennium of Christian Platonism: Augustine, Anselm and Ficino', *Anselm Studies* 2 (1988): 527–557, describes Anselm as a 'theocentric Platonist' (536), and summarizes his position on reality, psychology, cognition and morality, concluding that throughout the millennium Platonic philosophy as represented by these three thinkers exerted a considerable influence. Anselm's works were printed in Nuremberg as early as 1491. The second edition was Basel 1497, and the third Strasbourg after 1496 (Goldschmidt 122–123).

79 The version is 'of metropolitan provenance': *Manual*(2), Vol. 7, 2374–2375.

80 'Sawles Warde', *The Katherine Group: Edited from MS Bodley 34*, ed. S. T. R. O. d'Ardenne, Bibliothèque de la Faculté de Philosophie et Lettres, Fasc. 215 (Paris: Société d'Edition 'Les Belles Lettres', 1977) 165–185.

81 *Manual*(2), Vol. 7, 2296.

82 *Manual*(2), Vol. 7, 2376.

83 *Manual*(2), Vol. 7, 2346.

84 *Old English Homilies and Homiletic Treatises (Sawles Warde, and Þe Wohunge of Ure Lauerd: Ureisuns of Ur Louerd and of Ure Lefdi, &c). of the Thirteenth and Fourteenth Centuries*, 1st Series, Parts 1–2, EETS os 29 and 34 (London: Oxford UP for EETS, 1867–1868, repr. New York: Greenwood, 1969) 230–241.

85 Robbins and Cutler no. 3938.

86 *Manual*(2), Vol. 7, 2269.

87 *Manual*(1), Vol. 8, 274, 285, 520. This information may, of course, be revised in the forthcoming mystics volume of the revised *Manual*.

88 'Sermo de conceptione Beatae Mariae Virginis', *PL* CLIX 319–324.

89 *Cursor Mundi (The Cursur o the World): A Northumbrian Poem of the 14th Century in Four Versions, Two of them Midland*, ed. Richard Morris, Part 5, EETS os 68 (London: Oxford UP for EETS, 1878) 1416.

90 *Manual*(2), Vol. 2, 431, 451.

91 See, for example, the poems in *The Anglo-Norman Lyric: An Anthology*, ed. David L. Jeffrey and Brian J. Levy (Toronto: Pontifical Institute of Mediaeval Studies, 1990).

92 Riehle 13–15.

93 See the regulations, in French, for the priories of Polsloe (1319) and Canonsleigh (1314) in *The Register of Walter de Stapeldon, Bishop of Exeter (A.D. 1307–1326)*, ed. F. C. Hingeston-Randolph (London and Exeter, 1892) 316–318 and 95–96. We are indebted to Professor Christopher Holdsworth for drawing our attention to these regulations, and indeed to the important, and

neglected, information on the use of French in ecclesiastical circles which the Exeter bishops' registers contain.

94 N. Ker, *Medieval Manuscripts in British Libraries*, Vol. 3 (Oxford: Clarendon Press, 1983) 116–117; B. S. Benedikz, *Lichfield Cathedral Library: A Catalogue of the Cathedral Library Manuscripts*, 3rd ed. (Birmingham: Birmingham U Library, 1986) under the entry for Lichfield MS 16.

95 See n.6 above.

96 Ker assigns the hands to the early fifteenth century, but Dr Ian Doyle has suggested orally that the hand of LL is late fourteenth-century, the annotator's being early fifteenth-century.

97 Letter to the author, 6.10.1991. We are most grateful to Dr Scott for her habitual generosity in sharing her expertise to confirm, from colour prints sent to her, our interpretation of the dates and hands of borders in AN, ME, LL. The opinions expressed with regard to the three others are ours.

98 Kathleen Scott, 'Design, Decoration and Illustration', Griffiths and Pearsall 49.

99 AN, however, which unlike ME does not retain sections' opening Latin sentences, naturally has no equivalent on f.239^r for the large illuminated initial of 'Igitur' which at the beginning of §10, *De sapiencia*, extends for 12 lines outside the margin on ME f.215^v and on LL f.204^v.

100 Ker (116–117) seems to have missed this (and the interpolations). The misbinding is, however, remarked on, though not accounted for, by Benedikz.

101 L. C. Hector, *The Handwriting of English Documents*, 2nd ed. (London: Edward Arnold, 1966) 44–45; P. A. Grun, *Leseschlüssel zu unserer alten Schrift* (Görlitz: Starte, 1935), Tables X–XI.

102 Lichfield Cathedral Library, 60: 'A Catalogue of her Grace þe Dutchesse of Somersett's Great Library Taken August MDCLXXI', on the unpaginated page that would be p.123, describes Lichfield MS 16 briefly (under the shelfmark F.1.18). The implications of the description are discussed in the article mentioned in n.6 above. See also n.52 above.

103 *Memorials* 127–141.

104 *DA* 26.

105 *S. Anselmi Cantuariensis Archiepiscopi opera omnia* 1:117–122.

106 'Meditation 21', *PL*, CLVIII, 817C–820B.

107 *Auteurs spirituels et textes dévots du moyen âge: Études d'histoire littéraire* (Paris: Bloud & Gay, 1932) 199.

108 See Wilmart, introduction to Dom A. Castel, *Méditations et prières de saint Anselme* (Maredsous: Abbaye de Maredsous, 1923) xlvii n.6.

109 See *A Concordance to the Works of Saint Anselm*, ed. G. R. Evans (Millwood, NY: Kraus, 1984).

110 The material in this paragraph is based on *Memorials* 19–30. A summary of *DA* is in *Memorials* 108, which offer an edition of the second recension, noting the readings of the first recension in the critical apparatus.

111 *Memorials* 27–28, 15.

112 The evidence (*Memorials* 20) relies on interpretation of medieval authorial modesty and use of the first and third persons. The preface of *DA* shows one writer to be responsible for both it and the following *De miraculis*, but the writer of the latter could be neither the 'frater quidam nomine Baldewinus, vir strenuus et bene circumspectus, haec quae dico narrare consuevit' mentioned at the start of *De miraculis* chapter 37 (*Memorials* 234), nor the man mentioned at the start of *De miraculis* chapter 35: 'Vir quidam boni testimonii, Eustachius nomine, quem multi nostrorum veridici sermonis magnaeque eloquentiae fuisse noverunt, beatae memoriae Anselmo archiepiscopo me audient narravit quae dico' (*Memorials* 227). That the writer is Alexander, not Eadmer, is suggested by two of the miracle stories, the second recension of which describes Alexander as Anselm's sole companion, while the first recension is written by this companion in the first person.

113 *Memorials* 20.

114 Evans (1982) 160, which draws on and develops R. W. Southern, *Saint Anselm and His Biographer: A Study of Monastic Life and Thought* (Cambridge: Cambridge UP, 1963), and *Memorials*.

115 Evans (1982) 163.

116 The dates were generously confirmed by Dr Malcolm Parkes.

117 Westlake 125–126.

118 To avoid cumbersome reference to both sexes, translator and scribe are referred to throughout as male, though either or both might have been female.

119 There is an interesting area here for research. In spite of claims like that made by William Flete in his *Remedies Against Temptations*: 'quan I speke of man in þis wrytinge, take it boþe for man and woman, for so it is ment in alle suche writinges, for al is mankende' (cited by Riehle 16), more than one medieval writer is careful to make the inclusion of women explicit. Another case is found in *La Voie de Paradis* as opposed to the Middle English *Weye of Paradys* (q.v.): its prologue, preserved in the French only, suggests (§3) that the anonymous translator envisaged a public which might well contain the uneducated (those who are 'poy de la Sainte Escriture letrés') as well as 'grans clers' (§4). The French text is frequently concerned to address both men and women, the English text men only (see, for example, §§7.14, 80.1, 83.1, 155.4, 190.1, 215.4, 258.8, 260.1, 262.1, etc.). There is no compelling linguistic reason for the semi-systematic mention of 'honme et fame' in French: it is not just a stylistic quirk, since the indefinite pronoun *on* (or *en*) is often used instead (e.g. §§96.1, 240.1). We must assume that the French *Voie de Paradis* had in mind mixed audiences, or (perhaps) use in female as well as male religious communities.

120 *DA* 27–28.

121 This is the case, for example, in Cambridge University Library, Ff.5.30 (see *The Pilgrimage of the Lyfe of the Manhode*, ed. Avril Henry, Vol. 1, EETS os 288 (London: Oxford UP for EETS, 1985) xci).

122 See *AND*, *s.vv.* **cum** (126b) and **sicum** (709a) for forms attested elsewhere.

123 Cf. Mildred K. Pope, *From Latin to Modern French, with Especial Consideration of Anglo-Norman* (Manchester: Manchester UP, 1934) §§1173, 1290.

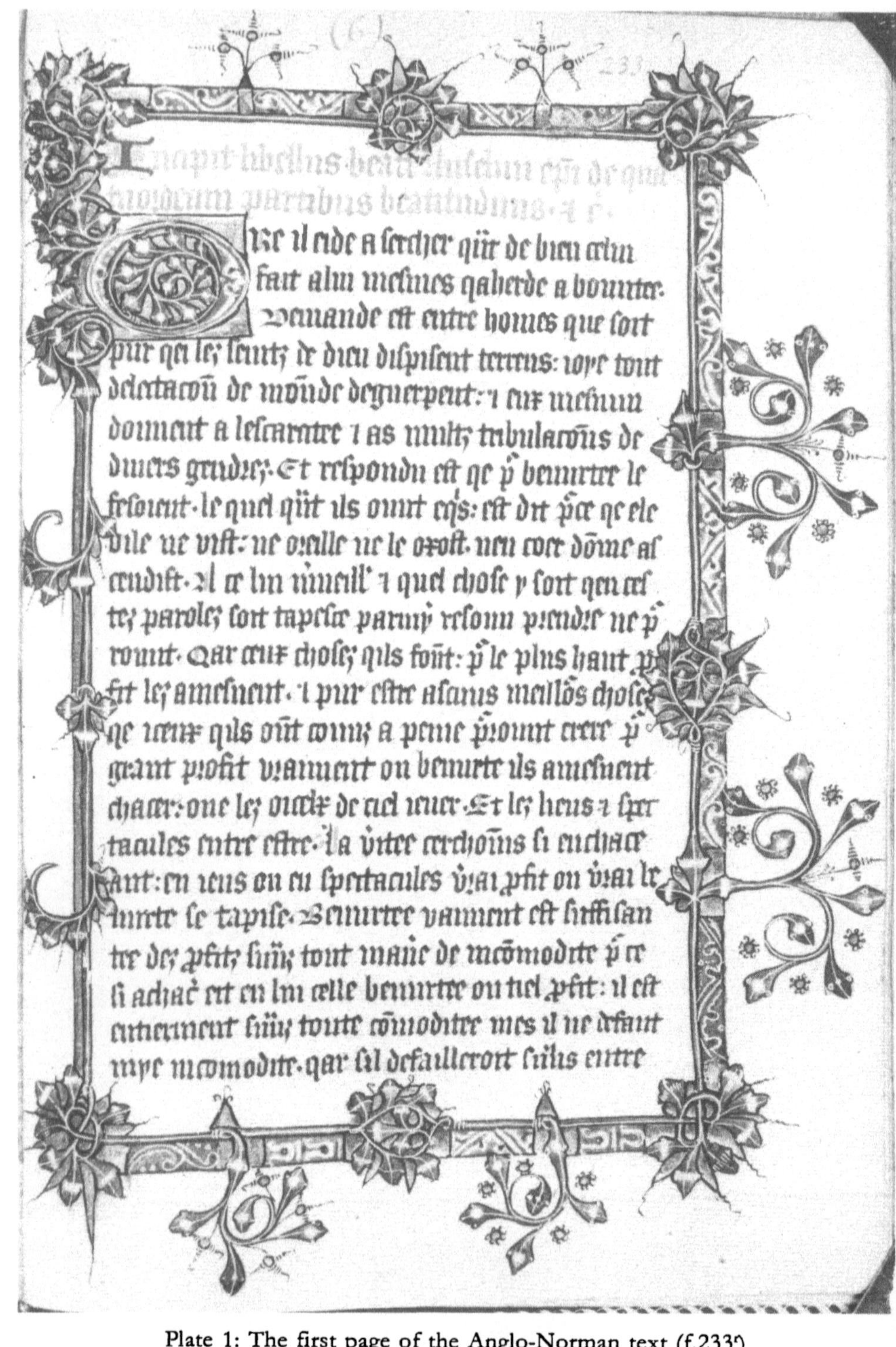

Plate 1: The first page of the Anglo-Norman text (f.233r)
(Reduced)

DE QUATUORDECIM PARTIBUS BEATITUDINIS: THE ANGLO-NORMAN

[f.233r]

1 **<Incipit libellus beati Anselmi episcopi de quatuordecim partibus beatitudinis etc.>**
Ore[1] il eide a sercher quant[2] de bien celui fait a lui mesmes q'aherde a bountee. Demandé est entre homes que soit pur qei lez seintz de Dieu dispisent terrens, joye [et] tout delectacioun de mounde deguerpent, et eux mesmes[3] donnent a l'escarcitee[4] et as multz tribulaciouns de divers gendrez. Et respondu est qe pur benurtee le fesoient, le quel quant ils ount e[n]quis, est dit pur ce qe ele 'oile ne vist, ne oreille ne le oÿst,[5] n'en coer d'omme ascendist'. A celui merveille; et quel chose y soit q'en cestez parolez soit tapescé,[6] parmy resoun prendre ne purrount. Qar ceux chosez q'ils fount, pur le plus haut profit lez amesnent, et pur estre ascuns meillours chosez qe iceux q'ils ount conuz, a peine purrount crere; pur grant profit vraiment ou benurté ils amesnent chacer, ové[7] lez oicelx de ciel jeuer, et[8] lez jeus[9] et spectacules[10] entreestre.[11] La veritee cerchonms, si en chaceant, en jeus ou en spectacules verrai profit ou verrai benurté se tapise. Benurtee v[r]aiment est suffisantee[12] dez profitz saunz tout manere de incommodité;[13] pur ce, si a chacer eit en lui celle benurtee ou tiel profit, il est entierment saunz toute [in]commoditee,[14] mes il ne defaut mye incomodité, qar s'il defailleroit sauns entre[f.233v]mettre,[15] chescun purroit chacer: pur [ce] noun est cest profit ou benurté illoeqes. En semblable manere en jeu des oyselx n'est my trové cest benurtee, nient en chescun[16] spectacule. Et pur ce ou est il? Per aventure en grauntz edificac[i]ouns, en chastellez tresbien gardez, en or et argent, en chivalx et grauntz possessiounis; mes si soit en icestez, et qi cestez chosez a, beneit est ille. Donque de tout solitari,[17] charge et travaille il est delivré, et certes nous veoms[18] qe ceux qi icestez ount, sount grevés ové greindre cure, solitarie et labour: non aussi en icestez est vrai profit ou benurtee. Et pur ce en ces chosez vrai profit ou benurtee n'est point. Et pur ce ou la cercheroms? Aillours cerchoms se trover la vuilloms, qar en cestez ne le purroms. A notefier[19] est deux estre benurtees et deux cheitiftees. Une benurtee est quel Adam avoit en

parais et la perdist, l'autre en ciel quel ount les angelis et les seintz quex Nostre Seignour a suspris.[20] Une cheitiftee est en terre quel nos toutzdiz suffroms; l'autre cheitiftee est en le puit d'enfren,[21] quel ceux perduz aprés la mort suffreront. Ceste benurtee quel Adam avoit en parais estoit temporel. Celui vraiment celestre, pur quel il est fait, perpetuel. Celui cheiftee[22] ou tri[f.234r]bulacion, quel nous suffroms en present, ad fin. Celui vraiment q'[en] enfern est, saunz fin est, et la quele 'mort' est appellé, pur quel est prié, ne le baptizee[23] eit 'la secounde mort'.

2 <Quod beatitudo proposita gracius sapiat si per partes lacius dirivatur.>

Pur ce cell' benurtee q'est promys as seyntz est taunt graunt et merveillous qe 'oile ele ne verra ne oreille orra, et en le coer d'omme ne descendra point'.[24] Cum ceste benurtee pur sa greindure[25] ne purrom veer. Consideroms que chose en ceste present vie nous naturelment delite: quel chose ce soit qe bon ou honeste soit veu,[26] si par aventure ascum chose soit trové, dount est celle merveilous q'est dit 'oile n'eit pas veu, n'orelle n'eit pas oye', apperge[27] [et] plus gracious savour[28] eit. Certes en trope poi dez paroles est compris tout cella q'est[29] as esluz promys. Et pur ce [qe] chose est ensi privé, ensi clos et multz dez almes maladez departez, nous environs[30] de si excellent joye [chose] extraire auquele soioms ententis, et ce en plusours parties ordeigner[31] en departant, parount il puisse vraiment le pluis lusant clarer[32] et confirmer. Posee[33] si un gros pomme soi[34] doné a un enfaunt a manger, par cause de trop tendretee[35] de soun petit bouche, il ne poit mye mordre; le[f.234v]quel si en parcelles soit trenché, l'enfaunt est en replez; et le quel pardevant il ne purroit mye entendre de quel sovour[36] il estoit, ore, par les gobetz[37] severalment ové le savour, il a mangé. Pur ce celle[38] invisible promission de Diu soit observez en tanque nous lui veioms, 'sicom il est': ententifment cerchoms qui[39] a nos corps, quei a nos almes, puet accorder; quel chose ils purront franchement s[a]unz offens affecter,[40] ou qe deliter; nous tenantz fermement, rien faillant a toutz iceulx d'onour ou d'ascum bountee qeux il aviendra d'estre en icelle benuretee. Pur ce sept chosez me semble etre qe sont ables[41] au corps et sont tresavenantz[42] et a benurtee suffisantz: et cestez chosez aussi sont beautee, vistesse, force, liberalitee,[43] sanitee, delite, repose; et a tantz en nombre de l'alme sont veus acorder, lez qeux en ceste nombre sont acompt[e]z: Sagesse, Amysté, Acorde, Honour, Poair, Seurtee, Joye. I n'est[44] poynt de doubte as esluz de Dieu en celle beneit roialme toutz iceux chosez pur avoir, puis qe Dieu eux enhabite et en eulx est resident. De qui est toute chose quel qe bon est, et puissant et glorious il est sur toutz chosez ineffablement.[45] Mes ore poi et poi realoms,[46] et en court raciuncle[47] ce que nous avoms dit, enviorons[48] a demonstrer, et comensantz as meindres en degré et[49] asscendantz as greindres.

3 <De pulchritudine [f.235r] sanctorum que est prima[50] pars beatitudinis ad corpora eorum pertinencis.>

Ici demaundez de beautee. Escotez q'est escript: 'lez droiturelx[51] serront lussantz com le solail'. Donque 'la lune lusera sicom le solail, et le solail sept foitz double sicom le lumer de sept jours'; pur ce si 'nos corps luserent[52] si com le solail' q'avera le lumer multeplié de sept jours, graunt et incomparablement[53] tresgraunt serra provez[54] cella. 'Et le Savour[55] attendoms Nostre Seignour Jhesu Crist qui reformera le corps de nostre humilitee, configuré al[56] corps de sa clertee.'[57] Certes quant Nostre Seignour en le montaigne est transfiguré devant sez disciples, 'resplendoit sa face sicom le solail'. Parmy la j[o]cunditee[58] de quel clertee, Petre fust delités et disoit: 'Seingnour, bon a nous est icy estre.' Et auxi 'le regarde' de l'angel qi seoit al sepulcre Nostre Seignour apparust 'sicom le foudre de ciel'. Et pur ce qe taunt de clertee icy fuist d'un angel, qe creiez vous come graunt, come glorious, la veant[59] serra quant millers dez angles et saunz nombre assemblez[60] al cleer corps Nostre Signour Jhesu Crist ov lui appareront? Cest benurtee et beneite beautee considera cil qe disoit, 'une chose du Signour j'ay demandé, celle je cerchera,[61] issint qe je demure en la meson du Signour'. De ceste beautee, que pur vrai[62] est graunt benurtee, plusuros[63] en seint escripture [f.235v] sont trovés. A cest beneit beauté nos avioms souzjoinez[64] la velocitee.[65]

4 <De velocitate[66] sanctorum que est secunda pars beatitudinis eorum etc.>

Vistessee[67] ataunt averont ceux qui ové Dieu serront, qant[68] a le ray del solail, ou l'oile d'ascum homme clerment veiant; le solail verament quant en l'orient vient sur la terre, tantos en l'occident son ray espande; en mesme le manere le ray de oille quant le surcille soit overee, en ciel ou en loigne est drescee, si nule obstacle ou ascum i soit qe le destourbe. Issint auxi quant nos corps serront espirituels et an manere dez angels nul charge ou grevance ne senterent; treslegerment[69] trespasserent en queconque lieu q'ils vuillent. Qar en resureccioun de[70] corps, toutz et chescun part de chescun homme ensemble serront unez, issint qe si la main eu le pee, ou ascum autre membre d'un homme ensemle, soit[71] en l'orient [enseveli], ou soit devorés dez bestes, et la remanant del corps en l'occident ou en le tombe giseit, ou en divers parties del mounde soit departies,[72] auxi tost tout le corps serra coillez ensemble si tost come l'oille serra clos ou overé. Babiloigne de Judé multez terres de loigne est assis et nientmeins[73] l'angel en un moment susporta[74] Abacuc de Juda en Babilon, lequel il metta desur le lieu dez leons,[75] qi bailla viande a Danyel; laquel chose [f.236r] fait, Abacuc tauntost estoit restitut en son lieu. Certein ille purroit amerveiller ou il fust, quant en soun propre lieu il soi trova si tost. Tiel auxi legertee ou agilitee[76] chescum homme avera, nientmeins icest beneit homme ne serra my content par cest soul felicitee.[77]

5 <De fortitudine sanctorum que est tercia pars beatitudinis eorum.>

Force ensiut,[78] quel chescun benuree a taunt avera quant cent mille hommes ensemble en cest present vie no[n] [a]verount,[79] qar la mesure de mesme dignité a tant serra, com cesti avera, qe ele a chosé.[80] Si tout la roundesse de tout la terre ov un dey vodroit mover, certes legerment le poet fere: unquore plus legerment purroit le deable, l'enemy de Diu, par force de sa nature mover l'eyer,[81] exciter lez ventz et tempestez, et ascum foiz fait la terre mover et plusours autrez merveillez assez; dount il est appellé 'fort armé'; et Dieu ne durra mye a sez esluz ou egal force ou, certein, mult greindre et meillour? Dieu defende cella qe ascum le sentirent, que ové sain teste chescun homme la saveroit. Vraiment Nostre Seignour fra 'la voluntee de ceux que lui dotent'. Asquex, com il est dit aillours, 'rien en ne faudra'. Si rien ne faille, ne force ne faudra mye; mes il aherdra[82] et nemy poi.

6 <De libertate sanctorum que est .iiij.[a] [f.236v] pars beatitudinis eorum etc.>

Vraiment pur ce qe ne force ne veloceté ne beauté de rien est prisee a lui qe n'est mye franke,[83] qar celle beneit multitude serra franc, ce n'est pas[84] doubte. Car nulle mater, nulle fu ou ew ou nulle autre mater qeqonque eux desto[r]bera,[85] q'ils ne entrent et isserent a qeconque lieu qe lour plerra entrer ou issir. Franchement Nostre Signour issit, le sepulcre estant closee.[86] Franchement il dispoilla enferne. Franchement 'lez portz overtz' a sez disciplez il entra. Franchement lez seintz de Dieu, s'ils vuillent, entrerent. Franchement par le fu et lez picz ardantz passerent. Franchement, quant ils vuillent, illoeqs demurent saunz blessure, qar de lour[87] en icelle flamme enfernelle[88] rien n'ardra forsque soulement pecchez. Et quant lez seintz de Dieu a tout ordure de pecché serront purgez par freidure et echalure,[89] par divers tormentis et estankes vaporantez,[90] ils passeront saunz blessure. Aux icelle tormentz ou la consideracioun de mesmez lez lieus serra en l'arbitriment[91] dez benurez, et al confusion dez reprovez;[92] a tant[93] serra lour libertee, quant[94] serra a avoir lour voluntee.

7 <De sanitate sanctorum que est quinta pars beatitudinis eorum pertinencis etc.>

[f.237r] Benoiez auxi sont les enfranchisez[95] et auxi franc benurtee, au quel le plus greable[96] sanitee serra comys; sanitee pur ce mult[97] serra, qar 'Dieu essura toutz lez lermes dez oilles dez seintz, et mort ne torment ne serra a eux d'illoqes en avaunt, ne clamour ne dolour, qar lez premers ils sount trespassez.' Qi bien considerer vodra, nulle sanitee en ce present sciecle[98] en nos est. Qar <en qeconque lieu nos eioms dolour en corps, si ascum[99] touche cele part un poi durement, pur dolour nos crioms. Issint auxi> en toutz autrez parties de nos membres, si ascum foiz plus durement nos soioms tocheez, tantost soioms[100] blessez: nos compleindronms. Et pur qoi cella, mes pur ce q'en chescun lieu fleblez[101] nos sumus[102] et maladez. Vraiment as esluz Nostre Seignour nulle blessure surveignir[103] purra, ne ferre ne fu ne ewe a eux noiera.[104] Nulle damage qe l'em a passé icy, chescun d'eaux q'illoeqs serra, rien ne purra noier,[105] qar atant[106] d'abundance de jocunditee illoeqs serra, qe de celle q'ore ils ount trespassez rien ne chargeront;[107] qar si cure a eux fusse de soi venger, a lour voluntee lieu averoient. Mes bosigne nul avera, qar le Seignour mesmes dist, 'A moi la vengeance, et je regardonraye.' De ce bien se abstenie[108] q'a Dieu plere desire, issint qe la vengeaunce de son tort [f.237v] a Crist baille.[109] Si vraiment lui mesmes vengeance preigne, il n'avera pas Diu vengeour[110] de mesme le tort, qar celle il a pris sur[111] lui presumptuousement;[112] a qi Nostre Signour dirra, 'Pur ce q'avoiez plus talent de toi venger qe moi attendre, ne moi enavaunt[113] de vengeance devez entrepeller.'[114] Bien a vous coveyne.[115] Si vraiment le conseil du Seignour eust[116] suy,[117] la venjaunce a suspendu, benuré il serra. Qar si nulle offence, nul serra a lui bosoign,[118] nu[l] fieblesse, mes sain[119] felicitee et tresbenuré[120] sanitee; toutes icestez chosez qe sount avaunt ditez, trop bons y sont, mes si sovour n'eient, sicom outrement saunz fruit i[121] sont. Si vraiment savour averoient, saunz doubte bouns incomparablement serroient.

8 <**De voluptate sanctorum que est sexta pars beatitudinis eorum.**>
Pur ce necessarie est delyt aherder, q'a celx benurés dorra sovour qe sont esluz ou beneiez, issint q'ils sachent et entendent 'combien amez' et jocundez[122] sount 'tabernacules'[123] Nostre Seignour, et coment 'un jour est meillour sur mylle jours en lez alleys[124] ou entrees de Jerusalem'; pur ce delectacioun serra plus graunt, et toutz gentz replera[125] en la tabul[126] de jocunditee. Le prophete crie: 'Tez mesons serront repleez[127] de plentevousté,[128] et del [f.238r] russel de ta delectacioun vous eux enbeverez, qar a toi est la fontaigne de vie.' Vraiment merveillous est celle reicin,[129] merveillous est celle meson. Sicom la rivere en descendant deffleue,[130] issint Diu toutpuissan nos emplera[131] ové sa merveilous douçour de sa mesoun. Et pur ce qe convenient[132] ensample de tant sweftee,[133] taunt de douçour et taunt de bounté trover ne purroms, consideroms le tresamer[134] dolour quel les reprovez averont, encountre le tresjocoundite[135] sweftee[136] quel avront lez prodez hommes; tresadecertes[137] qe, si ascum a moy ovesque un fer ardant enfoweroit[138] le purnelle de l'oille, graunt dolour j'avroy. Et si un autre ové semblale turment m'enficheroit, mult graunt dolour a moi serroit. Et si par toutz membris mesme la peine a moi serroit fait, mesme[139] tiendroit, quei creyez[140] vous serreit, ne qe je arrageray,[141] ne qe outrement hors de memoyre je serroi? En chescun part ardra, en [chescun] part la peyne constreindroit. Qe creiez vous? De quel memoire m'alme serroit? Issint auxi certein et plus large nous serons repleez ové la jocunditee de la face de Dieu. Auxi nos serroms replez del plentevoustee del meson de Nostre Seignoure. Nous serroms enyverez ou repleez del river ou [f.238v] russel de la delectacioun[142] ou de l'afectioun de Dieu mesmes; temporel delectacioun, passant[143] desire, en chescun partie du corps soulement est sentue:[144] vrément celle delitacioun[145] si com feu par tout est sentuz; ensiut[146] par toutez lez partiez du corps et alme serra senti; sicom tout le corps serroit en goule,[147] issint serra delit en icelle seintissme jocunditee. Si vraiment ils eient ma[l], maveis sount en toutz les parties de lour corps, qar bien faire ils ne vodront mye. Mult plus droiturelement lez bons bien avront en toutz lour membres, qar ils ount bien fait. Auxi lez seintz de Dieu avront ceste beneite delectacioun, la quel vraiment est delectable[148] et graunde benurtee. Mes poi est avoir iceste et autrez suisditz,

si non cella ovesque autrez saunz defaute ils purrount avoir.

9 **<De diuturnitate sanctorum que est .vij.[a] pars beatitudinis eorum.>**

Puur ce aveigne longe duree qe de nulle fin conu[149] la merke.[150] Ceste longeur nulle fin conust. Car la[151] beautee, la vistessee, la force, la libertee, la sanitee, la delectacioun dez seintz n'ad nulle fin. Celliu[152] q'ad iceux, ové lee[153] bouche purra chaunter 'Jerusalem, loiez toun Seignour, Syon loiez toun Dieux, qar il a conforté lez serures de tez[154] portez, il a benedit tez fez[155] en toy'; qar il sont benoiez [f.239r] qi ové tiel benecioun serront benoiez.

10 **<De sapiencia sanctorum que est .viij.[a] pars beatitudinis eorum ad animas pertinentis etc.>**

Pur ce considerés et briefement regardez lez partyes de benurtee quex au corps sont veuuez aparteignir, et auxi ceux partiez quex nous avonms avauntditz[156] a lez almez accorder, regardoms, eidant Nostre Signour. Pur ce dez iceux parties la premer est sagesse, quel lez benurez hommes pleinement avront, et rien a eux ne defaunte[157] dez toutz chosez queux ils vuillent conustre. Qar vraiment toutz chosez presentz et a veners[158] ils sacherent,[159] ne nulle serra qe de lour notice serra subtrait; ne bosoigne serra que ascum homme demaunde l'autre, qi fust soun basaiel,[160] de qi progenie[161] fust issu, qi il ou ele soit; de toutes langegez, de toutes creaturos, de toutz artz ils avront lez sciencez,[162] et lez pensees l'un de l'autre apertement verra; qeconques chosez j'ay fait, ou face en ce present vie, toutz yceux verront qeconque chose ascun d'ewx a fait; et je le verai si illoeqe je serrai, ne nulle labour[163] en ascum[164] avera, si en ceste vie a Dieu par mercy face satisfaccioun. Nous trestoutes savoms qe Petre l'apostoille soun Signour denya, et qe Mari Magdalene fust pecchere, le qe[l] est conuz a eux qe nous le sachoms. Qar s'il fusse muscé [f.239v], atante cella en lisant et en chantant nos le pronu[ncioms] issint qe muscer ne purra, et nientmeins rien de rougesse ou damage eient. <Mes lez angles ne despisent lez seintz, qar ascum foiz par temptacioun sount convictz;[165] ne lez seintz despisent lez angels, qar ils ne suffrent nulle temptacioun quel ils deussent venquer.[166] Si Michael a Petir dirroit, 'Tu as denyé toun Seignour', Petre purroit respondre: 'Veir est que tu dis; mes tu pur toun Seignour jammés rien ou un coup as sustenuz.' Quel toutz foiz ils ne fount, mes issint ils sount concordez, sicom ils fuissent toutz angels ou hommes.>[167] Pur qoi? Certes pur ce q'ils de lour fait ount repentaunce, et remissioun ount[168] suez. Mes si nous pur nos trespassez[169] eussonms sué remissioun [...] passez, veire 'qant j'estoi petit enfaunt, je savoi[170] com petit enfaunt, et pensoi come enfaunte; et quant j'estoi fait homme, je voida[171] lez maners d'enfaunt'; issint auxi q'en icele beneite vie, rien de hounte ne serra, si celui par satisfacioun, Dieu grauntaunt, viendra illoeques, le qel Dieu comaunda qe nulle jugera le mounde,[172] nulle homme quidra d'estre [...].[173]

11 <**De amicicia sanctorum que est nova pars beatitudinis eorum.**>

Et par entre lez compaignies dez seintz serra amysté parfet et nunt[174] faillant; qar [f.240^r] chescun par soi, trestoutz ensemble, Dieu lour Signour plus qe eux mesmes aymera; [ne lui mesmez aymera][175] plus qe l'autre, ne l'autre plus qe lui mesmez; en owel manere, lui et toutes maners autrez il aymera. Dieu, veire, il aymera sur lui et sur toutz autrez. Qe si ascum die, plus outre soi vuille amer soun pere ou sez parentz devant autrez,[176] lez[177] lui regarder a lui mesmez qei il dist. Et pur ce q'il ne sente pas bien vraiment, lesse lui entendre. Et qeconque qe tu soiez, qe dis ce, qe tu ové vrai et plus fervent amour aymez toun parent, tu desires qe toutz lui ayment[178] et en nulle meindre amour qe tu lui aymez; la mesme chose je sente de mon amy, vuille auxi et je desire. Et le[179] mesme desirent toutz autrez. Pur quoi quant tu coveitez qe toun amy j'ayme si com moi mesme, de necessitee tu aymes moy et toutz autrez si com toi, issint qe toutz autrez ayment toi si com eux mesmes: le quel quant il soit, il serra graunt et parfet amyst[é], qar en chescun singlerment,[180] et en toutz communalment, serra desir de parfecte amour. Pur ce l'amysté est benoie, qe couple lez espiritez de toutz beneiez en perp[et]uel joye.[181]

12 <**De concordia sanctorum que est decima pars beatitudinis eorum.**>

Dount est neez amyable acorde, qe[182] al semblance d'acord q'est en nos membres main[f.240^v]dra diligealment,[183] ne nient ordez.[184] Nos membres[185] vraiment a taunt[186] entre sei[187] d'acord isont[188] sicom sount les oylez, q'en nul manere l'un saunz l'autre rien voet overe.[189] Qar l'un oyle suis ou jus, dextrez[190] et leg[e]res[191] vodra entendre,[192] i[193] ne bosoigne pas q'il move l'autre pur regarder ov lui, qar naturalment nul d'eux voet regarder[194] saunz la compaignable[195] inspeccioun de l'autre; tant acord ils ount entre eaux mesmes, qe[196] qeconque chose l'un vorra, celle mesme chose l'autre desire. Et lez autres membres, ov mult acord ils sount entre[197] eux couplez;[198] qar lez mains overount pur lees pees et pur tout le corps, et pur lez mains et tout le corps regardent lez oylez. Pur lé mains et toutz le[199] corps va le pee entre deux ou unes paas. Ne dit le pee, tout soit qe ascum foiz il soit blessé ovesque lez creuls fichurez[200] d'espines, q'il ne voet plus oultre avaunt; ne lez mains, tout soit q'il soient plaiez, ne dien pas q'ils ne vuillen plus oultre over[e]. Ne s'il aveigne qe la main ovesque un hache blesse ou plaie le pee, unquore le pee n'est pas envers la main mové de ire. Vraiment ov taunt d'acord d'amour entre eux sount assemblez qe par nul reson ils ne purront entre eux [f.241r][201] aver[202] discencion parmi nulle occasion; a touz et a chescun d'eaux est il empenduz.[203] Toutz lez membres servent al teste et pur luy se mettent en perils, et par quei il pert overtement, q'ils plus aiment[204] le teste qe eux mesmez. Pur ce tiel sera l'acorde en icelle beneit pais dez benurez[205] qe nulle esperit[206] de discencion y serra trové, ou Dieu en touz et outre toutz serra, et sur toutz en toutz cher sera. ¶ Illoeqes, certein, nulle meindre accorde serra fermé parentre toutz qi serront lez membrez de Crist, q'a present n'est trové en le corruptible corps d'un homme corruptible; mes en tant[207] il sera greindre et plus precious, en quant q'il est constaunt; et jammés n'avera fyn.

13 **<De honore sanctorum qui est undecima pars beatitudinis eorum.>**

Graunt honour auxi a iceux benurez serra. 'Quia nimis[208] honorati sunt amici tui, Deus': qar, Dieux, tez[209] amys sont trop honurer. ¶ Ceste honour auxi graunt serra, que de sen humaine ne purra mye estre compris. Nepurquant mettouns par ensample qe ascun servant soit honurez del seignour. ¶ Certein si emper[er]s ou ascun roy soun servant honura, issint q'il lui deliroit[210] de soun villenage[211] et lui mettroit en ordre dez chivalers, celui servant mult sei quideroit estre debtour de soun seignour. ¶ Et si lui entre sez primates[212] enhaunceroit,[213] en quant pur l'amour de soun seignour deust estre [f.241v] [...] empenduz?[214] Toutz a lui servirent, ne indignacion du seignour qe lui honuroit devoient encurrer.[215] Si verament seignour froit unqore, en tant lui aymeroit q'il lui come en soun [filz] coverteroit,[216] et soun heir ordeigneroit, ne saveroit le manere; par quel chose y[217] poet estre pensez merveilous celle honour q'ascun y est donez par Dieux, le factour[218] de toutz choses.[219] Qui a lui servant, non soulement vivere touz jours en perpetuel pees fra,[220] ne soulement yceulz sez amys a lui appellera, mes lez fiz et heirs du roialme de ciel ordeigner[o]it. Quei est a quider comebien d'onour de toute creature il avera, soun [frere] il appellera, soun fiz il tiendra? Chescune creature a lui sera subjet, lequel sera graunt et incomparable[221] honour.

14 <De potestate sanctorum que est xij.[a] pars beatitudinis eorum.>

Pousté auxi a iceux benurez a taunt sera, quant[222] chescun aver voudra. Qar queconque chose ascun de eux, en ciel ou en terre, en mer ou en le parfounde[223] d'enferne, coveitra estre fait, s[a]unz contredit il sera fait. Merveillous poet estre veuz[224] ce qe nous diouns. Mes sibien soit consideré ou adonqes nous serons allower,[225] ou de qi corps adonqes nous seronms lez menbrez, et pur ce qe rien ne faudra a eux que Dieux ayment, ne sera ceo my incredible;[226] ar aventure il sera vew a ascune[227] poair estre, ce que nous avaunt nomez[228] forteresse,[229] mes non est [f.242r] forteresse; ce q'est desus parlez verai[230] il est vertu[231] d'overage; poiar certes icy moustré est vertu de comander. ¶ Ceste poiar verament averont lez seintz de Dieu, qar certes touz chosez ils averont ovesque le fiz de Dieu: yceste poiar serra pousté perpetuel; et pur ce ne mye petit benurté serra a yceux qui cele poair averont; assez graundez et gloriousez sount yceux donnes[232] de Dieu, sicome toutz jours purrount endurer. Auxi covient q'ils eient seurté, issint que ce q'ils ount, ils purront tut diz garder.

15 <De securitate sanctorum que est xiij.[a] pars beatitudinis eorum.>

Pur ce seurté serra suffisaunt, qar 'nul turment ne dolour plus avaunt ne sera jammés'; ne purra[233] perdre si graunde benurtee, si je verray, ou si Dieu de moi ouster le voudroit, ou si ascun plus fort qe luy surviendroit qi ele oustroi. Mes je su bien seur qe si je ele ay gainé,[234] je ele perdre ne voille. Auxi je su seur qe Dieux, 'a qi est nulle variance[235] ne enumbre',[236] ele non oustra puis q'il est une foiz doné. Auxi je su seur que nulle plus fort qe lui purra survenir, qar puis q'il est ensi, y[237] n'est nulle doute q'illoeqes est plener seurtee.

16 <De gaudio sanctorum que est xiiij.[a] pars beatitudinis eorum.>

Pur ce serra pur toutz iceux joy inestimable,[238] quel outrement surmonte sen humaine; qar qi poet penser la joye [f.242v] quel chescun avera de lui mesme, quant taunt beauté, vestesse, force, liberaltee, sainté, delit, repose, sapience, amysté, [concorde], honour, poair et seurté il avera? ¶ Nulle homme veraiment poet dire quant il est, qar nulle homme en ceste [vie][239] de ce est expert. Veraiment si Dieu dorroit ascun toun amy mesme le joye, q'a toi est veu, a quel tu es a veners,[240] qi qe tu soiez, ou qe tu ne mult enjoyereiez?[241] Et si deux, trois ou plusours et autrez, quex tu ne meyns amez qe toi mesme, quei deussz tu dire? Veraiment graunde joye en averez, et plus outre qe l'em ne poet dire tu joyeraiez,[242] la quel doin[243] en nulle manere faudra; mes mesme celle joye Nostre Seignour durra a nous, treschers amys et parentz, qi illoqes par la mercy de Dieux seronms. ¶ Issint que nous enjoyons de lui qi suz[244] nous sera, de nous mesmez joyonms et de nos veisyns joyonms, qi il prendra touz e[n] lui. Il surhabundra[245] trestoutz. A toutz environera,[246] en toutz de chescun part il sera, sicome pessoun en chescun lieu entour le mere se[247] ount. Issint lez seintz de Dieu celle tres graunt douceté de joye entour eux de chescun part averont, de qi[248] est dit: 'Entre en joye de toun Seignour.' <Joye parfet lui soul poet aver, qi lez ditz parties de toute benurté purra avoir. Et pur ce, qi est plus benuré que cesti cy q'est de taunt joye replené?[249] ¶ Unqore nientmains a le cumble de sa benuretee: un autre il avera dount [f.243r] plus purra joyer. ¶ Qar veraiment chescun homme aymera l'autre com soi mesme. Pur ce, combien et quantz de joyes chescun avera qi de benurté de taunz dez seintz enjoyera? Qe s'il enjoyera taunt dez autrez [qu']il aymera com li mesme, quant ou combien de Dieu, qui il aimera plus qe sei mesme,[250] il enjoyera? Pur ce, a taunt de benurté il avera, quant le memoire d'omme ne purra mye suffir a remembre.[251]

17 **Quod deum timentibus erit sufficiencia in omnibus.>**
Brefement regarder[252] lez xiiij parties de benurté ou de comoditee, par aventure sera qi demaundera: A qui[253] taunt de beauté, vetesse et autrez plusours parties devient,[254] puis qe soulement benu[r]ement vivre et ceux chosez avoir queux la vie ne poet my fayler, assez il purra suffire. Mes il est assaver qe Dieu en nulle chose est nonvaillant, et sicom il est en toutz sufficiant, issint sez amys et servantz en toutez chosez serrount suffisauntz. Veray si ascun de eux en chescune chose soi sentireit estre impotent, il ne joieroit my ataunt come il fra quant[255] il sei conustera estre en toutez choses toutpuissant; pur qoi, sicome[256] nostre joie soit plein, rien ne faudra a ceux que doutent Dieux.

18 <Excitacio mentis ad contemplandum summum bonum et coniectacio quale et quantum sit hoc bonum.>

Que ma alme excite et susleve tout toun entendement, et pense quant tu purras, [f.243v] et comme maveis soit celle bounté,[257] de quei en ist[258] taunt plenté[259] de biens. Veirement si toutz chosez soient delitablez, pense et remembre com delitable soit celle bountee qe contient la jocunditee de toutz biens; et noun tiel quel nous sumus[260] expert en chosez creez, mes de tant difference quant[261] le creatur differt[262] de creature. ¶ Et si la vie soit boun q'est formé, come bon soit la vie q'est creatrice?[263] Si la sanitee qu'est fait soit jocunde, quant jocunde est celle sanitee qe fait toute sanitee? Si amyable soit le sen qe toutz chosez fiist de nient, verai si mult et grauntz lez delytz soient es choses delitablez, quel et quant est la delit en lui qi fist ceux delitz?

19 Que et quanta sunt bona fruentibus Deo.

Ke qi ceste bountee usera,[264] quei a lui sera et quei a [lui] noun[265] sera? Certein[266] queconque il voudra serra, et quei il ne voudra mye, non sera. ¶ Illoeqes, verray, seront biens du corps et alme, queles 'ne oile vist ne orelle oit, ne coer d'omme pensa': pur ceo, pur qoi voisez[267] tu par multz chosez, petit hom,[268] encerchant lez biens de toun alme et de toun corps? Ayme tu un bon [en] qi sount toutz biens, et il suffist; desire tu un simple bon q'est sur toutz biens, et il est assez: ma char, quei vrai aymez tu? ma alme, quei desire tu? Illoeqes est, la est queconque chose vous aymez, queconque chose vous desirez; si beauté delite,[269] 'lez droiturelx lucerent sicom le so[f.244r]laile'; si vestesse ou force ou liberté de corps, a qi rien ne purra resister, 'seront semblablez as angelis[270] de Dieu', qar 'ille est seminé[271] corps bestial, et l'en ra corps espirituel' vraiment par poaire, nemy par nature. ¶ Si la vie soit longe et salubre,[272] illoeqes est sain perpetueltee[273] et sanitee perpetuel, qar 'lez droiturelx viverunt perpetuelment', et 'sanité dez droiturelx de Nostre Seignour' est. ¶ Si[274] saciesté,[275] 'sera saciez ou paremplez quant la glorie de Dieu[276] apparura'. ¶ Si iveresse ou plentevousté, 'sera enyverez ou replez del plent[e]vousté[277] del mesoun de Dieu'; si la melodie, le[s] choer[s][278] dez angelis illoeqes chaunterunt[279] a Dieu saunz fin. ¶ Si chescun soit innette, lour delit soit nette;[280] si 'Dieu eaux[281] enbevera ov le ryver de lour delit'. ¶ Si la sagesse, soit celle[282] sagesse de Dieu q'a eux sei mesme moustera. ¶ Si[283] [amysté], ils aymerent[284] Dieu plus qe eux mesmes et aymerent ensemble[285] sicom eaux mesmes; et Dieu aymera celx plus q'ils ayment eaux mesmes; qar ils ayment celui et sei et ensemble par lui; et il ayme sei et ceulx par lui[286] mesme. ¶ Si concorde soit, a toutz iceulx serra une[287] volunté; a eux sera, qar nulle volunté a eux ne sera forsque la soul volunté de Dieu.[288] S[i poair], ils seront tout puissantz de lour poair et de lour volunté, sicome Dieu de la soen; qar sicome Dieu purra ce q'il voudra par soi mesme, issint purront ils ce q'ils vuillent par lui; qar [f.244v] sicom ils nulle autre chose ne vuillent mes[289] sicom il voet, issint ille vuille quanque ils vuillent;[290] et si q'il voet ne purrest[291] my non estre: c'est assaver il covient[292] estre. ¶ Si honour et richesse, Dieux cez[293] servauntz[294] bones et loiax desur multz ordeignera; mes lez fiz Dieux 'dieues' seront 'appellees'[295] et seront; et ou[296] sera soun fiz, certes et illoeqes seront ceulx 'heirs de Dieu, veray coheirs de Crist'. ¶ Si come veray surtee[297] est veray et certein, ensi certeins seront le corps et l'alme, lez queux jammés n'en nulle manere l'un ne l'autre faudra de bountee, et auxi certein come ils seront par lour gree celle bountee [ne mye] perdre; en mesme le manere Dieux ne oustra mye celle seurtee de qui lui aymerent encontre lour volunté, ne nulle chose sera plus puissant que Dieu pur departir[298] eux de Dieu contre lour voluntee. ¶ Joie vrayment quel ou quant, illoeqes tiel et taunt bon est. Coer humayne, coer bosoignable,[299] coer expert dez meschiefs,[300] mes oppressez dez meschiefs, combien enjoyroiez si plenté de touz iceulx averoiez? Demandez cez[301] entiertees[302] s'ils purront prendre lour joyes de lour tant benurtee. Mes, certein, si que autre et auxi toutez sicom toi mesme ameroiez, mesme la benurtee il avroit, et toun joye serreit double; qar [ne] meyns joyeroiez pur lui que pur toi mesme. ¶ Si [f.245r] vray deux ou treis ou mult plusours le mesme joye avroyent, au darrein pur chescun de eux sicome pur toi mesme enjoieroiez, si chescun d'eaux sicome toi mesme ameroiez. ¶ Pur ce en icelle parfet charité dez innumerables[303] benurez angelis et hommes, ou nul d'eaux meyns aymera l'autre qe lui mesme, non autrement joyera checun pur toutz autrez qe pur lui mesme; pur ce, si coer d'omme de taunt soun bountee a peine prendra soun joye, coment sera preignant de tauntz des joyes? Et vrament en tant chescun ayme l'autre, en tant de sa bountee il enjoye; sicome en nulle parfet felicitee chescun par lui plus aymera Dieu saunz comparison qe soi et toutz autrez ovesque lui; issint il plus joyera saunz estimacion de felicitee de Dieu qe de sa propre benirtee, et de chescuns[304] autrez ovesque luy. Mes si Dieu issint ils aymerent ové tout lour coer, tout lour memoire, tout lour alme qe si bien tout lour coer, tout lour memoire, tout lour alme ne suffisent pas a dignitee d'amour; issint parfetement joyeront ové tout lour coer, tout lour memoire et tout lour alme: ne sufficent[305] mye a la plenertee de joye.

20 **An hoc sit gaudium plenum quod promittit Dominus se servis suis daturum.**

Moun Dieu[306] et moun Seignour, ma espoir et joye de moun coer, ditez a m'alme si ceste [soit] joye[307] de quei a nous tu dis par toun fiz: 'Dema[n]der[308] [f.245v] et vous receyverez; qe vostre joye soit plein', qar j'ay trové une plene joye et plus qe pleyn; vrayment ov plein coer, plein memoire, plein alme, tout l'omme plein de celle joye, unqore de autre mesure joy survindra; pur ce nemy tout icelle joye entrera en lez joyantz,[309] mes toutz les joyantz entrerent en le joye. Ditez, Seignour, ditez a toun servantz dedeins[310] en soun coer si ceo soit joye en quel tez servantz entreront, lez queux entrerent 'en le joye de lour Seignour'? Mes certein ycelle joye quel tez esluz joyerent, 'oyle ne verra ne [orelle] orra ne en coer d'omme descendra';[311] pur ceo, moun Seignour, unquore n'ay je pas dit ou pensé combien yceux cez benurez joyerent. Vraiment, taunt ils aymerent quant ils connuscerent, Seignour, combien ils adonque toi conuscerent, et combien toi aymeren? Certein 'ne oyle ne vera,[312] ne orelle ne ora,[313] n'en coer d'omme descendra'[314] en ceste vie, combien ils toi cognuscerent et aymere[n]t[315] en ycelle vie.

21 **Oracio pro hoc gaudio impetrando.**

O Dieux, jeo prie que jeo puisse toi conustre, toi amer, issint que[316] puisse joyer de toy. Et si jeo ne puisse my en ceste [vie] venir au plein,[317] ou qe jeo profite de jour en jour, en tanque cella vigne au plein; la conisaunce de toi profite icy en moy, et illoeqes soit fait plein, et encresce toun amour,[318] et illoeqes soit en espoir graund et illoeqes en chose plein. Moun Seignour, par toun fiz tu comandez, et auxi tu conseilles a deman[f.246r]der, et promettez prendre, issint que nostre joye soit plein. Sire, requere qe tu conseillez par le merveillous nostre conseiler qe je puisse prendre ce qe tu as promys par ta verité, issint que mun joye soit plein; sicom Dieu soit veray, je demande qe jeo puisse prendre que moun joye soit plein. Et en mesme le temps, ma memoire de ce pense; ma langue de ce parle; moun coer celle ayme; moun bouche de ce sermonize;[319] m'alme ce enfayme;[320] ma char ce enseyve;[321] toute ma substance le desire, en tanque j'entre en la maisoun de moun Seignour qu'est treis et un, Dieu benuré en sciecles.[322] Amen.

22 Recapitulacio brevis de partibus predic[t]arum beatitudinum bonorum et de perfecta miseria[323] malorum.[324]

Puis auxi qe tant soit la benuretee dez amys de[325] Nostre Seignour Jhesu, quei sera de sez ennemys? Certein, noun pas ensi malurez,[326] noun pas ensi. Mes countre ce qe lez seintez de Dieu seront plus bealx, ils serront plus puantz. <¶ Lez seintz lucerent sicome le solail; ils serront parmy lour ordure, plus ordez[327] serront.> ¶ Ne en lour resurreccioun ne serront \my changez en meilour, mes sicome lez seintz de Dieu en jour de revelacion Nostre Seignour seront/[328] glorifier, issint yceux en perdicion seront dampnez.[329]

Ils serront benurez a tout ceo q'ils vuilent plus vestessez,[330] ou legers; lez malurez seront plus pigrez.[331] <Ils seront si legers sicome le reye du solail q'en un moment d'orient passe en l'occident; lez autrez vraiment ov taunt charche[332] [f.246v] dez peynes sount oppresser q'a peine le pee purront mover.>[333]

Encontre la vaillant force dez benurez, lez caitive[s] averont le plus graunt fieblesse. <Ils seront aussi fortz q'ils purront mover la terre; lez autrez seront aussi fiebles q'ils ne purront my ouster lez vermes de lour oyles.>[334]

Lez droiturelx avront libertee de passer la ou ils vouilent; lez torceousez[335] dampnez ne purront aler[336] hors de perpetuel cloos.[337] <¶ Ils rien ne suffrent qui la ne vouilent, mes y sont suffrez[338] a faire quecounque ils vuillent; lez autrez vrament constraintz a toute q'ils ne voudroient.>[339]

Lez esluz de Dieu ové continuel sanité[340] seront pechez;[341] les dampnez vrament ov langour perpetu[e]l seront crucifiez. <¶ Iceux si sains q'ils ne purront my estre maladez, lez autrez seront[342] q'ils ne purront estre gariz.>[343]

Lez bones seront saciez ov le delit del mesoun de Nostre Seignour; lez mavez seront replez ové le plus amer bevereche[344] del mesoun del deable. <Ils, certein, sicome ferre ardant que contient \fu en chescun partie de lui, lez maveis vrament sentirent/ anguys.>[345]

En bountee les bouns avront longe durance, en malez chosez lez maveys jammés fyn n'avront. <¶ Iceux vraiment viverent taunt come Dieux; lez autrez vraiment ne purront mye vivere forsque en moriant.>[346]

Et sicome lez bouns serount av[au]ntdez[347] ové le plus graunt sagesse,[348] issint les maveis seront confunduz [f.247r] en lour nient sagesse. <Iceux vrament serront replez ovesque le sagesse quel Dieux,[349] et ele regarderent face a face. Iceux vraiment, de toute manere

vrai sagesse oustez, ou privez,[350] ov tauntz grevez dolours,[351] q'ils seront noun soulement nient sachauntz vraiment et en toute manere hors de memoire.>

Lez amys de Dieu la plus haut amysté averont, lez enemys vraiment de Dieu plus graunt enemyté[352] entre eux avront. <¶ Et vraiment chescun boun homme Dieu aymera, et issint \toutz lez autrez bones lui aymerount, par issint/[353] qe plus oultre[354] luy aver ou haye[355] ne purront mye. ¶ Et le maveis, chescun veraiment Dieu ly haye, et issint touz lez bouns lui hayent, par issint qe le fiz n'avra point de pitee de soun pere, en peynes lui regardant.>[356]

Lez benurez serount concorder en perpetuel pees, et lez caitives en continuel discencion decordés.[357] <¶ Le corps vraiment et l'alme de checun seint et touz altrez esluz seront de taunt acorder, quant en present sont nos oilles. ¶ Et les maveys vraiment en taunt discorde seront qe lour corps et almes toutz jours sount en dissencion. Car le [corps] avra l'alme en haye pur ceo qu'ele jammés male ne pensa. ¶ Et l'alme hayra le corps pur ceo qe lez maveis penser[358] en ovre ad acompli, pur touz quels ils serront en peyns tormenter.>[359]

Lez seintz de Dieu ové graunt honour seront enhauncer. ¶ Lez dampnez[360] vrai[f.247v]ment ové mult graunt hounte[361] sunt oppressez. <Sicome vraiment ascun emper[er]e eiant soun servaunt malade, et lui ferroit garer,[362] et sain ové preccius vesture lui vestiroit, et honereit[363] delés soun filz seier ferroit. Sicome lui q'il honoureit, issint[364] Dieu le pere honurera chescun boun homme purgez de tout corrupcioun, sicome lui en [im]mortalité[365] vestitut[366] ferreit seier[367] de par soun [filz]. Issint vraiment chescun maveys en countrere[368] sera honuree, issint[369] q'en tout temps[370] degetté[371] al dominacioun dez vermez soit subiect.>

Lez droiturelx avront roial poair de commander; lez torceonous[372] failleront[373] poair d'eaux mesmes ascunement. <¶ Iceux vrament purrount faire qeconque chose ils vuillent. Lez autrez vraiment rien[374] ne purront faire q'il voudrent.>[375]

Lez bones seront seurer,[376] qe lour bounté jammés ne perira. ¶ Et lez maveys averon pour de cheyer[377] toutz jours de male en pys. <¶ Iceulx vrament avront qeconque chose q'ils voudront et rien de ce lesser ne douterent. ¶ Et les autrez veraiment toutdiz avront pour de lour tormentz q'ils suffrent,[378] et jammés de eaux ne purrount eschaper.[379]

Chescun boun homme parfetement purra joyer, qar toutz les ditz parties de benurtee il avera parfetement. Le maveys vraiment encountre ové le plus haut tristesse sera repleez, qar toutz [parties][380] de tout manere caitifetee[381] il suffrera. Pur ce en y [...][382]

NOTES

1 Initial with gold leaf (as at the beginning of each main paragraph or section).

2 As is often the case in AN, 'how much' (= LL 'quantum'): *AND*, *s.v.* **quant**[1].

3 MS 'mesnun'.

4 'Hardship, shortage' (= LL 'parcitas'): *AND s.v.* **escharseté**.

5 MS 'oxost'.

6 This p.p. implies an infinitive *tapescer*, not otherwise attested in Anglo-Norman (*AND* 769a), nor in continental French (Gdf, TL): the verb is clearly related to *AND*'s **tapir** (1) (*ibid.*), a well-attested verb, used reflexively a few lines later on.

7 Or read 'ove' (and hereafter), since there are 10 instances of 'ov' without final '-e' (against 20 with).

8 Rubricated capital 'E', not retained.

9 MS 'lieus'.

10 'Spectacle, entertainment': *AND s.v.* **spectacle**, of which this is a latinized form, unattested in Gdf (X:708b), TL (IX:1038) or *FEW* (XII:159a).

11 An obvious calque of the Latin 'interesse' ('to attend, be present at'); not in *AND*, but given by Gdf III:285b; TL III:684.

12 'Sufficiency' (= LL 'sufficiencia'): *AND s.v.* **suffisance**.

13 'Inconvenience, disadvantage' (= LL 'incommoditas'): not given in *AND*. See, however, Gdf X:4b (dated 1389).

14 MS 'commoditee', which would mean 'ease, fortune': this meaning is not given in *AND s.v.* **commoditee** (given in Gdf IX:134b). The correction is suggested by LL (which makes more sense).

15 'Without interruption' (= LL 'sine intermissione'): *AND s.v.* **entremettre**.

16 (As elsewhere) 'chu' (with superscript nasal bar).

17 It seems that the AN scribe, or author, has misread 'sollicitudine' (perhaps abbreviated in his exemplar) as 'solitudine'. Not much sense can be made of 'solitari' in this context (*AND s.v.* **solitaire**).

18 Here as elsewhere in the case of ind.pr.4 endings, the scribe (of this part of the manuscript) seems to write '-onis' (with a clear stroke on the 'i', in which matter he is careful and consistent throughout. Such endings have been edited throughout as '-oms'. They do not occur after the apparent change of scribe at f. 241[r] (cf. AN n.201); but ind.pr.4 endings are rare thereafter in any case. In both parts of the manuscript, the ending '-is' is also used for post-tonic syllables (e.g. 'angelis' ff. 233[v], 244[r], 245[r]; 'tormentis' f. 236[v]; 'membris' f. 238[r]).

19 'Let it be known, noted that' (= LL 'notandum est'): *AND s.v.* **notifier.**

20 Literally 'taken up' (= LL 'assumpsit'): *AND s.v.* **susprendre.**

21 Metathesized form of *enfern: AND s.v.*

22 'Wretchedness' (= LL 'miseria'): *AND s.v.* **chaitiveté.**

23 If we follow LL, this must be p.p. of *baptizer* (*AND s.v.* **baptiser**) used as substantive and here the direct object of 'eit': 'lest the "second death" should possess the reborn (baptized) person'.

24 N.B. the divergence from LL (and the Vulgate). Read 'ascendra'? The inclusion of the apparently redundant 'ele' may also be scribal error.

25 MS 'cum pur ceste benurtee sa greindure'. For 'greindure', 'large size, magnitude' (= LL 'magnitudo'), cf. *AND s.v.* **graignur** (this sense not given *ibid.* under (2) s.).

26 'Might seem', a literal translation of the Latin (= LL 'videatur'). Cf. *AND s.v.* **veer**[1] (847a), for *estre vu* in the sense of the passive use of *videre.*

27 Sbj.pr.3 of *AND* **aparer,** 'to appear' (= LL 'appareat').

28 Here as later (sometimes spelt 'sovour'), 'savour, flavour, taste': *AND s.v.* **savur.**

29 Superscript 'e'.

30 MS 'environoms'. The verb here is *envi(o)rer* (this form being fut.4), 'to try, endeavour': *AND s.v.* **envier**[2]; the scribe seems to have confused it with *environer* (here and later in the paragraph). *Envirer* is attested from an early date, in *Les Proverbes de Salemon*, ed. C. Claire Isoz, ANTS, 44–45 (London: ANTS, 1988) v. 3085, 'to emulate': 'N'envirer ome torçonier, Lai ses veies e sun sentier' (= LL: 'Ne emuleris hominem iniustum'). The substantive *envire* (listed as a variant form *s.v.* **envie** in *AND* 246b) is also found in *Salemon* (v. 642), and in Philippe de Thaon's *Bestiaire*: cf. *Le Livre de Sibile*, ed. Hugh Shields, ANTS, 37 (London: ANTS, 1979) n. to vv. 700–704 (p.102). For the anomalous development of *envire* < INVIDIA, cf. TL III:713.

31 MS 'ordergner'.

32 Aphetic form of *AND* **esclarer,** 'to explain'. Cf. H. G. Richardson, 'Letters of the Oxford Dictatores', Oxford History Society, n.s., 5, 1942, 360–416 (p.422), where 'soit claree' translates 'clareat'.

33 An auxiliary ('soit') would be normal here: 'posé soit', translating *ponatur*, 'supposing that'. LL has 'profecto': AN may be corrupt.

34 i.e. 'soit': perhaps read 'soi[t]'? Cf., *infra*, 'oustroi' (cond.3 of *o(u)ster*). But there are numerous cases in this manuscript where final '-t' is omitted from verb forms.

35 'Tenderness, softness'. Not apparently attested elsewhere in Anglo-Norman (cf. the palaeographically similar forms *tendresse, tendresce*: *AND*, 779b). Gdf has it (X:751a).

36 'Flavour' (= LL 'sapor'): *AND s.v.* **savur.**

37 'Small portions, pieces' (= LL 'frusta'): *AND s.v.* **gobet.**

38 Capital 'C', not retained.

39 Read 'quei' (= LL 'quid')? Cf. AN n.248.

40 'To seek after, be attracted to' (= LL 'appetere'); not given in *AND*. Gdf I:135c, VIII:39a, TL I:176 have quotations with this sense.

41 'Appropriate, applicable'; LL uses a rather different construction. Cf. *AND s.v.* **able**.

42 'Most fitting' (= LL 'decentissima'). Not otherwise attested in Anglo-Norman. Cf. *AND s.v.* **avenant, avenir**. Not in Gdf or TL.

43 'Freedom', or possibly 'generosity' (*infra*, 'liberaltee'; = LL 'libertas'): not given in *AND*, but cf. *ibid. s.v.* **liberal** (387a). Except for these two instances, 'libertas' is rendered by 'liberté' (e.g. para. 6). Cf. Gdf IV:772 (dated 1369); TL V:395 (which suggests both of the senses indicated).

44 MS 'este'.

45 'Ineffably' (= LL 'ineffabiliter'), in the etymological sense of 'unsayably': one of a number of latinisms not given in *AND*. Cf. Gdf X:10b.

46 'Go back' (= LL 'redeamus'): *AND s.v.* **raler**.

47 MS 'ramucle' (?), 'brief argument, demonstration', = Latin 'ratiuncula'. Our suggestion assumes that AN has created an otherwise unattested latinism. Cf. LL n.19 to the corresponding passage. The text is corrupt in both LL and AN.

48 MS 'envioronoms'. See AN n.30.

49 MS 'es'.

50 MS 'primi'.

51 'The just [people]' (= LL 'Iusti'): *AND s.v.* **dreiturel**.

52 LL ('fulgebunt') suggests this must be fut.6. Numerous fut.6 endings in AN are in '-erent'.

53 MS 'incorporablement' (= LL 'incomparabiliter'). Not given in *AND*. Given in Gdf X:4b.

54 This seems to mean 'demonstrated' (cf. *AND s.v.* **prover**[1]), but interpretation is not helped by the discrepancy between AN and LL.

55 'Saviour' (*AND s.v.* **salveour**); not to be confused with *savour* <SAPOREM (*AND s.v.* **savur**).

56 'Fashioned after, according to' (= LL 'configuratum' + dat.); *configurer* is not attested in *AND*. Cf. Gdf IX:152a (**configuré a**); TL II:679 (**configurer**).

57 'Clarity': *AND s.v.* **clarté**.

58 'Joy, happiness'; not in *AND* (= LL 'iocunditas'). Cf. Gdf IV:645a.

59 Otherwise unattested substantival use of p.pres. of *veer* (cf. *AND s.v.* **veer**[1], 847a), to mean 'sight, spectacle'; AN does not follow LL closely, so there is no corresponding noun in LL. This meaning is not in Gdf VIII:155c; TL has 'veant pc.prs. sehend, subst. oder adj.' (XI:225).

60 MS 'assemblablez'.

61 Fut.1. Fut.1 forms in '-a' are not infrequent in later Anglo-Norman, particularly outside the literary register: cf. 'Letters of the Oxford Dictatores' 362: 'jeo luy [*sc.* a pupil] trovera choses bosoignables et l'senfornera'; *Anonimalle Chronicle 1333–81*, ed. V. H. Galbraith, Publications of the University of Manchester, History Series, 45 (Manchester: Manchester UP, 1927) 87: 'jeo n'esparnera', etc.; see also *Der anglonormannische Boeve de Haumtone*, ed. A. Stimming, Bibliotheca Normannica, 7 (Halle: M. Niemeyer, 1899) xxvii and 195, for evidence of their use within the literary canon (none at the assonance).

62 Adverbial locution meaning 'in truth' (= LL 'vere'): *AND s.v.* **verai.**

63 = *plusurs* (*AND s.v.* **plusur**, with a comparable plural form, *plusourus*, showing the same unstable orthography of post-tonic vowels).

64 Pluperfect, which (oddly) corresponds to LL's perfect tense 'subiunximus'; p.p. implies a first-conjugation *souzjoiner*, 'to subjoin, follow with, append to' (not in *AND*, Gdf or TL). *AND s.v.* **joindre** has no '-er' infinitive.

65 'Rapidity, alacrity' (= LL 'velocitas'); only quotation in *AND s.v.* **velocitee.** Not in Gdf or TL; cf. *FEW* XIV:468a.

66 MS 'volocitate'.

67 'Alacrity, speed' (= 'velocitas'): *AND s.v.* **vistesse.** The scribe of AN spells this word, variously, 'vistessee' (here and f.238v), 'vistesse' (f.234v), 'vestesse' (f.242v), (f.244r) and 'vetesse' (f.243r). There might be a case for printing 'vistesse' here; but we might also be dealing with the type of scribal problems with final '-e' which are discussed at length in, e.g., *Fouke le Fitz Waryn*, ed. E. J. Hathaway, P. T. Ricketts, C. A. Robson and A. D. Wilshere, ANTS, 26–28 (London: ANTS, 1975) lxvi–lxviii.

68 'As much as (the sun's ray has)'. Cf. *AND s.v.* **quant[1]**.

69 MS 'treslegeriment' or 'treslegermient', 'most easily, lightly' (= LL 'facillime'). Only quotation in *AND s.v.* **treslegerment.**

70 MS 'dz'. Read 'dez'?

71 MS '7 [= *et*] soit'.

72 'To distribute, disperse' (= LL 'dispersum'): *AND s.v.* **departir.**

73 MS 'niencmeins'(?).

74 'Removed, transported' (= LL 'sustulit'); sense not listed in *AND s.v.* **supporter.** Gdf does not give it *s.v.* **sousporter** (VII:555b), **suporter** (VII:597b) or **supporter** (X:728b); but does *s.v.* **sourporter** (VII: 538b).

75 The error in AN corresponds exactly to that in LL: MS 'supra locum leonum', which we have corrected to 'lacum' on the basis of the relevant Vulgate texts and of *DA* 131.

76 LL's 'agilitas' corresponds to AN's doublet, 'legertee ou agilitee', the latter a latinism meaning 'agility, dexterity'; it is not in *AND*. Given in Gdf VIII:46c; TL I:208.

77 AN seems to have omitted part of its exemplar: in LL, 'magnum munus, magnam proculdubio felicitatem habebit'.

78 'Follows': *AND s.v.* **ensivre**.

79 MS 'noveroount'.

80 'Chosen' (= LL 'elegerit'): *AND s.v.* **choisir**.

81 'Air' (*AND s.v.* **air**[1]).

82 MS 'ahordra'.

83 Here and subsequently, 'free, not servile' (*AND s.v.* **franc**[1]).

84 MS 'pars'.

85 MS 'dest°bera'.

86 The p.p. 'closee' suggests a first-conjugation infinitive *closer*. With the exception of 'vistessee' twice, on f.235v and f.238v, all cases of final '-ee' in AN seem to correspond to tonic [e]; this form may, however, be simply *close* (cf. *AND s.v.* **clore**). It would not, of course, be at all surprising to find a first-conjugation remodelling of *clore* in an Anglo-Norman text of this type. TL (II:502) suggests an infinitive *closir*.

87 Literally 'of their', i.e. 'of them(selves)', without any direct equivalent in LL.

88 There is a short erasure at this point in the manuscript, but there is no obvious lacuna in the text.

89 'Heat': cf. *AND s.v.* **chalur**. It is possible that, at some stage in the transmission of the text, 'e chalure' has been miscopied as 'e e chalure' ('et' is in fact abbreviated in this manuscript); read '(e)chalure'?

90 Participial adj. (here plural), 'steaming', calqued on LL 'vaporancia'. Cf. TL XI:116 *s.v.* **vaporer** (p.p.), and *FEW* XIV:167a.

91 'Judgement', = LL 'arbitrium'. *AND s.v.* **arbitrement** only has the sense 'arbitration, award'. Cf. Gdf I:377c with sense akin to AN.

92 'Reprobates', i.e. 'those rejected by God'; p.p. as substantive (*AND s.v.* **reprover**, only gives p.p. as adj., and not in this specifically religious sense). LL has 'reproborum', and (*infra* §8) opposes 'probi' to 'reprobi', where AN has 'lez prodez hommes' and 'les reprovez'. For *reprobus*, cf. *RMLWL s.v.* **reprob/atio** (403a).

93 MS 'atant': *AND s.v.* **atant**[1], **autant, tant**.

94 'Tant ... quant' (= LL 'tanta ... quanta'): 'as much ... as much': *AND s.v.* **quant**[1], **tant**.

95 'Free men, freed men'. LL's 'libertati', at first sight an error for 'liberati', may stand: *liberto* is attested in (late) British medieval Latin: *RMLWL s.v.* **2 liber** (276a).

96 'Pleasing, agreeable': *AND s.v.* **greable**.

97 MS 'multa'.

98 'This world' (= LL 'seculum'): *AND s.v.* **secle**.

99 MS 'sique'.

100 MS 's soiomoms'.

101 'Feeble' (= LL 'debiles'): *AND s.v.* **feble**.

102 MS has a 9-shaped abbreviation mark. This scribal form is found in, e.g., *Boeve de Haumtoune*, vv. 1858, 2003, 2537 (no unabbreviated forms; Stimming prints 'sumus'); *Mirour de Seinte Eglyse*, ed. A. D. Wilshere, ANTS, 40 (London: ANTS, 1982), 6.43 (A-text only: B has 'sumes'; edition gives no indication of whether this is an expanded abbreviation); *La Vie de Seint Auban*, ed. A. R. Harden, ANTS, 19 (Oxford: ANTS, 1968), where the word is also written in full as 'sumes': the editor regards the abbreviated 'sumus' as 'an inadvertent latinism', and prints 'sumes' (n. to v.457, p.68). There is no case of unabbreviated 'sumes' in AN.

103 MS 'survergnir'.

104 i.e. fut.3 of *AND* **nuisir,** 'to harm' (= LL 'nocebit').

105 = LL 'nocere': read 'noi[s]er'?

106 'So much': *AND s.v.* **autant**.

107 This verb, which corresponds to the impersonal construction in LL ('curet'), seems to mean 'to care about, attach importance to', supported by *AND s.v.* **charger**.

108 Read 'absteine'?

109 MS 'la vengeaunce de son tort / a Christ le ou baille'. The verb is *bailler*, 'to give'. The manuscript may preserve the corrupt remains of a synonymic doublet here ('le' = 'le[sse]'?).

110 'Avenger' (= LL 'vindicem'); the texts quoted in *AND s.v.* **vengeor** (i.e. various psalters and AN) suggest that this word is particular to the religious register, but in fact it is attested in, for example, Jean Bodel's *Chanson des Saisnes* as well (cf. Gdf X:838c; TL XI:159a).

111 MS 'sui'; perhaps read 'sus'?

112 'Arrogantly, presumptuously' (= LL 'presumptuose'); not in *AND*. Cf. Gdf *s.v.* **presompcieusement** (VI:391a).

113 'Henceforth' (= LL 'amodo'): *AND s.v.* **enavant**.

114 'To call on' (= LL 'interpellare'); not in *AND*, nor otherwise attested in medieval French. Gdf (IV:600b and X:25c) and *FEW* (IV:785b) have the 'learned' *interpeller*.

115 'So be it', 'on your own head be it' (?). This looks suspiciously like a formula: cf. LL 'Bene vobis conveniat'. TL (II:982) has various quotations which suggest that just such a formula was alive and well in the vernacular.

116 MS 'eux'.

117 Apparently p.p. (*AND s.v.* **sivre**) 'followed' (= LL 'secutus', with no auxiliary). This assumes that the proposed correction of MS 'eux' to 'eust' is right.

118 MS 'bosoign', with superscript nasal bar over 'n'.

119 MS 'sani'; read 'san[e]', 'sain[e]'?

120 MS 'tersbenure', 'most blessed, most blissful' (= LL 'felicissima'): *AND s.v.* **tresbenuré**.

121 The absence of any direct equivalent in LL makes it impossible to determine

whether this is the adverb < IBI (*AND* **i**[2]), the personal pronoun *il* with final consonant effaced before following consonant (cf. M. K. Pope, *From Latin to Modern French* (Manchester: Manchester UP, 1934) §841), or the meaningless 'i-' attached to the beginning of monosyllabic verb forms (*AND s.v.* **i**[1]).

122 'Joyful' (= LL 'iocunda'): *AND s.v.* **jocunde**.

123 'Dwelling-places' (= LL 'tabernacula'): *AND s.v.* **tabernacle**.

124 The initial is a rubricated capital, which has not been retained. 'Hall(-way)s, entrance halls': *AND s.v.* **alee**. A synonymic pair 'en lez alleys ou entrees' corresponds to LL's 'in atriis'.

125 'Will fill up, replenish' (= LL 'inebriabit'), apparently from a reflex of Latin REPLEO (not in *AND*), which, to judge by the p.p. 'repleez' (and 'replez', *infra*), seems to be *repleer*. See, however, Gdf VII:60a (*s.v.* **repletir**); TL VIII:901 (adj. **replet** only); *FEW* X:267b *s.v.* **repletus, replere**.

126 'Table' (*AND s.v.* **table**), with no direct equivalent in LL.

127 See AN n.125.

128 'Plenty, abundance'; not in *AND*, but cf. adj. **plentivus** and adv. **plentivusement** (532b), for which also cf. TL VII:1150 and *FEW* IX:58a.

129 MS 'reiton'.

130 MS 'descendant comandant deffleue'. 'Comandant' makes no sense here. 'Deffleue' is ind.pr.3 of *deffl(e)uer* (not in *AND*), 'to flow down' (= LL 'defluit'). Cf. Gdf II:462; TL II:1289.

131 'Will fill up' (LL 'replebit'): *AND s.v.* **emplir**. Cf. AN n.125.

132 Latinism: 'fitting, suitable' (= LL 'conveniens'). Not given in *AND*. Given in Gdf II:286b (s. xv).

133 MS 'swestee' (?) 'sweetness, gentleness' (= LL 'suavitas'): *AND s.v.* **sueftee**.

134 'Very bitter' (= LL 'amarissimum'): *AND s.v.* **tresamer**.

135 Read 'tresjocounde'? A very long shot: read 'tresjocounditė', which assumes that AN's exemplar had (or, more likely, was taken to have) not the superlative adj. 'iocundissimam' (as in LL) but a p.p. of post-classical IOCUNDARE (cf. *RMLWL s.v.* **jocund/itas**) used as an adjective. This is the only quotation in *AND s.v.* **tresjocoundite**. Not in Gdf or TL.

136 MS 'swestee'(?).

137 'Most certainly' (= LL 'profecto'); only quotation in *AND s.v.* **tresadecertes**. Not in Gdf or TL.

138 Cond.3 of *enfower*, 'to embed, dig' (= LL 'transfoderet'): *AND s.v.* **enfuir**[2].

139 The syntax really needs a noun to be supplied here ('[dolour]'?): cf. LL 'idem dolor teneret'.

140 MS 'quei crey vous'.

141 'I should go mad' (= LL 'insanirem'): *AND s.v.* **esrager**, where the form with prefix 'a-' is given.

142 'Pleasure, delectation' (= LL 'voluptas'): cf. *AND s.v.* **delectation**. Corresponds to both 'voluptas' and 'delectacio' in LL.

143 'Passing, transient' (= LL 'transitoria'): *AND s.v.* **passant**[1], where this figurative sense is not found. Cf. TL (VII:437) *s.v.* **passer** ('tempor. vorübergehen, verstreichen') and gerundive use of *passant* (VII:450).

144 MS 'sentur'.

145 'Delectation' (= LL 'delectacio'): the latinism is not in *AND*, but cf. *ibid. s.v.* **delectation.** Given in Gdf II:485c; TL II:1335. On the development (or lack of development) of the DILIGERE family, see D. A. Trotter, 'The Vocabulary of the Love of God in Anglo-Norman', paper given at '*Amour sans frontières': Colloquium in honour of Alfred Karnein*, University of Exeter, April 1991. The substantives and adjectives evidently existed in a complete series of doublets in *delit-* and *delect-*; the proximity of both forms in AN suggests that these are not as readily assigned to the categories of 'popular' and 'learned' as we like to think.

146 Adverb 'then, subsequently' (= LL 'ita'); not in *AND*, but cf. *s.v.* **ensivre**[2].

147 'Just as all the body shall be in [the form] of a mouth ...', a literal translation of the image in LL, 'Quasi totum corpus esset gula'. Cf. *AND s.v.* **en**[1] (c) for this use of the preposition, and *s.v.* **gule** for figurative uses of the noun (some of which are already present in classical Latin).

148 'Delightful' (= LL 'delectabilis'): *AND s.v.* **delitable** for the 'popular' reflex of DELECTABILIS. Cf. Gdf II:485a (*deletable, s.v.* **delitable**) and IX:295a (*delectable, s.v.* **delitable**); TL II:1329 (*delectable*, from Wace, *Roman de Rou*). Cf. AN n.145.

149 Despite appearances, this must presumably be pret.3 (= LL 'novit'): cf. 'conust' in the next sentence. Absence of final '-t' is a common feature of verb forms in AN (and in Anglo-Norman in general).

150 'Boundary, limit' (sing. for LL 'metas' pl.): *AND s.v.* **merche**[1].

151 MS 'lar'.

152 Read 'cellui'?

153 'Happy' (= LL 'leto'): *AND s.v.* **lé**[2].

154 MS 'toz'.

155 Unusual plural of *filz* 'son' (= LL 'filiis'), which is, however, attested elsewhere in Anglo-Norman (*AND s.v.* **fiz**[1]).

156 Otherwise unattested use of the verb *avantdire* (here in compound past tense); the p.p. *avantdit* is of course common (cf. *AND s.v.*; unattested Gdf, TL). The text of AN is made more stilted by the use of a calqued accusative-and-infinitive construction (though, for the view that the construction is found in Middle French independently of translations, see Charles Brucker, 'La valeur du témoignage linguistique des traductions médiévales: les constructions infinitives en moyen français', *Linguistique et philologie (applications aux textes médiévaux). Actes du colloque des 29 et 30 avril 1977*, ed. Danielle Buschinger (Amiens: Université d'Amiens, Centre d'études médiévales, 1977) 325–344).

157 Read 'defaute'? But it is not just a matter of a superfluous nasal bar: the word is written in full. This must be ind.pr.3 of *AND*'s **defaillir** (= LL 'desit', sbj.pr.), 'to lack'.

158 This is an inflected infinitive, *vener* (i.e. *venir*), used quasi-adjectivally to mean 'future' (cf. *AND s.v.* **venir**, 854b), common in later Anglo-Norman. LL's 'preterita, presencia et futura' has been reduced in AN to 'presentz et a veners'.

159 Logically, a future tense (= LL 'scient'), but formally a strange hybrid future-cum-present-subjunctive of *saver*; not listed under the forms of the verb in *AND* (679b).

160 'Ancestor, great-grandfather' (= LL 'proavus'): *AND s.v.* **besael**.

161 Not used with the sense of *progenie* given in *AND s.v.* ('progeny'), but meaning 'lineage' (cf. LL: 'de cuius stirpe'), as in Gdf VI:427c; TL VII:1958.

162 This curious plural usage (cf. LL 'scienciam') is not otherwise attested in Anglo-Norman (cf. *AND s.v.* **science**). It is just possible that it is scribal for 'l'escience(z)'. No plural usage is given in Gdf X:640a or TL IX:274.

163 This reading can stand if it is taken to mean 'suffering' (*AND s.v.* **labur**), and thus by extension 'anguish'. LL has 'ruborem' ('shame, disgrace'). In the light of 'rougesse ou damage', a few lines below, perhaps read 'ruvour' or 'rovour' (cf. *AND s.v.* **ruvur**)?

164 MS 'ascum ascum'.

165 = LL 'victi sunt': latinized p.p. of *convencre* (cf. *AND s.v.* **cunvencre**).

166 'Which they would have to overcome, defeat ("venquer")' (= LL 'vincerent'): *AND s.v.* **veintre**.

167 The section from 'Mes lez angles ne despisent lez seintz ...' to '... sicom ils fuissent toutz angels ou hommes' is not found in *DA* (p.134).

168 MS 'fount'; perhaps read 'sount', if a calque of the Latin is possible here. The AN text seems to be corrupt: 'suez' appears to be p.p. of *suer* = *sivre* (cf. *AND s.v.* **sivre**), so that 'remissioun (f)ount suez' = LL 'veniam consequuti sunt', but this does not explain the garbled syntax which follows. A section is evidently missing after 'eussonms sue (read 'sué') remissioun' (= 'veniam consequuti fuerimus'?) and before 'passez, veire' (= 'pertransiret'), since LL, from 'nichil de perpetratis' to 'illa iam', is not translated.

169 Not p.p. of *AND* **trespasser**, but plural of *ibid.* **trespas** substantive, 'sins'.

170 MS 'savroi'.

171 Pret.1 of *AND* **voider**^{2}. Perhaps read 'voida[i]'; but there is enough evidence, here and elsewhere, of 'irregularities' in verb morphology to support the conservative solution. 'Letters of the Oxford Dictatores' (p.362) provides examples of two possible pret.1 forms in '-a' ('jeo pensa', 'poia'); *Boeve de Haumtone* also has them. See AN n.61.

172 Not quite the same as LL: AN may have taken (abbreviated?) 'inmundum' ('the unclean person') to be *mundum*, 'the world'.

173 Something seems to be lacking here, corresponding to LL's 'improperandum'.

174 A form of *nun*, used here as a negative prefix (cf. *AND s.v.* **nun**^{1}).

175 These words, or similar, are needed if any sense is to be made of this complicated passage. LL seems to be comprehensible: the emendation is based on

the corresponding phrase there, 'Nec se diliget plus quam alium, nec alium plus quam se'.

176 MS 'auntrez'.

177 Sbj.pr.3 of *lesser*, used as 3rd-person imperative with 'regarder' (= LL 'videat'), 'let him see, look' (cf. *AND s.v.* **lesser**[1]).

178 MS 'axment'.

179 MS 'lez'.

180 'Individually, severally' (= LL 'singulariter'): *AND s.v.* **singulerement.**

181 This looks like the result of a misreading: an abbreviated 'gloria' has been taken for 'gaudia'. ME agrees with AN; and they perhaps make more sense than LL (or *DA* 136).

182 MS 'qo'.

183 Not an obvious equivalent of LL 'iugiter', although 'assiduously, steadfastly' is plausible enough as an extension of the meaning of 'diligeaument'.

184 i.e. p.p. of *order* 'sullied, besmirched' ('nient ordez' = LL 'inviolata'): *AND s.v.* **order.**

185 MS 'memembres'.

186 'So much ... as ('sicum')' (= LL 'tantam'): *AND s.v.* **tant** (3), adverbial loc. **a tant ... cum.** AN demonstrates very clearly the difficulty of successfully distinguishing between *autant*, *atant* and *tant* in Anglo-Norman.

187 MS 'entresse'.

188 MS 'i sont'; but here there seems to be no obvious explanation except to see this as the meaningless 'i-' prefix attached to verb forms (cf. *AND s.v.* **i**[1] and AN n.121).

189 'Work': *AND* **ovrer**[1].

190 'Right-hand': *AND s.v.* **destre**[1]. The latinate spelling may well be a result of the translation process. Gdf II:669b has orthography *dextre s.v.* **destre** subst.; TL II:1786 has it as adj. (*Girart de Roussillon*).

191 MS 'legres', which makes no sense at all, even when corrected; LL 'levaque'. Presumably the AN translator has confused LAEVA with LEVIS. There is no obvious emendation, other than the radical solution of 'senestre'.

192 'To direct its attention': *AND s.v.* **entendre**[1].

193 = 'Il', with lost final consonant (Pope §841 and AN n.121.)

194 MS 'radarder'.

195 The adverb *cumpaignablement* is given in *AND*, but not the adjective (128a). Given in Gdf II:200b; TL II:612.

196 MS 'q^{i}'.

197 MS 'entrez'.

198 MS 'complez'.

199 MS 'lez'.

200 'Cruel pricks, thorns' (cf. *AND s.v.* **cruel, fichure**; the latter only with the

sense of 'fixture, fastening'). The senses given in *AND s.v.* **ficher** confirm that the sense suggested here for 'fichurez' (= LL 'aculeis') is semantically possible. Neither Gdf *s.v.* **ficheure** (III:782b) nor TL *s.v.* **ficheure** (III:507a–b) has exactly the sense of 'thorn'.

201 There is some evidence (e.g. the formation of the letter 'y') to suggest a change of scribe at this point, which coincides with a change of quire.

202 MS 'avera'.

203 Passive construction involving what is presumably p.p. of v.impers. *empendre* (= LL 'impenditur'), 'to be incumbent, be a duty' (not in *AND*). Cf. Gdf IV:57b (not in this sense) and *FEW s.v.* **impendere** (IV:583b), 'aufwenden'.

204 MS 'vraiment'.

205 MS 'bemurez'.

206 MS 'espot'.

207 Partly because of the following 'en quant', the word division in the manuscript has not been altered to 'entant' (see *AND s.v.* **quant**[1]; although cf. *ibid. s.v.* **entant**).

208 MS 'minus'. This quotation (the only one in Latin in the AN text) is rubricated.

209 MS 'cez' (?).

210 = LL 'liberaret': most likely to be cond.3 of *deliverer* (in which case, read 'deli[v]roit'?), but just possibly part of *delier*, 'to release' (cf. *AND s.v.* **deliverer, deslier**). Semantically, there seems to be some overlap between the two verbs in Anglo-Norman.

211 'Serfdom' (= LL 'servitudo'): *AND s.v.* **vileinage.**

212 'Leaders, rulers, nobility': *AND s.v.* **primat;** *RMLWL s.v.* **prim/a (primatus** 372a). This sense is not given by Gdf (VI:405a; X:417b) or by TL (VII:1855).

213 'Raise, exalt' (= LL 'exaltaret'): *AND s.v.* **enhaucer.**

214 It looks suspiciously as if AN has omitted a section of its exemplar here, via an eyeskip from 'flagraretur' to 'impenderetur'. This coincides, in Lichfield MS 16, with a turning-over of the folio.

215 'To incur' (= LL 'incurreret'): *AND s.v.* **encurre.**

216 MS 'coveiteroit'(?): *AND s.v.* **convertir** (includes variant without nasal, *covertire*).

217 Apparently = 'il': see AN nn.193 and 121.

218 'Creator'; slightly surprisingly, the equivalent of LL 'conditor'. Not in *AND* (but cf. **faitour** and variant forms thereof); *AND s.v.* **faiture** has a doublet in **facture** (*ibid.* 291a and 293b). Not (with this sense) in Gdf (IX:591b); but given in TL III:1604 and *FEW* III:361a.

219 MS 'choser'.

220 MS 'Qui a lui fra servant non soulement vivere touz jours en perpetuel pees'. The text perhaps needs 'Qui [ceux] a lui servant' to make sense; the translator has just followed the Latin: i.e. 'who [*sc.* God] will make ('fra' at the end of the clause) [those] who serve him live in perpetual peace'.

221 MS 'incorporable'.

222 'Tant ... quant' again; see AN n.94.

223 Additional superscript 'o' over the 'o'.

224 MS 'velez', or 'vebez' (?).

225 Apparently = LL 'locati': despite appearances, 'allower' (cf. *AND s.v.* **aluer**, 'to hire') is p.p. (as frequently in this text, final [e] is variously spelt '-ez', '-er', with scant regard for morphological regularity).

226 'Incredible' (= LL 'incredibile'); not in *AND*; not, according to TL (IV:1369–1370) found with this sense until Deschamps, although it appears meaning 'unbelieving' in Froissart (cf. Gdf IV:568b). Also attested in Jean de Vignay's translation (*c.* 1331–1333) of Odoric of Pordenone, *Les Merveilles de la Terre d'Outremer*, ed. D.A. Trotter (Exeter: University of Exeter, 1990), p.83.1 (*var.* imposible a croire); cf. *ibid.* p.xxix and n.70.

227 There is no obvious reason for the feminine here (cf. LL 'alicui'): correct to 'ascun', or is this simply a spelling for final 'n'?

228 If LL were to be followed ('superius nominavimus') for the establishment of AN, there would be a strong case for emendation to '[avons] avaunt nomez'. An alternative (accepting that 'superius' is not translated) would be 'avons nomez'. Cf. AN n.230 for the punctuation in AN.

229 At first sight, an odd choice of word to correspond to LL's 'fortitudo', elsewhere (notably §5) rendered by 'force'. One explanation is that here (as in the next line) the abbreviation mark is redundant: read 'fortesse', as per *AND s.v.* **fortece**. It is, however, possible that the author of AN did intend 'forteresse', in the sense of 'force, strength'. Gdf IV:99c gives *only* this sense *s.v.* **forteresce**; the first sense given in TL II:2160 is this one. For figurative meanings of the word in Anglo-Norman see *AND s.v.* **fortelesce**.

230 Capital not retained. AN's punctuation here would make the words 'ce q'est desuz parlez' part of the previous clause; this would make equally good sense, but would follow LL less satisfactorily.

231 'Capacity, power' (= LL 'virtus'): *AND s.v.* **vertu**.

232 'Gifts' (= LL 'dona'), plural of *AND* **don**[1]; or (less plausibly) read 'donnés', p.p. as substantive of **doner**[1] (not given in *AND* 194b).

233 i.e. fut.1 of *poer*. Not listed as form in *AND s.v.* **poer**. Cf. AN n.61.

234 'Earned, won': *AND s.v.* **gainer**.

235 'Variation' (= LL 'transmutacio'): *AND s.v.* **variance**.

236 MS 'enumbre de ele': 'de' is redundant, unless (which seems likely) a word is missing (corresponding to LL genitive 'vicissitudinis'): for the possibility that the common Latin source for AN and ME lacked this word, see ME n.200. 'Enumbre' means 'shadow' (cf. LL 'obumbracio'); not in *AND*. The substantive is not in Gdf or TL, but both have a verb *enombrer* (Gdf III:212c; TL III:47b).

237 Corresponding to LL 'ibi': i.e. *AND* **i**[2] (cf. AN n.121).

238 Not in *AND*; = LL 'inestimabile'. Cf. Gdf X:11a; TL IV:1381.

239 MS 'ceste de ce'.

240 MS abbreviation suggests 'avenus'. The sense, and LL ('futurus'), both point to 'a veners'; cf. AN n.158.

241 'Enjoy': *AND s.v.* **esjoir**. The forms of the verb in this text (ind.pr.3 'enjoye'; ind.pr.4 'enjoyons'; fut.3 'enjoyera'; cond.5 'enjoyereiez', 'enjoieroiez', 'enjoyroiez') all indicate an infinitive *enjoier*; modification of both prefix and conjugation is of course typical of Anglo-Norman. The word order of this sentence is chaotic in AN.

242 'Enjoy' (= LL 'exultares'): *AND s.v.* **joir**.

243 'Gift' (= LL 'donacio'): *AND s.v.* **don**[1] (this spelling is not given).

244 MS 'sut'; read 'sur'?

245 Only listed as v.n. in *AND*, meaning 'to abound': transitive here, despite LL ('he will be bountiful to all').

246 *AND*'s **enviruner** is v.a. only. Both Gdf (III:318a) and TL (III:723) give it as v.n. as well.

247 The unexpected word order in the manuscript could just about be defended if 'se ount' is taken as *aver* v.refl., meaning 'to have for themselves' (a sense absent from *AND s.v.* **aver**[2]), and 'entur' as adverb not preposition: 'as fishes have the sea everywhere around'. Or read 'entour sé le mere', 'they have the sea all around them', where 'sé' (= LL 'se') is object pronoun (*AND s.v.* **sei**[2]) and 'entur' is prepositional. Note, however, that 'entour eux' corresponds to 'circa se' in the next sentence.

248 'Qi' in Anglo-Norman can refer to things as well as to people: cf. *AND s.v.* **qui**[1], so there is no pressing need to alter to 'q[ue]i'. Cf. AN n.39.

249 'Filled' (= LL 'replebitur'): *AND s.v.* **replenir**.

250 There is a space in the manuscript here, but no apparent erasure or omission.

251 'Remember'; an unusual choice for LL's 'estimare'. This form of the infinitive is not given in *AND*, Gdf or TL (*s.v.* **remembrer** in each case). There might be a case for 'remembre[r]'.

252 The syntax (and the ablative absolute in LL) implies that this must be p.p. of *regarder*: 'having considered the fourteen parts of blessedness ...'.

253 See AN n.248 (= LL 'quid'). The abbreviation, however, suggests that 'qu[e]i' is possible.

254 A plural verb would be logical here (= LL 'debeant'); read 'devien[en]t'?

255 MS 'quant quant'.

256 'In order that' (= LL 'ut'); not given in *AND s.v.* **sicum**.

257 The nonsensical MS reading here presumably derives from an error in the Latin original, i.e. (presumably) 'quantum et male' as in LL, where 'male' clearly stands for 'quale' (cf. LL n.78). Perhaps one might substitute 'et combien' for 'maveis'.

258 'Ist' (ind.pr.3 of *issir*, 'to issue') is an odd translation of 'manat', although it makes sense here; 'est' would be closer to LL.

259 'Plenty' (= LL 'copia'): *AND s.v.* **plenté**.

260 MS again has a 9-shaped abbreviation mark.

261 There is a hole and a space in the manuscript here, but nothing apparently omitted or erased.

262 'Differs' (= LL 'differt'); ind.pr.3 implying (in theory) infinitive *differir*; not in *AND*, but cf. Gdf *s.v.* **differer** (II:712b); TL *s.v.* **diferer** (II:1924).

263 Latinism: 'creative, generative' or subst. 'creatrix' (= LL 'creatrix', which according to *DMLBS* can be adj. or subst.); *AND* only has **creatur**, as subst.

264 'Will benefit from, make (profitable) use of' (= LL 'fruetur'); not amongst the meanings given in *AND s.v.* **user**. Cf. TL XI:64 (v.n. 'Gebrauch machen von'), and the (related) legal usage in Gdf VIII:122a.

265 MS 'quei a nous sera'.

266 No capital in the manuscript.

267 Ind.pr.2 of *aler* (*AND s.v.* **aler**[1]: this form not listed).

268 MS 'petit hor', with a nasal bar over the 'o'.

269 'Gives (you) delight' (= LL 'delectat'): *AND s.v.* **deliter**.

270 The spelling 'i' for post-tonic mute 'e' may well be encouraged (here) by 'angelis' in the exemplar (as in LL). See AN n.18.

271 Translates the Latin passive 'seminatur', 'shall be sown (born)', just as 'il est veu' translates 'videtur'. *AND* has *seminer* in both literal and figurative senses.

272 'Healthy, salubrious' (= LL 'salubris'); not in *AND*; cf. Gdf X:620b; TL IX:125 (*Quatre Livres des Reis*); *FEW* XI:125a.

273 'Diuturnitas' written in R.H. margin at end of line opposite the first syllable of this word.

274 'Sacietas' written in R.H. margin at end of line opposite this word.

275 'Satiety': *AND s.v.* **sacieté**.

276 'Ebrietas' written in R.H. margin at end of line opposite this word.

277 MS 'plentvousté'. 'Plentuousté' is a less likely reading, but only because AN has several examples of the otherwise unattested 'plentevousté' (see AN n.128). Gdf, however, has a headword **plentuoseté** (the form actually attested seems to be *plantuousseté*), VI:217b, to which TL refers; cf. *FEW* IX:58b.

278 MS 'de le choer'. The translator has taken 'chori', nom. pl., 'the choirs', for a gen. sg. Cf. *AND s.v.* **queor**[1].

279 'Melodie' written in R.H. margin at end of line opposite this word.

280 MS 'Si chescun lour delit soit nette et nemy innette'. Something is obviously wrong with this phrase: the MS reading does not make sense. The suggestion in our printed text is based on LL. 'Innette' means 'unclean'; not in *AND*; = LL 'immunda', just as 'nette' corresponds to 'munda'. Both *monde* and *immonde* are given in *AND* (436b and 361a). 'Innette' is not given in any dictionary consulted (cf. *FEW s.v.* **nitidus** for full range of reflexes and derivatives).

281 Initial 'e' is superscript.

282 'Voluptas' written in R.H. margin at end of line opposite this word.

283 'Sapiencia' written in R.H. margin at end of line opposite this word. The emendation is necessary if the text is to make sense.

284 Fut.6.

285 'Amicicia' written in R.H. margin at end of line opposite first syllable of this word.

286 'Concordia' written in R.H. margin at end of line opposite this word.

287 'Potestas' written in R.H. margin at end of line opposite this word.

288 It may be that the opening 'a eux sera' is a scribal error, which should be deleted.

289 The comparison with LL ('sicut illi non aliud volent quam quod ille') perhaps suggests that this is not *voleir mes* 'to prefer', but *mes* as an exceptive preposition, i.e. 'they do not want anything except [that which] he wants' (for both possibilities, cf. *AND s.v.* **mes**[4], (1) and (2) respectively).

290 MS 'issint ille ne vuille quanque ils ne vuillent'.

291 Cond.3 of *poer.*

292 'Honor' written in L.H. margin opposite the first syllable of this word.

293 Despite spelling, possessive adj., not demonstrative (= LL 'suos').

294 'Divitie' written in L.H. margin opposite the first syllable of this word.

295 MS 'appelleres'.

296 MS 'l'ou'.

297 'Securitas' written in L.H. margin opposite this word.

298 MS 'departie'.

299 'Needy' (= LL 'indigens'): *AND s.v.* **bosoignable.**

300 'Gaudium' written in L.H. margin opposite this word.

301 Read 'tez' (LL 'tua')?

302 This word is plainly wrong: what is needed is something meaning 'intimate friends' (cf. LL 'intima').

303 MS 'innumerabler'.

304 Final 's' is superscript, intruding into the R.H. margin.

305 The heart, mind and soul are understood as the subject of the verb (LL repeats them).

306 'Dieu' is a superscript addition, apparently in the same hand.

307 Supplied on the basis that the Latin 'si hoc est gaudium' is rendered, a few lines later, by 'si ceo soit joye'. A more plausible emendation, from a palaeographical point of view, might be to 'si ceste [est] joye'.

308 Imperative. See AN n.225.

309 *AND* lists *joiant* adj., but not substantive as here. Cf. Gdf IV:646; TL IV:1714 (both adj. only).

310 This use of 'dedeins' (= LL 'intus') with 'en' is not given in *AND s.v.* **dedenz.** TL has a possible use of it (*an mere dedanz*, adv.), II:1264.

311 Note the change of tense from the Latin, and the error of 'descendre' for 'ascendere', also found above (cf. AN n.24).

312 MS 'veia'.

313 MS 'oia'.

314 N.B. both of these biblical quotations contain the same error.

315 MS 'aymeret'. It is possible that this form, where the nasal has been omitted (cf. MS 'equis' for enquis, §1; possibly 'defaunte' for 'defaute', cf. AN n.157), provides evidence of denasalization in later Anglo-Norman, and that the manuscript reading should stand uncorrected.

316 MS 'que q puisse', with superscript abbreviation mark over 'q'.

317 'Venir au plein' seems to be calqued on the Latin (cf. LL), and apparently means something like 'to enjoy (it) fully, to have full enjoyment (of it)'. The expression is not in *AND s.v.* **plein** or *s.v.* **venir.** Gdf does not give it *s.v.* 2 **plein** (VI:212c; X:355a); TL has various verbs used with *a plein* and *tot a plein* (VII:1132), as does *FEW* IX:59b.

318 'Amour' is the subject; the verb is sbj.pr.3: 'and may your love increase' (= LL 'crescat amor tuus'). Cf. *AND s.v.* **acreistre.**

319 'Speaks, preaches', apparently ind.pr.3 or sbj.pr.3 of *sermonizer*, not given in *AND*, Gdf or TL. LL has 'sermocinetur'. This entire series of verbs is in the subjunctive in LL. Most of the Anglo-Norman verbs here could be either subjunctive or indicative: 'sermonize' could conceivably be taken as sbj.pr. 3 of *sermonir*. *AND s.v.* **sermuner**[2], gives the form *sermunier.*

320 'Hungers after' (= LL 'esuriat'), ind.pr.3 (or sbj.pr.3) of *enfaymer*: cf. *AND s.v.* **enfamer** (?), **enfaminer,** and TL *s.v.* **enfaminer** (III:315).

321 'Thirsts after' (= LL 'siciat'), ind.pr.3 (or sbj.pr.3) of *enseyver*: *AND*, **sei**[1]. There is no reflex of the verb SITIO (with or without any prefix) given in *AND*, Gdf or TL. *FEW* XI:662b has p.p. *essévé* (s. xiii) and p.p. *essoyvé* (1582). *Assoiffer*, a vernacular formation from *soif* < SITIS, is given from 1607 only.

322 'Forever', i.e. Latin formula 'in secula' (as LL); the expression is not given in *AND s.v.* **secle,** but cf. *en pardurable secle (ibid.)*. Gdf VII:418a quotes a translation of a sermon by St Bernard where the expression 'ens seules des seules' is used; cf. TL IX:629.

323 MS 'miserie'.

324 For paragraph divisions in this part of the text, see the Introduction, pp.39–40.

325 Small hole in the manuscript after this word, through which 'en' (from line 15 of f.247[r]) can be read.

326 'Wicked, impious', here (and in the first sentence of the next paragraph) a substantive (= LL 'impii'): *AND s.v.* **maluré** (adj. only). Several of the quotations in both Gdf (V:117a) and TL (V:985) could be regarded as substantival uses of p.p. *maleuré.*

327 Either plural adj. 'dirty' (*AND s.v.* **ord**), which LL 'turpiores' adj. supports, or possibly p.p. of *order* 'to dirty' (*AND s.v.*; cf. AN n.184). LL's 'fuligine' (figuratively, 'blackness'?) is translated rather prosaically by 'ordure'.

328 The section between oblique strokes \my ... seront/ is written in the R.H. margin, opposite 'y' of 'yceux', apparently in the same hand, and is presumably meant to be inserted at the inverted caret mark following 'serront'. Cf. LL. The corrected eyeskip ('serront'/'seront') could, equally, arise from two consecutive 3rd-person passive plurals ('-untur'), perhaps abbreviated, in a Latin exemplar, and is thus inconclusive as evidence that AN derives from an Anglo-Norman exemplar.

329 'Pulchri' and 'Fedi' are written opposite this paragraph in the R.H. margin.

330 Adj. meaning 'rapid, speedy' (consigned by *AND s.v.* **[vistessé]**); not in Gdf; AN has a synonymic pair ('vestessez, ou legers') corresponding to LL 'velocissimi'.

331 Latinism (= LL 'pigirrimi'), 'slow'; not in *AND*. The author of AN may or may not have understood the Latin of his exemplar: his version is barely comprehensible. The word is in Gdf *s.v.* **paresseux** (VI:157b) and in *FEW* VIII:445.

332 'Weight, burden' (= LL 'pondus'): *AND s.v.* **charge**.

333 The pair of marginal words (to correspond to 'Veloces' – 'Pigri' in LL f.196[r]) is lacking in the AN version.

334 'Fortes' and 'Debiles' are written opposite this paragraph in the L.H. margin.

335 'Unjust, sinful' (= LL 'iniusti'): *AND s.v.* **torcious**.

336 'Estre', expuncted and crossed out, is written at the beginning of the line in the manuscript, before 'aler'.

337 'Enclosed place' (= LL 'clausura'): *AND s.v.* **clos**; Gdf IX:114a–b (**clos, close**); TL II:502 (**clos**).

338 'Allowed to, suffered to' (= LL 'permittentur'): *AND s.v.* **suffrir** (same usage in ROUGH 15 quotation, top of 737a).

339 'Liberi' and 'Clausi' are written opposite this paragraph in the L.H. margin. The last clause of LL ('et ab omnibus que voluerint prohibebuntur') is not in AN.

340 Or 'sainté'?

341 The text is not clear here, and seems not to translate the Latin. 'Continuel' has no equivalent in LL, and 'seront pechez' makes no sense at all. If LL 'pocientur' is taken to mean 'to receive, acquire' (i.e. *pocior/potior*), a possible suggestion for AN might be 'purveez', 'provided with' (*AND s.v.* **purveer**[1]).

342 Possibly add '[si maladez]' (cf. LL 'infirmi')?

343 'Sani' and 'Languidi' are written opposite this paragraph in the L.H. margin. 'Ga' (at end of line) written next to a hole in the manuscript, through which 'me' (from line 15 of f.245[v]) is visible.

344 'Drink' (*AND s.v.* **beverage**); LL does not correspond exactly.

345 'Voluptas' and 'Anxietas' are written opposite this paragraph in the L.H.

margin. An obelisk in the manuscript refers to a line of text added below this page and marked by a cross (the material between oblique strokes here); it is in the same, or a similar, hand. The omission is most easily explicable as eyeskip between either 'continet' and 'sencient' in a presumed Latin exemplar, or as the same process between the corresponding AN verbs 'contient' and 'sentirent'.

346 'Diuturnitas' and 'Brevitas' are written in L.H. margin opposite this paragraph.

347 The suggestion assumes that this is p.p. of *AND* **avancer**[1], here 'avauntder' (= *avanter*), 'to help, advance' (= LL 'prediti', i.e. adj. *preditus*). Cf. Gdf **3 avancier** (I:509b); TL I:701 and 709 (**avancir**).

348 'Sapientes' and 'Incipientes' are written in L.H. margin opposite this paragraph.

349 The sense, presumably, is 'the wisdom which is from (or of) God'; the relative (?) 'quel' does not convey this clearly.

350 'Privati' in LL corresponds to a synonymic pair 'oustez, ou privez', 'deprived (of)' in AN (cf. *AND s.v.* **oster**[1], **priver**), although normal expansion of the manuscript abbreviation would in fact suggest 'prenez', which makes no sense at all.

351 The manuscript word order can be retained if 'grevez' is taken as fem. pl. adj., 'grievous' (*AND s.v.* **gref**). But, if 'grevez' is p.p. of *AND* **grever**[1], 'to oppress, distress' (which would correspond better to LL 'urgebuntur'), the word order in the manuscript is wrong, and the text should read 'grevez ov tauntz dolours'.

352 'Enmity' (= LL 'inimiciciam'): *AND s.v.* **enemisté**.

353 The words 'toutz lez autrez bones lui aymerount, par issint' (between oblique strokes here) are written in the R.H. margin, with a caret mark opposite '... Dieu ly haye'; the passage seems, however, to fit best here.

354 MS 'aultre'.

355 The construction is 'aver ou (=en) haye', 'to hate'; cf. LL 'habere odio' (for the noun 'haye', *AND s.v.* **hé**[1]). It is used again ('le [corps] avra l'alme en haye') in the next paragraph. The expression is attested in continental French (two quotations *s.v.* **hé** in TL IV:1044), and may be compared to the more common *cuillir, prendre en hé* (cf. TL *ibid.*; Gdf IV:445c).

356 'Amici' and 'Inimici' are written in the R.H. margin opposite this paragraph.

357 This phrase is the equivalent of LL's 'erunt miseri iugi dissencione discordes'. AN makes sense as it stands only if MS 'decordes' is taken as p.p. of *decorder*, i.e. *AND*'s **descorder**, meaning 'disagreeing, in disagreement'. Alternatively, read '[en] decorde(s)' (the locution 'en descord' ('in disagreement') is used two lines below in AN: *AND s.v.* **descord, desacord**).

358 This seems to be plural (read 'penser[s]'?), since it is followed by the relative clause 'pur touz quels ...'.

359 'Concordes' and 'Discordes' are written in the R.H. margin opposite this paragraph.

360 'Honorati' and 'Inhonorati' are written in the R.H. margin opposite this paragraph.

361 The manuscript is badly stained here.

362 'Heal': *AND s.v.* **garir**[1].

363 This must be p.p., to judge by LL ('adornatum'), though cond.3 is also syntactically possible (with corresponding changes to punctuation: remove comma after 'vestiroit', insert comma after 'honereit').

364 MS 'sicome' (no capital), 'Issint' (capital not retained).

365 MS 'en mortalité'. Or read '[ové] enmortalité'? The sense obviously requires 'immortality' not 'mortality', and LL has 'cum enim inmortalite'. *Immortalité* is not given in *AND*, although both *immortel* and *mortalité* are (361a and 432b). For *immortalité* cf. Gdf IX:784c; TL IV:1348; *FEW* IV:574a.

366 Classified by *AND* as p.p. of *vestir*, i.e. (figuratively) 'clothed, vested' (= LL 'indueret'). Other possibilities include a verb *vestituir*, or scribal error (dittography), in which case read 'vest(it)ut'.

367 MS 'feire', which does not make sense. 'To sit' is what is needed; the suggestion here is supported by LL as well as by the virtually identical passage a few lines above in AN. This whole passage is evidently corrupt in AN.

368 'On the other hand' (= LL 'econtra': *AND s.v.* **contraire** and also Gdf *s.v.* **encontraire** adj. (III:113c)).

369 Initial capital, not retained.

370 'Fetore' in the Latin may at some stage have been misread as 'tempore' to produce 'temps'. A reflex of *fetor* is presumably what is needed for the text to make sense, perhaps 'feteur' (cf. Gdf III:775a; TL III:1784; *FEW* III:677a).

371 'Rejected, thrown down' (= LL 'deiectus'): *AND s.v.* **degeter**.

372 'Wrong-doers' (= LL 'iniusti'): *AND s.v.* **torcenus**.

373 *Faillir* as v.a., 'to lack', is not common in Anglo-Norman (though given in *AND s.v.* **faillir**); the syntax here may well be influenced by Latin (LL: 'iniusti carebunt potestate').

374 Initial 'r' seems to be written over 'a'.

375 'Potentes' and 'Impotentes' are written in the L.H. margin opposite this paragraph.

376 i.e. p.p. of *AND* **seurer**; or read 'seures', adj.?

377 'Of falling', infinitive used where LL has a gerundive, 'cadendi'. Cf. *AND s.v.* **chair**.

378 A future tense would be logical here: an (abbreviated?) syllable may have been omitted.

379 'Securi' and 'Invidi' are written in the L.H. margin opposite this paragraph.

380 MS 'toutz maneres parties de tout manere caitifetee'.

381 'Wretchedness' (= LL 'miseria'): *AND s.v.* **chaitiveté**.

382 The AN text, which is incomplete, ends here. 'Gaudentes' and 'Tristes' are written in the L.H. margin opposite this paragraph.

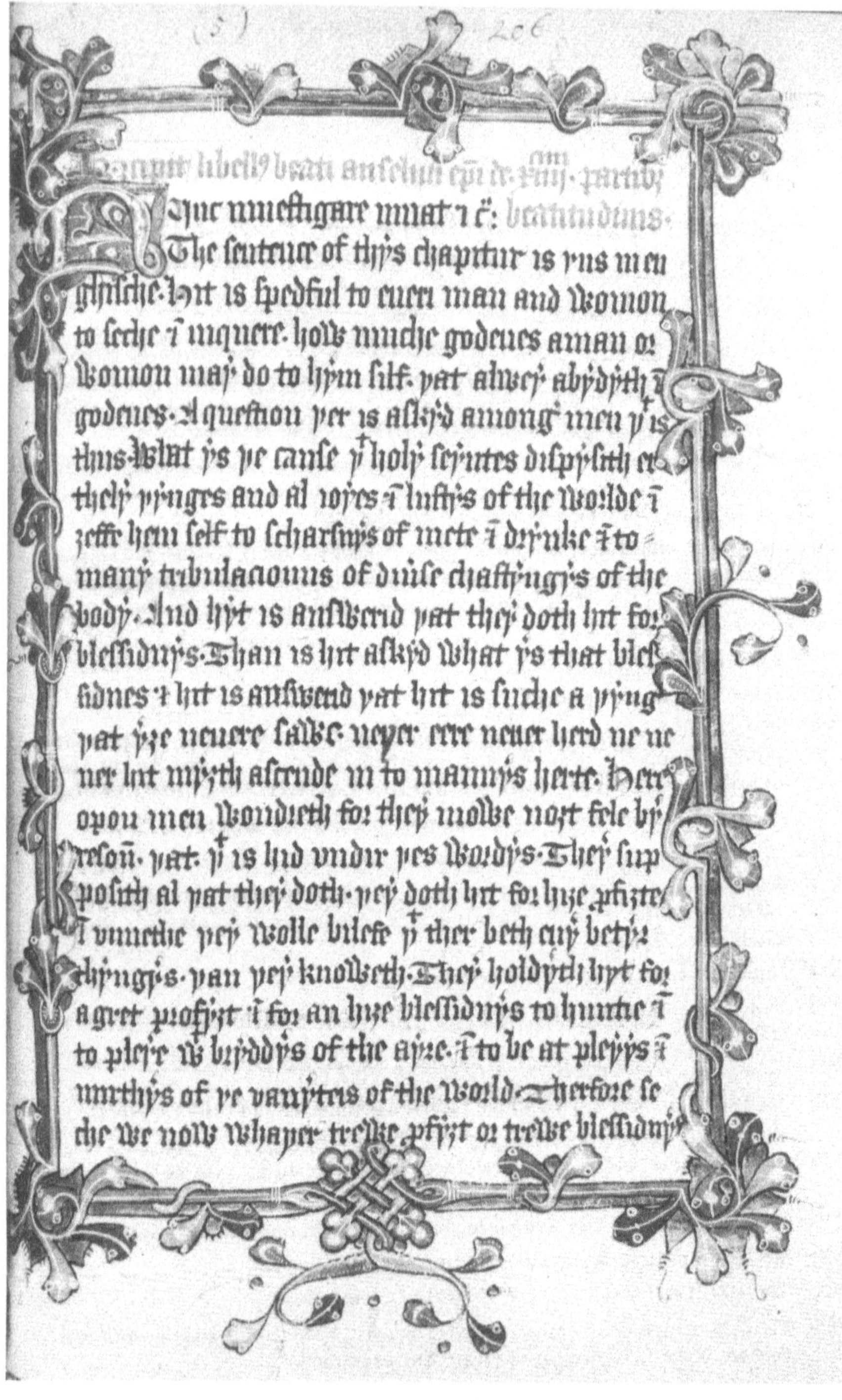

Incipit libell9 beati anselmi epi de ·xiiij· partibus
Hunc inuestigare iuuat i c: beatitudinis·
The sentence of thys chapitur is þus in en
glische· hyt is spedful to euery man and womon
to seche & inquere· how muche godenes a man or
womon may do to hym silf· þat alwey abydyth &
godenes· A question þer is askyd among men þt is
thus· What ys þe cause þt holy seyntes dispysith er
thely þynges and al ioyes & lustys of the worlde &
ȝeffe hem self to scharsnys of mete & drynke & to
many tribulacioums of diuse chastyngys of the
body· And hyt is answerd þat they doth hit for
blessidnys· Than is hyt askyd what ys that bles
sidnes & hyt is answerd þat hyt is suche a þyng
þat yȝe neuere sawe· neyer eere neuer herd ne ne
uer hit myȝth ascende in to mannys herte· Here
opon men wondreth for they mowe noȝt fele by
reson· þat· þt is hid vndir þes wordys· They sup
posith al þat they doth· þey doth hit for hiȝe profite
& muche þey wolle bileue þt ther beth euy betyr
thyngys· þan þey knoweth· They holdyth hyt for
a gret profyȝt & for an hiȝe blessidnys to hunte &
to pleye wt byrddys of the ayre· & to be at pleyys &
merthys of þe vanytees of the world· Therfore se
che we now whaþer treuwe profyȝt or treuwe blessidnys

Plate 2: The first page of the Middle English text (f.206r)
(Reduced)

DE QUATUORDECIM PARTIBUS BEATITUDINIS: THE MIDDLE ENGLISH

<Incipit libellus beati Anselmi episcopi de ·xiiii·^{cim} partibus beatitudinis.>

Nunc investigare iuvat et cetera. The sentence of thys chapitur is þus in Englisch.[1] Hit is spedful to everi man and womon[2] to seche and inquere how muche godenes a man or womon may do to hym silf, þat alwey abydyth godenes.[3] A question þer is askyd amonge men, þat is thus: 'What ys þe cause þat holy seyntes dispysith erþely þynges and al joyes and lustys of the worlde, and ȝeffe hem self to scharsnys[4] of mete and drynke, and to many tribulaciouns of diverse chastyngys[5] of the body?', and hyt is answerid þat they doth hit for blessidnys. Than is hit askyd: 'What ys that blessidnes?', and hit is answerid þat hit is suche a þyng 'þat yȝe nevere sawe, neþer eere never herd ne never hit myȝth ascende in to mannys herte'.[6] Here opon men wondreth, for they mowe noȝt fele by resoun þat þat is hid undir þes wordys. They supposith al þat they doth, þey doth hit for hiȝe profiȝte, and unnethe þey wolle bilefe þat ther beth eny betyr thyngys þan þey knoweth. They holdyth hyt for a gret profyȝt and for an hiȝe blessidnys to huntie[7] and to pleye with bryddys of the ayre, and to be at pleyys and mirthys of þe vanyteis of the world.[8] Therfore seche we now whaþer trewe profyȝtf[9] or trewe blessidnys [f.206^{v}] be hit[10] in huntynge, on pleyes and murthis and vayne syȝtys of the world. Trewe blessidnys is a sufficiens[11] of profiȝtys, whytoute al manere inprofyȝte.[12] Therfore if huntynge have on hym silf þis blesidnys or this profyȝte, þan hit is worþy to be usyd; but huntynge is withoute a profyȝt (for if hyt were profytable, every man myȝt hunte wiþoute reprefe) and therfore þys blessydnys or profyt is noȝt in huntynge; neþer þys blessydnes is noȝt founde in pleyynge wiþ bryddes neþer in murthis neþer in eny vanyteys of the world. Than whare ys hit? Haply hit is in grette bildyngys and in gret wardyd[13] castellys, and in gold and in silvore, and in horse of gret valoure, and in gret possessyons of temperal[14] godys: and if þis blessidnys be in suche[15] þynges, ful blessid is he þan þat havyth hem, if he be delivered ther þrowe fro al besynys and charge and laboure of the world; but we seeth in certeyne þat þey that havyth suche þyngys in possession beth more ygrevyd with besynes and laboure and kepynge þer of, þan þey be þat have but lityl of worldely godys – and[16] þerfore trewe profiȝt and blessidnys[17] is noȝt yfounde in suche þyngys. Than whare schul we seche þat blessydnys? We most nedys seche hit in oþyr þyngys if we desire [f.207r] to fynde hit. ¶ I know be hit þat ther beth twey[18] maneres of blessidnes, and twey maneres of wrecchidnis. On blessidnys is the weche blessidnys Adam had in paradise, and lost hit; and another blessidnys is þat is in hevyn, þe weche angelis, and Goddys s[e]ynttys[19] þat God hath take to hym, havyth in possession. On wrecchidnys is here in eorthe þe weche we suffreth in everi houre, and anoþer wrecchidnys is in the preson[20] of helle the weche soulys schul suffre aftir here deth. Thilke blessidnys þat Adam had in paradise duryd but for[21] a tyme, but þylke hevynly blessidnys for the cause of wham Adam was made is everemore lastynge. The wrecchidnys and sorowe and tribulacioun þat we suffreth here in oure life hath an ende, but þat wrecchidnys þat ys in helle haþ nevere an ende, the wycche wrecchidnys is callyd 'deth': wharefore hit \ys/[22] prayyd in holy chirche þat 'þe secunde deth'[23] schuld have no powere on him that is baptisid, and bilevyth on Crist.

2 <**Quod beatitudo proposita gracius sapiat si per partes[24] lacius dividatur.**>

Beatitudo igitur illa que promittitur sanctis et cetera. The sentence of þis chapitur is þus in Englische. The blessidnys þat ys behote to seyntys is so gret and mervelous þat 'yȝe never sawe hit, neþer eere hirde [f.207v] hit ne nevere hit miȝt ascende in to mannys hert';[25] and siþþe we mowe noȝt see thys blessidnys bicause of þe magnytude þer of, biholde we and considere we þan þat þynge that may delyte us in þys life, and biholde we what hit is, þat semeth gode and honeste, if haply eny manere þynge may be founde of þat wondirful wordis þat ys sayd abofe (whare on hit is seid þat hevynly blessidnys is so mervelous þat 'yȝe nevere sawe hit ne ere nevere hird hit')[26] if hit myȝt be seid more clerere and have more esioure savoure[27] to mannys undirstondynge. Alle þys blessidnys þat ys behote to Goddys seyntys is comprehendyd[28] in ful fewe wordys, an for[29] by cause þes wordys beth yseid so derke and so close and so harde to mannys underestandynge, enforse we ure silf[30] to drawe oute sumwhate of so excellent grace of þilke byheste of Goddys seyntys, and departe[31] we hit in to mony partyes, þat hit may be seid and isey[32] more cleroure to mannys underestandynge. Dowȝtelese if ther be a gret appul yȝyve[33] to a ȝonge[34] childe for the child schuld ete hit, the chylde schal noȝt have my3t forto bite hyt for the grette tendirnys of his mowthe: but if þe apul is kut in to smale parties, þan may þe child ete hit savely[35] withowte grevance of hys mowthe; [f.208r] and so may þe childe ete the apul with the savoure þer of, whan þe apul is kutte in to smale pecis, þat my3t no3t afore tyme undirstond of whate savoure þe appul whas[36] whan he was hole. Therfore, þe promisse of God þat is unvisibile ysavyd and ikepte hole[37] to þe disposicioun of God, enserche[38] we bisily, or we com thedir whare we may see God 'ry3t as he ys'[39] in his maieste, what þynge belongeth to oure bodyes and what bilongeth to oure soulys,[40] and what þynge we mowe coveytye and desire freely withoute synne – knowynge and undirstondynge þat no manere þynge of worschip or of eny godenys wantyth to hem þat beth isette in þat blessidnys þat is in hevyn. Sevyn þyngys ther beeth þat mowe be acordynge to mannys body, and they beth ful comenabile[41] and suffi\ci/ent[42] ynow to blessidnys, þe wycche beth þes in Latyn: Pulcritudo,[43] Velocitas, Fortitudo, Libertas, Sanitas, Voluptas, Diuturnitas; and other vii þyngis þer beth þat perteyneth to þe soule þat beth this: Sapiencia, Amicicia, Concordia, Honor, Potestas, Securitas, Gaudium. The first vii, þat bilongyþ to the body, beth thes in Englysche: Fayrnes, Swyftnes, Strengthe, Freenes, Helthe, Lust, and longnys of tyme; and þe other vii, þat [f.208v] perteyneth to þe soule, beþ þes in Englische: Whysdome, Frendschip, Acorde to gedere, Worschip, Power, Sykyrnes, and Blysse. Hit is no dowte þat seyntes þat ben in hevyn havyth al thys blessidnis, siþþe þat he duelleth on hym[44] and is president[45] on hym of whom al godenys comy3th, þat ys ful of my3t and ful of joye, al þynge havynge Crist him silf.[46] Therfore go we a3ene a litil to oure first purpose, and enforse we us silf[47] to schewe, with a schort reson, þes wordys þat we seyd afore: and bygynne we at þe lowyst partye of hem and so ascende we up by grecys.[48]

3 <**De pulcritudine sanctorum que est prima pars beatitudinis ad corpora eorum pertinens.**>[49]

Queris de pulcritudine. The sentence of þys chapitur is þus in Englische. Thow askys haply what feyrnys seyntys havyth in hevyn, and if þow wolt knowe how hit is, huyre þow and take gode hede to þus ywryte[50]: 'Ri3tful men schul schyne as the sonne',[51] and þan 'schal þe mone schyne as clere as the sonne doth nowe, and the sonne schal schyne[52] sevynfold cleroure þan he doth nowe';[53] and þo3 hit my3\t/[54] be þat þe schynnynge of the sonne of vii dayes my3t be gadered to gadere on a day, 3ut schal þe sonne have at tha\t/ tyme as mucche clernes as have now vii dayys, þoȝ þey [f.209r] myȝ\t/ be had on one day. Therfore seþþe oure bodyes 'schul schyne as bryȝt as the sonne',[55] the wycche sonne schal have þe clernys on hym silf of vii daies, þan withowte dowte, ful gret and withoute comparison þat feyrnes schal be and overepassynge gret; and fortheremore underestonde we whare hit is wrete þus: ¶ 'Salvatorem expectamus dominum Jhesum Christum qui reformabit corpus humilitatis nostre configuratum corpori claritatis sue.' ¶ That is to seie: 'We abydeth Oure Lord Jhesu Crist oure savyoure weche schal reforme[56] þe body of owre mekenys[57], and make hit evyn licke to the body of his owne clernys.'[58] ¶ What tyme Oure Lord whas transfiguryd afore his discipulis in the montayne, as the Gospel makyþ mension, 'his face schone as bryȝt as the sonne',[59] þrow þe gladnys of the weche bryȝtnys seynt \Petir/[60] was so delyȝtyd for joye þat he seid to Oure Lord þus: ¶ 'Domine bonum est nos hic esse', ¶ that is to seie: 'Lord, hit is gode to us to be here stille.'[61] Also þe 'lykenys' of the angel þat sate and kepte þe[62] sepulcre of Owre Lord, appered and schone as 'briȝt as the bryȝtnes' of hevyn.[63] Therfore syþþe þe bryȝtnys of on angele was so gret schynynge, what trowist þou how glorious and gret schal þilke feyrnys be whan þowsandys withoute noumbre [f.209v] of seyntys schul be imade evyn ylike on clernys and bryȝ\t/ nys to the body of Oure Lord Jhesu Crist, and schul apere with hym in hevyn?[64] The holy man David considerit wel and sawe wel this feire blessidnys and this blessid feyrnys, whan he seid thus: ¶ 'Unam pecii a Domino hanc requiram ut inhabitem in domo Domini', ¶ that is to seie: 'I aske on thynge of Oure Lord, and I wole seche the same thynge, that is that I myȝt duelle in the house of Oure Lord.'[65] ¶ Ful many places in Holy Scripture make mension of this feyrnys, weche is truly a gret blessidnys. Nexte to this blessid feyrnes we have sette swyftnys, the weche is the secunde partye of blessidnys that seyntes havyth.

4 <**De velocitate sanctorum que est secunda pars beatitudinis ipsorum.**>

Velocitatem tantam habebunt hii qui cum deo erunt. ¶ The sentence of this chapitur is thus in Englissch. The seyntys that schul be with God schul have so muche swyftnys as hath the sonne beme, or as muche as eny yȝen havyth of eny creature that may see most clerest; ȝee schul undirstonde that anone as the sonne comyth in the este upon the eorthe, anon he streccheth his [f.210r] lemys[66] in to the west, and in the same maner the leme of a mannys yȝe, as sone as the browe[67] of the yȝe is openyd, is sende up in to hevyn or in to ferre contreye, whodir a man lust, if ther be none obstacul[68] that lette hit. In the same manere, whan oure bodyes schul be made spiritual and schul fele[69] no birthyn nether hevynes no more than angelis doth, þan þey schul[70] passe ful liȝtly whodir they have lust. At the generalle resurreccioun whan al eorthely men and wemen schul arise, than schal every partye þat bilongeth to every man and woman be knyȝtte to gedere in sucche manere – [71] þoȝ that hit be that an honde or a fote or eny membre of eny man or woman be buryed in the este party of the worlde, or thoȝ that hit be devouryd[72] with bestys, and the partye of the bodye lefte lyynge on the west or in the northe, or be disparkeled[73] abrode in to diverse partyes of the worlde – al the hole bodye schal so swyftely and in so litel tyme be gadered to gadere as the yȝe of a man or woman closeth and openyth. Babilon is a cite ful ferre fro the londe of Jude, and ȝut naȝt withstandynge that, an angelle brouȝt the prophete Abacuk in a moment fro the lond of Jude in to the cite of[74] [f.210v] Babilon, and put him upon the cafe[75] whare on liouns were ordeyned to devoure Danyel, whan Abacuk broȝt mete to hym;[76] ¶ and whan the prophete had fulfillid the comaundement of the angel, he was restoryd anone to his owne place. Withoute dowte he myȝt ful hyȝely wondrye ware he was whan he was brouȝt in to so ferre contre, siththe he was brouȝt so sone aȝene to his propir place; ¶ and siththe that everi seynte schal have so muche swyftnys, withoute dowte every seynte schal have a ful gret ȝifte and blessidnys of God, and ȝut thoȝ[77] the seyntys of God holde hem ful apayed with this blessidnys aforsaid, semynge to hem as thoȝ hit suffisid, noȝt wythstandynge that, they schul have more ther to, and that is strengthe.

5 <De fortitudine sanctorum que est tercia pars beatitudinis eorum.>[78]

Sequitur fortitudo et cetera. ¶ The sentence of this chapitur is thus in Englische. Strengthe[79] that every seynte schal have in the blisse of hevyn is more thane the strengthe of an hundrede thowsand men that here lyvyth in eorth, for the mesure of the myȝt of everyche of hem schal be so muche as eche [f.211r] of hem hath desire to have hit in strengthe; for if eny of hem hath desire to meofe al the eorthe with on fynger, withoute dowȝte he schal meof hit[80] after his owen desire. ȝe schul undirstonde þat[81] the devyl meovyth the ayre ofte tyme thorwe[82] strengthe of his owen kynde, and areryth grette whyndys and tempestys; and other whyles he maketh eorthe quavynges, and mony other thynges he doth that beth ful mervelous, and for that cause he is callid in Holy Wryȝt: 'fortis armatus' in Latyn, that is to seye in Englische: 'A stronge persone iarmyd';[83] and trowist thou that God wole noȝt ȝife as muche strengthe to his seyntis as he suffreth the devyl to have? Ȝus withoute dowȝte he schal ȝeve hem muche more strengthe, and muche bettur strengthe, than the devyl hath; and God forbede that eny man or woman havynge here ryȝt mynde undirstonde other wise, for as the holy prophete David seith:[84] ¶ 'Voluntatem etenim timencium se faciet Dominus',[85] ¶ that is to seye: ¶ 'Sothely', he seith, 'Oure Lord schal do and fulfille the wille of men and wemen that dredeth him'; and hit is seid of the same in another place, that 'nothynge schal wante'[86] to hem that dredeth God; and if 'no manere [f.211v] thynge schal want' nether lac to hem, than withoute dowȝte they schul not faile of strengthe but they schul have ful gret strengthe.

6 <**De libertate sanctorum que est quarta pars beatitudinis eorum.**>

Verum quia nec fortitudo et. ¶ The sentence of this chapitur is thus in Englische. Trewly neyther strengthe neyther swyftenys neyther feyrnys is but litel of price but he that had hit were free and nouȝ\t/ bonde; and therfore hit is no dowȝte but thylke blessid multitude of hevyn schul be ful fre and sikere fro al bondage, and they schul have so gret liberalte that non matere of substaunce of eny manere thynge – neyther fuyre, ne water, ne eny other mater – schal lette hem, but thei mowe entere in and go oute whather ever they luste to entre in or go oute; for ryȝt as Oure Lord God come oute frely of his sepulcre, and freely robbed helle and freely entred in to his discipulis 'the ȝatys beinge yclosyd and ischette',[87] ryȝt in the same manere seyntys of God, if they[88] wylle hit, they schul freely entre in to helle, and abide ther frely as longe tyme as thei wolle hem silf, withoute grevaunce or hurtynge or eny manere dissese,[89] for in the fuyre of helle schal no [f.212r] thynge ellys brenne, saffe only synnys and trespassis; and bycause that seyntes of God beth clene ypuryd for al manere fylthe of synne, they schul go wythoute eny grevaunce by the colde and hote brennynge forneycis and by stagnys[90] boylynge and al other diverse tormentis that ben in helle, withoute eny harme. Also the consideracioun in the byholdynge and the visitynge of seyntes þat wolle go to see the peynys of helle, schal be in choyse of the seyntes,[91] and to schame and confusion of hem that ben idampnyd; and the fredome and liberalte of hem schal be as muche as they schul have wylle to have hit. Next aftyr thys liberalte they schul have evere lastynge helthe, et cetera.

7 <**De sanitate sanctorum que est quinta pars beatitudinis eorum.**>

Beate itaque libertati et cetera. ¶ The sentence of thys chapitur is thus in Englysche. Nexte aftyr thys forsaid blessid liberalte and fredome, they schul have evere helthe withoute sekenes; and therfore that helthe schal be ful gret, for 'God schal wype awey al terys fro yȝen of his seyntes and aftyr that schal nevere no deth come to hem, neyther weylynge, ne wepynge, ne cryngе, ne no manere of sorowe, for al sucche [f.212v] thynges were ended afore tyme';[92] and ȝe schul understande that ho so wole wel consydere and see, he schal fynde none helthe on us that lyvyth in this present world, <for we havyth dissese on eche place of oure body. ¶ If a man towche and bruyse eny partye of the body that is sore, sumwhat harde, anone we cryeth for the dissese ther of; and also hit falleth the same> by al other partyes of oure membris, for if we be towched eny thyng[93] hard, anone we playneth us silf ihurte. And why is that trowyst thow? For noȝt ellys but tha\t/[94] we beth both sike and febil; but ther schal none hurtynge ne perschynge[95] come to the seyntys of God, neyther fuyre, ne yre,[96] ne watyr schal dissese hem. In that place schal no mynde of eny harme or lost[97] that eny of hem that schal be in hevyn hath suffred here in eorth dissese hem, for ther schal be so gret abundance of murthe and joye and blisse that they schul sette at nouȝt al sucche thyngys that ben passid; and if eny seynte wole take eny wreche[98] or veniaunce on eny thynge that hath grevyd him here in eorthe, he schal do hit aftyr his owen wille – but ȝut hit schal be no nede to hem to take veniaunce for hym silf, for Oure Lord seythe þus: [f.213r] 'michi vindictam, et ego retribuam'.[99] ¶ That is to seye: 'Put ȝe ȝowre veniaunce that ȝe wolle have do on myn handys and I wold do hit'; and be he that desireth to plese God welle awhare that he aske not veniaunce for his wrongis, but committe he his veniaunce for his unryȝt only to Crist, for withoute dowȝte if he take veniaunce for him silf, he schal noȝt have God to avenge him for his wronge, because that he toke hit presumptuosli[100] upon him silf; and therfore schal Oure Lord seie to him thus: 'By cause that þou haddist levere to avenge thy silf, than forto abyde in tyme that I wolde avenge the, therfore here aftyrward aske thow noȝt me to be avengyd for the.' Withoute dowte thys wordys of Owre Lord acordyth wel to us,[101] and therfore ho so that he be that foleweth the consaile of Oure Lord, and put his wronge to be avengyd throw him, whytoute dowȝte he schal be ful blessid, for to hym schal be none offense, neyȝther poverte, ne febilnis, but on hym schal be an hole blessidnys and ful blessid holnes. Al thes thyngys that beth aforsaid beth ful gode and gracious, but if hit be that men have no savoure ne lust on hem, than without dowte thei beth of no valowre and no [f.213v] thynge worthy; and if men have savoure[102] and gode velynge[103] on hem, than wythoute dowȝte they schul be passyngly and withoute comparison[104] gode. Next aftyr this blessyd helth, seyntes that schul be with God schul have lust and wille.

8 <**De voluptate sanctorum que est sexta pars beatitudinis eorum.**>

Necessario igitur adherit voluptas. ¶ The sentence of thys chapitur is thus in Englysche. Also seyntys þat schul be in hevyn with God schul have lust that schal ȝife hem savourynge and undirstondynge that they mowe savoure and undirstonde 'how delitable'[105] and how ful of joye the 'duellynge placys'[106] beth that beth in hevyn, and that they mowe undirstande that 'on daye is muche bettur for to be abydynge on in the blis of hevyn' then for to abide 'a thowsande dayys'[107] in eny murthes that beth made on erthe. Therfore schal here lust be ovyr passyngly muche, and hit schal fulfille al the seyntys of God with ovyrpassynge joye; and therfore seith the prophete thus: ¶ 'Inebriabuntur ab ubertate domus tue, et torrente voluptatis tue potabis eos',[108] ¶ that is to seie: ¶ 'They schul be fulfillid with the plentefulnys of thyn house, and thow schalt ȝyve hem drynke of the [f.214r] ryvere of thy lust, for with the is the welle of life.' Douȝtles this replecioun is ful wondirful, and thys plentefulnys is ful merveylous, and the hous of God is ful hyȝe wondirful to mannys mynde, for ryȝt as a ryvere falleth adoun fro an[109] hille and flueth forthe, on the same manere almyȝty God schal fulfille his seyntys with the wonderful suetnys of his house; and thoȝ we mowe noȝt fynde by oure undirstandynge a convenient[110] ensample of so muche suetnys and blessidnys in godenys as is in the hous of God, ȝut biholde we the overepassynge bitter sorwe that dampned creaturys schul have, aȝens the overepassynge gladnys that they schul have that schul be savyd. Withoute dowȝte, if hit so were that a man wolde drawe out the appul[111] of myn yȝe with a brennynge yre,[112] I schuld suffre ful gret sorwe ther throwe; and ȝif he wold drawe out myn other appul with the same turment, than were the sorowe muche the more to me; and if it were so that I schuld suffre the same peyne in al the membris of my body, and the grevans were evere more and more, how, trowyst thow, how sorwful and disesy[113] wold hit be to me? Trowist thow that we schuld \nouȝth/[114] be myndles and [f.214v] wixe wode[115] for sorwe? Than as thow trowist, what mynde schal my soule have whan lemys[116] and flammys of fuyre brennynge compassith me and brennyth me on every side, and peynys perschyth me on every side? And in that other syde,[117] whanne we schul come to hevyn we schul be fulfillid in another manere with gladnys and murthe of the syȝth of God, and we schul be replete of plentefulnys of the hous of Owre Lord, and we schul be yȝeve drinke of the ryvere of his lust and of his owen desyre. This temporale delyȝt and lust passynge awey[118] of this world is only yhadde and felyd whilys we lyvyth in eorth, in every part of oure body, but thylke delyte and lust that schal be in hevyn schul be felid in hem that schul be savid, as for as muche joye and gladnys as was the peyne of fuyre brennyn in here most sorwe; and seth that wyckyd creaturys schul suffre ful grevos turmentys and peynys[119] in al partyes of here bodyes bicause that they wolde not do aftir the plesauns of God, than by gret ryȝtfulnys[120] Godys seyntys that plesid him, and dede wele wylys they lyvyd, schul have ful muche joye and blesse in al here membris, seyth[121] they absteynyd [f.215r] hem from al wyckyd lustys; and in thys[122] manere schul Goddys seyntys have thus blessid lust the weche is trwly[123] delyȝtable, and a gret blessidnys. But ȝut hit were to hem ful litel to have this blessidnys that beth aforsaid, but[124] hit were so that[125] they myȝt have everemore abydynge and contynuaunce[126] on hem;[127] and therfore we have sette to thys another chapitur that is of everelastyngnys.

9 **<De diuturnitate sanctorum que est ·vii· pars beatitudinis eorum.>**

Accedat et[128] diuturnitas, que nullius finis, et cetera. ¶ The sentence of thys chapitur is thus in Englische. Next aftir thes forsaid blessidnys of lust commyth everelastyngnys and abydynge ther upon, þat nevere schal have an ende. The abydynge þat schal be ordeynyd for seyntys in hevyn schal nevere have ende, for here feyrenes, here swyftnys, here strengthe, here freedome, here helthe, and here lust schal nevere have ende; and therfore he that hath al this joye and blysse may wel seye thes wordys: ¶ 'Lauda jerusalem dominum lauda Deum[129] tuum Syon', that is to seye: 'Jerusalem preyse thow thy God, and thou Syon comende thou thy[130] Lord.' ¶ 'Quoniam confortavit seras [f.215v] portarum tuarum: benedixit filiis tuis in te', ¶ that is to seie, with that that is seid afore whare hit is seid, thus:[131] ¶ 'Jerusalem preyse thou thy Lord, for he hath confortyd the lokys of thy ȝatys, and hath blessid the children that were on the';[132] for truly schul they \be/[133] blessid, that schul be blessid with suche a benesoun.

10 <De sapiencia sanctorum que est ·viii· pars beatitudinis ad animas ipsorum pertinens.>[134]

Igitur consideratis et breviter insinuatis et cetera[135] ¶ The sentence of thys chapitur is thus in Englische. ¶ Whe[136] have schortely overe seye and in fwe[137] wordys comprehendyd thys vii blessidnys[sys][138] that ben rehersid afore, the weche bilongeth only to the body; ¶ and therfore now beholde we thylke blessidnys that perteyneyth only to oure soulys, of the weche the first partye ys wisdome, and that schul blessid seyntys have after here owen desyre, in so mucche that ther schal be no manere thynge be hid fro hem, but that they schul knowe al manere thynge that they have wille to knowe. They schul knowe al thynges that beth now to hem present, and suche[139] thyngys that schul come afterwarde, for ther schal no maner thynge be hidde nether withdrawe fro[140] here knowlyche; nether ther schal be no manere nede that eny [f.216r] man aske ho was hys graunte fadir, or of what lynage he come, or what he or sche is, for they þat schul be in that place schul have knowliche of al craftys and undirstandynge of al langagis, and al so they schul have knewliche of al creaturis; and eche of hem schal know al the thouȝtys of eche other, for ther schal no maner thynge be hidde fro hem; and they al that schul be in that place schul see al thyngys that I have do or do nowe lyvynge in eorth; and yf[141] I be in that place I schal see and knowe al thyngys that eche of hem hath do, and they schul noȝt be aschamyd ther of, if they have do comenabile satisfaccioun for here trespasses to God whylys[142] they lyvyd in eorth. We[143] knoweth wel, eche of us, that Petur the apostole forsoke Oure Lord thre tymes,[144] and we knoweth also that Marie Magdalene was a synful woman, and they knoweth hem silf that we knoweth hit, and thoȝ hit were so that we know hit noȝt, sethth we redeth and syngeth hit in Holy Scripture we most nedys knowe hyt, and ȝut they have no schame neyther harme ther throwe. <Angelys that beth in hevyn dyspisith noȝt seyntys, þoȝ that they have be overe come at sum tyme with temptaciouns; neyther seyntys dispisith nouȝt [f.216v] angelis thoȝ that they nevere suffred eny temptacioun, ne overecome no

temptacion. ¶ If hit were so that Michael wold seye to Petir: 'Thou forsokyst thy Lord, and so ded I never!' Petir myȝ[t][145] answere and seye thus: 'Sothe hit is that \y/[146] forsoke God, but thou suffredist nevere for him as muche as wold be on buffette'; but certeyn they doth nouȝt so, for they ben al acordynge to gederes as thoȝ they were al men or al angelys; and why is that as thou trowyst? Certeynly the cause is for they repentyd of here synnys, and therfore they have gete of God forȝyvnys;[147] and in the same manere, if we gete forȝyvnys[148] of God for oure synnys, than schul not we be aschamyd of oure trespassis that we dede before tyme; for why, what schame schul hit be to us, thou eny man or woman wold atwyte[149] us of that we dede whan we laye on oure cradelys? withoute douȝt hit were no schame to us, in so muche that thilke tyme and thilke age had none undirstandynge,[150] for as the apostole seyth: ¶ 'Cum enim essem parvulus sapiebam ut parvulus cogitabam ut parvulus. ¶ Quando autem factus sum vir evacu[f.217r]avi que erant parvuli', ¶ that is to seie: 'Whan I was a child I savouryd as a child, and I thouȝt as a child, but whan I was made a man I voyded awey al my childhode';[151] and ther in thilke blessid life of hevyn schal no manere thynge of schame be seye, and ȝyt every seynt[152] schal see eche otherys dedys withoute eny manere schame for ther schal no man deme eny thynge[153] unclene that God hath purgyd,[154] ne no man schal ther atwyte eny creature for here synnys afore don.

11 <**De amicicia sanctorum que est nova pars beatitudinis eorum.**>

Inter hec sanctorum agmina et cetera. ¶ The sentence of this chapitur is thus in Englis. ¶ Amonge this blessid companyue[155] of seyntys schal be another blessidnys, that is parfyȝt frenschyp[156] that nevere schal fayle, for eche of hem by hym silf, and they al in on, schul love here God more than hem silf; and eche of hem schul love eche other as muche as hem silf; and they schul love no more hem silf than they lovyth eche other, but they schul love to gadres evynyliche muche; but they schul love God abofe hem silf, and afore al oþer þengys;[157] and if[158] hit so be that eny man or woman that lyvyth nowe in eorthe [f.217v] sey that he wolle love his fadir and hir modir[159] more than eny other, be he awhare of that opynyoun and undirstande that he felith not truly in that that he seyd \so/;[160] and therfore what evere thou[161] be that seist so, that desyrist that al men schul love thy fadir and thy modir wham thou lovist specially afore al other – as muche as thou lovyst hem, thynke thou how muche thou woldist thy silfe forto be bylovyd in that place,[162] for haply I thynke[163] of my frende as thou thynkest on thy frende, and I have haply as gret desyre to my frende as thou hast to thy frende,[164] and the same havyth al other men and women also; and therfore, sithe thou coveytyst me forto love thy frende as muche as my silf, and I desyre that þou schuldest love my frende as muche as thou lovyst thyn owne persone, than thou schalt love me by thyn owen nede,[165] and al other as muche as thy silf, bycause that al seyntys schul love the as thou lovyst hem; and whan hit is thus[166] brouȝt to gedere than schal ful gret and parfyȝt frendeschyppe be amonge hem, for hit schal be in every seynt by hym silf; and in hem al, evyn commune and al ilyke, muche schal be par[f.218r]fyȝt love and charite. Therfore ful blessid schal thylke frenschippe be that the holy seyntys of God schul have in evere lastynge joye.

12 <**De concordia sanctorum que est decima pars beatitudinis ipsorum.**>

Hinc nascitur amica concordia et cetera ¶ The sentence of this chapitur is thus in Englische. Next aftyr thys forsaid blessidnys of frendschip of love, they schul have acordynge in on to gedere that schal alwey abyde and dw\e/lle[167] on hem ryȝth as the menbris[168] of oure bodyes acordyth eche with other. Oure membris here in eorth havyth so gret acordynge to gadere on eche other as thoȝ eche of hem were an yȝe, in so muche that on of hem may no manere thynge worche, neyther do withoute anoter;[169] for ȝif a man wole byhold upward or dounward with on yȝe,[170] he may not turne his syȝth thedirward \But hys boþe eyȝen turne to gedere þudyrward,/[171] for on yȝe wole noȝt kyndely[172] bihold in to no place withoute biholdynge of the other yȝe. They havyth so gret acordynge to gedere, that what so hit be that on yȝe desireth, the other disiryth the same. Also in the same maner al other membris of a man havyth bytwene hem ful gret acordynge to gadere, for mannys hande worchyth bothe for the feete and for al the [f.218v] body, and the yȝe biholdeth for the handis and al the body. The fot goth for the yȝe and al the body, other wile barefote, and the fote seith noȝt, thoȝ[173] that he be hurte and blede throw scharpe thornis and stonys, that he wolle no more go in to no place; neythere the honde seith, thoȝ he be hyȝe and sore wounded, that he wole no more worche therfore; and thoȝ hit falle þat the honde make a wounde in the fote with an axe, ȝut is the fote nothynge ymeovyd with wreche aȝens the honde, for they beth so yknytte to gedere with acordynge of love that they may not discordye bytwene hem silf by no maner weye, for that that is do to eny of hem, hit is do to eche of hem. They al do servys to God that ys here hedde, and they puttyth hem silf in perel for hym, and throw that hit may be opynly felid that they love God more than hem silf. This schal the acordynge be in thylke blessid contrey of hevyn, where schal no filthe of dissension be founde, whare God schal be sovereyn[174] abofe al, and ilovyd[175] most of hem alle abofe al other; for in certeyn, lasse a concorde schal noȝt be had amonge seyntys of God, weche beth Cristis membris, [f.219r] than is founde in the corruptibile body of men that lyveyth here in eorthe, but hit schal be muche bettur and more precious whan hit is ste\a/-bilid,[176] for hit schal nevere have ende.

13 <**De honore sanctorum que[177] est undecima pars beatitudinis eorum.**>

Honor quoque beatis illis magnus erit, et cetera. ¶ The sentence of this chapitur is thus in Englische. ¶ The worschip that seyntys schul have in hevyn schal be overepassynge gret, for as hit ys[178] wrete: 'Nimis honorati sunt amici tui, Deus', that is to seie: ¶ 'God, thy frendys beth hiȝely worthy to [be] worschipyd',[179] and therfore schal here worschip be so muche that hit may noȝt be comprehendid by mannys whytte. Put we now undir an ensaumple how eny servant myȝt be worschipid of his lord. ¶ Withoute douȝt, if an emperoure or a kynge wold make that eny of his servauntys schuld be worschiped in suche manere that if he[180] were bonde, that he wolde make hym fre and ordeyn hym to be a knyȝt – than were that servaunt hyȝely þer bounde to and in dette to hys lord that had so graciusly do to him; and if hit so were that the lord wolde put him and ordeyn hym [f.219v] to him to be principalle toward him,[181] how than, as thow supposist, were thys servaunt iholde to love hym?[182] Then reverence and worschip schul be of al men do, by cause of his lord, to hym, and they wold plese him, for they wold have hys love and noȝt hys wrethe;[183] and if hit were so that lord lovyd the same persone so muche as he were his owen sone, and wolde ordeyne hym[184] to be his ayre, than withoute dowte the joye and gladnes of thys servant wold be so overpassynge gret that he schul noȝt knowe hit him silf – thorwe[185] the weche ensaumple we mowe knowe that thilke ȝift that is ȝyfe of God is ful mervelous, and an overepassynge worschip to hym that God ȝyvyth hit, the weche God schal nouȝt only make his servantis to lyve evere lastyngly in evere durynge rest and pese, nether he schal nouȝt calle hem his owen frendys but he schal calle hem his owen children, and he schal ordeyne hem to be eyrys[186] of the kyndome of hevyn. Than, as thow trou\is/,[187] howe muche worschipe of every creature schal he have, wham God, fourme[188] of al creaturis, schal have as for a frende, and calle hym for his brother and holde him for sone his? And whan every creature schal be subiecte to hym for love [f.220r] of his Lord that is God, than douȝteles that schal be a gret worschip withoute eny comparison.[189]

14 <**De potestate sanctorum que est duodecima pars beatitudinis ipsorum.**>

Potestas eciam beatis illis tanta erit quanta[m quivis] eorum voluerit, et cetera. ¶ The sentence of this chapitur is thus in Englysche. The seyntys of God that schul be in hevyn schul have so muche power ygrauntyd to hem of God as they hem silf wille have and lust to have; for hit schal so stonde at that tyme, that what evere hit be that eny seynt commaunde to be do, be hit in hevyn or in eorth or in the see, or in the lowist partye of helle, hit schal be do withoute eny contradicioun. Withoute douȝte, thes wordys that I seye beth ful wondirful to many mennys undirstandynge, but if we consydere wel here intensioun, that is to seye, in what place schul we be at that tyme, and how we schul be transfigurid and purid in the siȝt of God (on the weche place schal no manere thynge wanti[190] neyther lacke to hem that lovyth him) than schul thes forsaid wordys be noȝt incredibile,[191] but sothe. Haply sum man wole suppose that this powere that I nowe seie to ȝowe, and make mension of [f.220v] afore, is strengthe (that I made in mensioun in the thred chapitur):[192] but hit is noȝt so, for the strengthe ware of I spake in the fowrth chapitur[193] is a vertu[194] and miȝt of worchynge and of dede doynge, but this power that I speke and make mensioun here is a vertue of commaundynge. Thys power schul truly the seyntys of God have, for they schul have al thyngys with God. Thys power that they schul have schal be power that evere schal last, and therfore hit schal be a ful hyȝe blessidnys to hem that havith hit. Withoute douȝt, thes forsaid ȝiftys of God beth glorious and sufficient ynow to seyntys of God, if hit so were that they myȝt have hem for evere, and have trewe sekyrnys of hem. Haply many man thynkyth[195] thys, and seyth thus in his mynde: 'Hit were litille joye to eny man to serve God but if he myȝth have sykyrnis of his joyes and blessidnissis that beth aforsayd.' Therfore hit byhovyth that seyntys have sykyrnys that they mowe kepe alwey that they haveth.

15 <De securitate sanctorum que est tercia decima pars beatitudinis eorum.>

Securitas ergo, sufficiens erit et cetera. ¶ The senten[f.221r]ce of this chapitur is thus in Englisce. ¶ Sykyrnys that Goddys seyntys schul have in hevyn schal be ynowe sufficient, for 'aftir tyme that a soule is thare he schal never aftyrward have weylynge nether sorwe';[196] and if I[197] schal be in that place I schal nevere lese that blessidnysse, but if I wolle lese hit be my owen wylle, or but ȝif God wold take hit fro me, or if eny that were more myȝty than God be wold come thyr and put me thennys; but I am sekyr that whan I have gete that place, that I schal nevere lese hit aftyrward, for I am sykyr that þere[198] ys in Goddys wordys[199] 'no transmutacioun'[200] neyther mys inquitynge[201] of mannys deservynge; and forthermore I am sykyr that ther may non come thedur that is strongour than he be. Wharefore sithe hit is thus, and schal be thus as I have seid, hit is no dowte that ther schal be evyn ful sykurnys, that nevyr schal have ende.

16 <De gaudio sanctorum quod est quartadecima[202] pars beatitudinis ipsorum.>

Erit igitur pro hys omnibus et cetera. ¶ The sentence of thys chapitur is thus in Englische. ¶ Abof al thys forsayd blessidnyssys schal be so [f.221v] muche joye that hit may not be comprehendit by mannys mynde, for hit passith mannys[203] undirstandynge to fele hit on his wyttys. Ho may thynke how muche joye a man schal have of him silf, whan \he schal have/[204] so muche Feyrnys, Swiftnys, Strengthe, Fredome, Helthe, Lust, Everelastyngnes, Wysdome, Frendschip,[205] Concordynge to gedres, Worschyp, Pouwer and Sykyrnys whan he comyth to hevyn? Truly ther may no man lyvynge here in eorth seie howe muche joye ther ys, for ther was never man[206] in thys present life that evere prevyd hit. Take thou, that hopyst to come to thylke place, go\od/[207] hede now to my wordis. If hit so were thou haddist[208] a frende that thou lovedist specialy, and God wold ȝif hym that joye, what semyth the, woldist thou noȝt be hily gladde therwith? And if hit were so that he wold ȝyve the same joye to tw\e/yne or thre or to mo of thy frendy\s/[209] that thou lovidist as muche as thy silf, what schuldest thou seye than? Withoute douȝt thou woldest have ful gret joye in thyn hert ther of, and thou woldes[210] have exultacioun and gladnys therfore, more than may be seyd with tonge – the weche ȝift of joye and gladnys schal [f.222r] noȝt fayle by no maner wey, but God schal ȝyve the same joye to oure frendys that brouȝt us in to thys world (that schulle be in that place by his mercy), so that we mowe joysy[211] and be glad on hym that schal be abofe us, that is God hym silf. Of us silf than mow we be gladyd, and of oure neyȝborys we mowe be ful joyeful. That joye and gladnys is so gret and huge as they that havyth desyreth to have hit.[212] Hit schal ȝyve superhabundance to hem al, and hit schal compasse hem al, and hit schal be to hem alle in every syde of hem al, for ryȝt as fisches that beth in the see havyth the see aboute hem on every syde, on the same manere Godys seyntys schul have aboute hem in every syde thylke overepassynge suetenys[213] of joye, of the weche is seyd to the gode servaunt[214] in Holy Wrytte thus: ¶ 'Intra in gaudium Domini tui', ¶ that is to seye: 'Entre thou in to the joye of thy Lord.'[215] <He alone may have ful parfyt joye and blisse, that may gete to hym al thes forsayd partyes of blessidnys. Ho may, or what thynge may be more blessed than is he, that schal be fulfillid with al thys forsaid joye and blisse? \And ȝyt he schal a noþer thyng[216] have to encrese of hys blessydnesse, where þorow he schal have more joye and blys./[217] Sith hit stant so that eche of hem schal love eche other as muche as hem silf, hit scheweth wel than that eche [f.222v] of hem schal have as muche gladnys of anotheres felicite as he schal have of his owen felicite. Than, as thow trowist, how many and how gret joyes schal eche of hem have, whan eche of hem schal have so gret joye of every otheris[218] blessidnys? And sethe he schal have so gret joye and gladnys of oþer men þat[219] he lovyth as muche as him silf, than howe muche blisse and gladnys and joye schal he have on God, wham[220] he schal love abofe him \self/?[221] withoute dowȝte he schal have so muche blessidnys that mannys mynde may noȝt suffice to undirstant hit.

17 **Quod Deum timentibus erit sufficiencia in omnibus.**>
Breviter perspectis,[222] quatuordecim partibus et cetera ¶ The sentence of this chapitur is thus in Englische. Seyth we have schortly overe seie and biholde the xiiii blessidnys[sys][223] or parfyȝtis[224] that beth found ther on, haply sum man wole aske and seye thus: 'What schul so muche feyrnis, swyftenys and al other-parteys aforesaid do to us, sethe that if a man or woman lyve welle and do wel, they schul have joye ynow that schal be sufficient ynowe to hem?'[225] But as toywchynge to that, ȝe schul underestande that God hath nede [f.223r] to no thynge, and ryȝth as he is sufficient in al thynges, on the same manere

schul al his mynystrys and his frendys have sufficiens in al thynges; and if hit were so that eny seynte that schal be in hevyn velyd hym silf impotent[226] and unmyȝty,[227] he wolde noȝt be so glad neyther so joyeful as he wold[228] be if he velid truly hym silf al myȝty[229] in al thynges. And why ys that? For his joye wolle nouȝt be so ful[230] that he schuld have sufficience ther[231] on if he were unnemyȝty[232] and impotent; and therfore syth[233] no manere thynge schal wanti neythe\r/[234] lacki to Goddys seyntys, here joye here gladnys and here murthe[235] schal evere be fulle to hem withoute ende. Amen.

18 <**Excitacio mentis ad contemplandum summum bonum et coniectacio quale et quantum sit[236] hoc bonum.**[237]
Excita nunc anima mea et cetera. ¶ The sentence of thys chapitur is thus in Englische. Nowe my soule arise up, and stere thou thyn underestandynge and thynke thou, in as muche as thou mayst, how muche and howe gret thilke godenes is, of wham so muche plen[f.223v]tethe[238] comyth of al blessidnys. Seththe hit is so, that al gode thyngys ben gode and delitabile eche ther of by hit silf,[239] than thynke[240] thou bisily, howe deliȝtabile is that godenys that conteyneth in hym silf murth and joye and jocundaunce of al godenissis. I speke noȝt of jocundaunce that we havyth here in erthe in erthely thynges, but I speke of that jocundaunce and godenys that is fro us in as muche difference as is bitwene him that ordeynyd al thynge, and his creature that he fourmyd. If life that is[241] ymade and ordeyned be gode on hym silf, than ful muche is he that first made life;[242] and if helthe be gode whan hit is ordeynned and made in mannys body, than ful blessid is that helthe that made al helthe; and if wysdome of thynges þat beth ymade is worthy to be lovid for the knewliche ther of, than how muche schuld thylke wysdome be ylovyd that made al thynges of nouȝt; and sethe hit is so that ful many and ful gret deliȝtes and gladnyssis beth in diverse thyngys that beth deliȝtabile, than, as thou supposist, how huge \schal/[243] the delite be on hym that made al deliȝtes?

19 **Que et quanta sint bona fruentibus deo et cetera.** [f.224r]
O qui hoc bono fruetur, quid illi erit et cetera. ¶ The sentence of thys chapitur is thus in Englische. ¶ O glorious God, what schal he have, that hath al this blessidnis, and what schal lacke to him? Certeynly he schal have al that he desiryth, and that he desiryth nouȝt, he schal noȝt have. Certeynly ther schal be al gode thyngys that belongyth bothe to

body and soule, the weche thynges mannys 'yȝe nevere sawe neythere ere never hird, ne hert never \þowȝt/'.[244] Than, man, whare to art thow so besy sechynge godenyssis that schuld be profyȝty both to thy body and to thy soule? Love thow on gode thynge, that is God on wham beth al gode thyngys, and hit sufficit to the. Desire thou hym that is only gode and is al gode withoute comparison, and hit is ynow to the. Thou that art my flesche, what lovyst thou? And thou that art my soule, what desirist thou? What that ȝe loveyth and desyryth, hit is in that plase of hevyn. **Pulcritudo**[245] If feyrenes delyȝtyth the, 'ryȝthful men schul schyne ther as the sonne'.[246] **velocitas·**,[247] **fortitudo**,[248] **libertas**[249] \ȝyf suyftnesse or strengthe or fredom of the body[250] to wham nothynge may withstande, deliȝteth to the, 'al men schul be ylyke to angelis of God',[251] for 'thoȝ oure body be sowe here bestly,[252] he schal arise aȝene a spi[f.224v]ritual body'[253] by powere of God and noȝt by hys owen kynde. **Diuturnitas**[254] If longe and hole life[255] delyȝte the, ther is everelastynge life and helthe that nevere schal have ende, \for 'ryȝtful men scullyþ[256] lyve for evere'[257] and[258] 'here/[259] helth schal come of God'.[260] ·**Sacietas, ebrietas**[261] 'If thou desirist, or they þat schul be in hevyn desyrith, to have replecion of eny manere thynge, they schul be fulfillyd whan the joye of God schal be openyd.'[262] ....[263] **Melodia**[264] If they desyre to have or huyre melodie, the quere of blessid angelis syngyth thare to God evere withoute ceessynge. **Voluptas** If they desire to have clene lust, 'God schal ȝeve hem drynke of the ryvere of his lust.'[265] Sapiencia If they deliȝtyth in wisdome, the wysdome of God schal schew here silf to hem. **Amicicia** If they delyȝte in love and frenschip, they schul love God more than hym silf, and eche other as muche as hem silf, and God schal love hem more than they lovyth hem silf, for they schul love hym, and hem silf to gedere by hym, and God schal love him silf, and hem also thrw[266] him silf. **Concordia** If they deliteth to be acordynge to gadere, they al schul have on manere wille, for to hem schal be non other wille but only the wille of God. **Potestas** If power deliȝteth [f.225r] hem, they schul be almyȝty of here wille, as God is of his wille, for ryȝt as God may have his owne[267] wille, and do what he lyketh bi hym silf, on the same manere they schul do what they lust by hym, for ryȝth as they wylnyth non other wyse, but as God wylnyth, ryȝt in the same maner God wy\l/nyth[268] as they wilnyth, and that God wilnyth most nedys be fulfillid. **Honor** and[269] **Divicie** And if worschip or rychesses delyȝteth hem, God schal ordeyne his gode and trwe servauntys to be governourys upon ful muche godys and richessis, for they schul be callyd Goddys owen childryn, and also 'they schul be callud'[270] goddys, \and þey schulle be goddys;/[271] and thare as is the sone of God, thare schul they be the ayrys of Crist Jhesus.[272] **Securitas** If trwe sykyrnys delyteth hem, they schul be so certeyn that the joyes of hevyn schal nevere fayle to hem, as they schul be certeyn þat they nevere wole lese hit by here owen wille; and certeyn they schul be, that God, that they lovyth so wel, schal nevere take that joye fro hem that he lovyth, aȝens ther wylle; and they schul be certey[n][273] þat noþyng þere[274] schal be so[275] stronge and myȝty that his power schal be strongour than Goddys power, that schal put [f.225v] God and hem both fro that place. **Gaudium** In that place schal be so gret joye and so muche blisse and so overepassynge gladnys, that nevere mannys yȝe sawe, ne nevere eeres hird, ne nevere mannys hert myȝt thynke hit.[276] O thou mannys hert that nedyst help, that hast suffryd many wrecchidnyssis and hast be overcome with sorwys, how glad and jocunde myȝttyst thou be, if thou haddist al the habundaunce in al thyngys of that joye. Aske thou and inquire thou the inmoste partyes of thyn undirstondynge if they mowe[277] vele and undirstande and know by reson the excellent joye of so muche blessidnys. In certeyn, ȝif hit were so, that eny man that thou lovyst as muche as thou dost thy[278] silf had that blessidnys that is aforesaid, than thy joye schuld be dowbelyd ther throw, for thou woldist be as glad of hys joye as thow woldist of thyn owen blisse; and if hit were so, that tweyn, or thre, or many mo of thy frendys had the same joye and blissydnys, and if thou lovedist eche of hem as muche as thy silf, thou woldys have as muche gladnys[279] for everych of hem as thou woldist have for thysilf. Therfore in thylke parfyȝth charite of blessid angelis and men that beth withoute [f.227r][280] noumbre, whare no creature schal love none other man ne woman lasse þan he[281] lovyth him silf, and none of hem schal have more joye of him silf than he schal have of every of hem,[282] and seth that a mannys hert may unnethe fele the joye of hys owen godenys, than how schuld he fele and underestande the magnitude of so many joyes comynge to gadere? And seth hit schal be so that everyche seynt schal be as glad of every other blisse as of his owen joye, than every of hem that schal be in that felicite schal love God withoute comparison more than him silf, and more than he schal love hem, al that beth with hym; and ȝut muche more joye he schal have withoute estimacioun,[283] of the felicite of God, than he schal have of his owen and of al that schal be with hym; and seth they schul love God so with al the hert, with al the mynde, and with al the soule, in so muche that al the hert, al the mynde, and al the soule may not suffice to that digni\te/ of love,[284] than withoute dowȝte they schul have so muche joye,[285] gladnys and blisse, with al the hert, wyth al the mynde and al the soule, that al the hert, al the mynde and al the soule may not suffice to underestande the plenitu[f.227v]de of that joye and blisse.

20 An hoc gaudium sit[286] plenum quod promittit Dominus se servis suis daturum.

Deus meus, et Dominus meus et cetera. ¶ The sentence of thys chapitur is thus in Englische. O glorious God my Lord, myn hope and the joye of myn hert, schewe thow to my soule, if this be the same joye of the weche joye thou seid to us by the Sone thus: ¶ 'Petite et accipietis, ut gaudium vestrum sit plenum', et cetera; that is to[287] seie: 'Aske ȝe and ȝe schul underefange,[288] that ȝowre joye may be fulle.'[289] I have founde a certeyne joye that is fulle and more than fulle, and ȝut abofe that schal be an overepassinge joye þat schal be with ful hert, ful mynde and ful soule, and al the body schal be ful with that joye. Thys joye schal not entre in to hem that schal be so[290] joysynge, but al they that beth so ful of joye schul entre in that joye. Glorious God, seye þow[291] to[292] thy servant in hys hert wythinforth, if thys is[293] that joye on the weche thy servantys schul entre[294] that schul entre 'in to the joye of here Lord';[295] but certeynly that joye whare on thyn[296] electe childryn schul joysy is so overepassynge that 'yȝe nevere sawe hit neyther eere [f.228r] nevere hirde hit, neyther hit myȝt nevere ascende[297] in to mannys hert'.[298] Therfore, glorious God and Lord, I seyd noȝt, ne nevere thouȝt hit, how muche joye thy blessid seyntys schul have. Certeynly they schul have as muche joysynge[299] as they schul have love, and they schal have[300] as muche love as they have knewliche. Than, glorious Lord, howe muche schul they knowe the, and how muche schul they love the? Certeynly they schul knowe the so muche, and so muche they schul love the in that live, that 'yȝe myȝt nevere se hit, ne eere myȝt nevere huyre hit, ne nevere hit myȝt[301] ascende in to mannys hert in hys lyfe'.

21 Oracio pro hoc gaudio inpetrando· Oracio.[302]

Oro Deus ... [303] ut gaudeam de te. ¶ I pray the, God, that I may have my joye in the; and thow I may nouȝt fully fele that joye,[304] ȝut, gracious Lord, ȝyve thou suche grace to me that I may profyȝty fro day to day, in to tyme that thylke tyme come whare ful joye and gladnys schal be. Graunte thou grace that thy knowliche may profyȝty here to me, and be hit had ful toward the,[305] and wexe thy love upon me,[306] and be hit ful toward the,[307] so that my joye may [f.228v] be here gret \in/[308] hope, and ful in dede in thy blisse. Glorious Lord, thou comaundist us by \þy/[309] Sone, and also thou conseilist us, that we schul aske[310] as thou[311] bihetist us that we schuld have oure askynge, that is, that oure joye myȝt be fulle. Therfore gracious Lord, I aske that thou conselist us to asky by thy mervelous conseiloure, that is, that I myȝt receife that as thou bihotist by thy trewthe, that my joye myȝt be fulle. Trew God and most gracious Lord, I aske nowȝt ellys but that I myȝt have that my joye myȝt be fulle. Therfore, in the tyme of my life, graunte thou to me that my mynde may thenke ther on, and that my tounge may speke ther of, and that myn hert may love \hyt/,[312] and myn mowthe may schewe hit, and that myn soule may desyre hit, and my body may coveyte[313] hit, and that al my substance may wylny hit, that I may entre in to the blisse of myn Lord – the weche Lord is withoute begynnynge and ende, in thre persouns and in on, that is God hym silf yblessid. AMEN.

22 **Recapitulacio brevis de partibus predictarum beatitudinum bonorum et de perfecta miseria malorum hoc modo et cetera.>** [f.229r]

Cum itaque tanta sit beatitudo et cetera. ¶ The sentence of thys chapitur is thus in Englische. ¶ Seth hyt[314] stant so that God schal ordeyne, to hys frendes that lovyth hym, so muche joye and blisse as afore is seid, than what, as thou supposist, schal be ordeyned to Goddys enemyes? Certeynly they schul nouȝt be unrewardyd, but aȝenst that that seyntys havyth, that schul be withoute comparison feyr ≈≈≈[315] they schul be withoute comparison foule and disfourmyd. ∞∞∞[316] <¶ Ryȝtful men schul schyne as the sonne, and they that schul be dampnyd schul be fouloure and blackoure than sowte of smoke that hangeth on bemys;>[317] and they schul not be changyd in to bettur and feyroure coloure whan they schul come to the dome, but ryȝt as the seyntys of God schul be glorifyed in the day of dome, evyn in the contrarie[318] they schul be dampnyd in to evere lastynge sorowe.

They that schul be savyd schul be wondirly swyfte ≈≈≈[319] and evyn the contrarie the other most slowist. ∞∞∞ <The seyntys schul be so swyfte as is the leme of the sonne, that strecche[th] hys lyȝt [f.229v] in a moment fro the est in to the west, but the dampnid soules schul so be thrast adoun with so gret charge of penys that they schul have no myȝt to move here fote.>

¶[320] And aȝenst the overepassynge strengthe[321] that Goddys seyntys schul have [≈≈≈][322] the dampnyd soulys overe wondirfulle febilnys[323] schul have. ∞∞∞∞∞[324] <¶ The seyntys schul be so strong that they schul have myȝt to meve al the erthe, and the other schul be so febil that they schul have no myȝt to meof the wormys that schul crepe on here yen, fro hem.>

Ryȝtful men schul have liberalte[325] to go whare that they lust ≈≈≈[326] but the dampnyd creaturys schul be schytte up with evere lastynge clausure and they schul nevere come thennys. ∞∞∞∞∞ <¶ The seyntys schul suffre no thynge that they have no wille to suffre, but they schul be suffred to do what evere they lust, but the dampnyd schul be constreynyd to al thyngys that they wolde nouȝt, and they schul be refreynyd of[327] al thyngys that they wolde have.>

Seyntys of God schul evere have helthe withoute sykenys ≈≈≈[328] [f.230r] but the dampnyd soulis schul brenne and be turment[329] with evere lastynge sycknys and sorowe. ∞∞∞∞∞ <¶ Goddis seyntys schul be so hole that they mowe nevere be sike, but the dampnyd soulys schul be so seke that they schul not have myȝt to underestond how muche hit schal be, for sorwe.>

Ryȝthful men schul be fulfillyd with the lust of the house of God ≈≈≈[330] but the dampnyd soulys schul be yȝeve drynke of the bittur replecioun of the sorwys of helle. ∞∞∞∞∞ <....>[331]

¶ Riȝtful men schul have[332] longe abydynge in here blisse [≈≈≈][333] but synful soulys schul nevere have ende in here sorwys. [∞∞∞∞∞][334] <Ryȝtful men schul lyve as God lyvyth, but the dampnyd soulys schul nevere lyve[335] but in deth with evere lastynge peyne.>

And ryȝth as ryȝtful men schul have al maner undirstandynge in al wysdome ≈≈≈[336] in the contrarye manere they that schul be dampnyd schul be confunded in here folye. ∞∞∞∞∞ <¶ They that schul be savyd schul be fulfillyd with the same wisdome that God hym silf is, and they [f.230v] schul[337] se God evere contynualy fro face to face, but they that schul be dampnyd schul be depriuyd fro[338] al manere wysdome, and they schul be brennyd with so huge sorwes and turmentys that they schul not only lese here mynde ther throwe, but also they schul wixe wodde[339] for sorwe.>[340]

Godes frendys schul have ful hyȝe frendeschippe and love bitwene eche other ≈≈≈[341] but Goddys ennemyes schul have overepassynge enmyte betwene hem silf. ∞∞∞∞∞ <¶ God schal love eche of hys seyntys, and they al schal so love God that aftyr that tyme they schul nevere hate God, neyther God hem, but God hym silf and al his seyntys schul have every dampnyd soule in so gret hate that the sone schal have no pyte of hys fadir that he schal se in peyne.>

¶ ¶[342] Goddys seyntys schul be acordynge to gadere in perpetual pes ≈≈≈[343] but the dampnyd soulys schul evere be discordynge in contynual dissensioun.∞∞∞ <¶ The body and soule of every seynt, and also seyntys, schul have so gret concordaunce to gadere[344] as oure y3en have in thy present life, but the dampnyd soulys schul stonde in so gret discorde [f.231r] that here body and here soule schal be overecome ther throwe.[345] The body of dampnyd soulys of eche of hem schal have the soule on hate, bycause the soule thou3t alwey evyl; and the soule schal have the body in hate bycause the body fulfillyd in dede the wickyd thou3tys that the soule tho3te: and therfore they schul be turmentyd in ful gret peynys.>[346]

Goddys seyntys schul be exaltyd with hy3e worschipe ≈≈≈[347] But the dampnyd soulis schul be thrast doun with muche schame; ∞∞∞ <¶ for ry3t as an emperoure that had a gode servant that were sike, and he desyred hym to be curyd of hys sykenys and wolde magnyfye him to worschip, whan he were hole he wold clothe hym with precious stonys and clothys and make him sitte so ryaly clothyd besidis his owen sone and so wolde he magnifie him – on the same manere, God fadir almy3ty schal magnifie his gode trewe servant whan he schal clothe[348] him, aftir he is clansid fro al corrupcioun, with the stole of immortalite,[349] and make hym sitte bysydes his owen Sone; but eche of hem that schal be dampnyd schul be evyn contrarie[350] ther a3ens yput at al dispute,[351] so that he [f.231v] schal be cast doun in al stynche, and foule wormys schul gnawe and have domynacioun on hym.

Ry3tful men schul have ryal powere[352] to commaunde what they have lust too[353] [≈≈≈][354] boote[355] the dampnyd soulis schul have no power to meof hem silf to no place. ∞∞∞ <¶ Ry3tful men schul have powere to do what evere they lust, but the dampnyd soulys schul have no power to do no manere thynge that they wilnyth to do.>

Ry3thful men schul be sekyr that here godenes schul nevere fayle ≈≈≈[356] but the dampnyd soulis schul evere have drede of here sorowys[357] in peynys[358] tha\t/[359] nevere schal have ende. ∞∞∞ ¶ <Ry3tful men schul have al thynges that they desyryth, and they schul[360] knowe that they schul nevere lese hit, but the dampnyd soulys schul evere drede thys turmentys that they schul suffre, for they schul nevere be delyveryd.

Every ry3tfulle man and woman may have, and schul have, ful

parfyʒt joye that schal gete al thys partyes of blissidnys aforsaide ≈≈≈[361] but the soulis that schal be dampnyd schal in the contrarye wyse be replete with [f.232r] ful hyʒe sorwe, ∞∞∞∞ ¶ for he schal suffre al the peynes of wrecchidnys on everysyde of hym. Therfore I conseyle that no man no[362] woman that thynketh to be savyd desyre ne coveyte no disseyvable[363] worschipis of thys world, but coveyte they only the blysse of hevyn:>[364] for they þat lovyth[365] only God schul have joye and blisse and gladnys that nevere schal have ende, but they that dispisith hym schul have sorowe, weylynge and wepynge for here deservynge, that evere schal last – whare fro God defende us.[366] A.M.E.N.[367]

NOTES

1 MS 'enghische'.

2 LL ('iuvat') does not mention women here. See p.27 for many other examples of this alteration.

3 LL 'bonitati adheserit', but *MED s.v.* **abiden** does not attest the sense 'persevere in'; the nearest appropriate senses cited are perhaps 8(a) 'hope for' and 10(a) 'experience, enjoy'.

4 'Insufficiency, want' ('snys' over erasure); the form is unrecorded in *MED s.v.* **scarsnes(se.**

5 'Castigations': *MED s.v.* **chastiinge** (**chasteing, chasting**) ger.

6 LL n.2.

7 (OE *huntian*): one of several occurrences in this text of the '-i(e)' inflexional suffix in the infinitive, which survived longest in southern Kentish and south Midland dialects: see *MED s.v.* **-i(e(n.**

8 LL 'avibus celi ludere, iocis et spectaculis interesse'. That the error 'locis' for 'iocis' is not echoed suggests that ME is not derived from LL.

9 'Benefit, advantage'.

10 LL 'latitet'; 'be hit' may be an inversion of 'hit be' ('[it] may be') in which case 'hit' is pleonastic (*MED s.v.* **hit** pron. 6.(a)); alternatively, it might be an error derived from misreading of a Middle English exemplar reading not 'be hit' but 'beit' (*MED s.v.* **ben** pr.3.sg., not attested as a subjunctive).

11 'Sufficiency': the earliest citation with this sense in *MED s.v.* **sufficience** n. is *c.* 1410.

12 'Disadvantage' (= LL 'incommoditate'); the word is not separately recorded in *MED*, and one would expect '-im' before 'p': *MED s.v.* **in-** pref. (2).

13 'Protected, guarded'.

14 In accordance with 'temporale' on f.214ᵛ, although the 'er/ar' abbreviation mark is used here.

15 MS 'sechue', but perhaps it is officious to emend a word so variously spelled. The scribe's form elsewhere is 'suche', whereas he used 'seche' for 'seek'.

16 Cramped and over erasure, hence its unusual use of a nasal bar.

17 MS 'bessidnys'.

18 The word 'wey' is over erasure; an illegible word in Hand B is erased from the R.H. margin.

19 Emendation has been kept to a minimum (and is perhaps officious even here), but the scribe's usual form is 'seynt(e/is/ys)' – with one 't'.

20 'prison' (?) – but the er abbreviation is used.

21 A final 'e' is erased.

22 In greenish ink in Hand C; 'y' in Hand B is erased from the R.H. margin.

23 LL n.6.

24 LL 'pater'.

25 LL n.8.

26 LL n.10.

27 Here 'appeal', though more usually 'taste'.

28 'Contained'.

29 This is the only example in the text of 'an' for 'and'.

30 The phrase 'enforse we ure silf' means 'let us undertake'.

31 'Divide'.

32 MS '·i·sey', each punctus with a red punctus under it.

33 MS 'y/ȝyve' originally written as one word, and then divided by a stroke.

34 MS 'ȝonge'.

35 This form of 'safely' is not recorded in *MED s.v.* **saufli**.

36 This form is not recorded in *MED s.v.* **ben**. v. p.sg.1 & 3, but the scribe uses it again on f.209ʳ (and cf. 'Whe' on f.215ᵛ).

37 *MED s.v.* **saven** 5(a): 'saven hole' means 'keep whole'; however, it is possible to construe 'hole' not as adj. but as adv., 'completely'. The former is perhaps more likely in view of the translator's clever echo of the 'hole' at the end of the previous sentence, where it refers to the whole apple that is too much for the child (the earthbound soul).

38 'Find out'.

39 LL n.14.

40 LL n.13. LL 'Servata igitur illa promissione invisibili Dei, donec veniamus ei "sicuti est", intente rimemur quid corporibus, quid animabus nostris conveniat ...' The translator expanded in order to clarify. The sense in ME is perhaps 'The promise of the invisible God having been reserved and preserved according to the will of God, let us, before we come to where we may see Him "as

he is", diligently find out what sort of thing is proper to our bodies and what to our souls.' It is interesting that, although the exemplar seems to have been corrupt, with 'promissione invisibili Dei' instead of 'promissione invisibilis Dei', the translator's 'þe promisse of God þat is unvisibile' is sufficiently ambiguous to allow either the sense his exemplar offered (the promise being invisible), or the sense that logic suggests (the invisible God making the promise).

41 'Appropriate': the form, not recorded in *MED s.v.* **covenable** 1(a), occurs again on f.216r.

42 The insertion is in greenish ink.

43 The capital initials of the names of the Properties are in red or blue; in most the scribe's guide-letter is visible.

44 The Latin (LL n.18) and the sense suggest that this = 'them' (*MED s.v.* **hem** pron.pl.) as in 'they schul love God more than hym silf' (f.224v); the scribe's usual form is 'hem'.

45 LL 'presideat'; *MED s.v.* **president** adj. 'superintending, overseeing' cites only two examples, both from manuscripts of *c.* 1450, which this example predates.

46 LL 'Hec omnia electos Dei in illo beato regno habituros dubium non est, cum illos inhabitet ac in illis presideat, de quo est quicquid usquam boni est et potens et gloriosus super omnia ineffabiliter est' ('There is no doubt that the chosen of God possess all these [blessednesses] in that blessed kingdom, for he from whom all goodness everywhere comes, who is full of power and joy, powerful and glorious and ineffably above everything, dwells in them and rules over them'); 'al þynge havynge Crist him silf' probably means 'every creature in heaven having access to Christ himself' rather than 'Christ himself possessing everything'.

47 *OED s.v.* **self** A.3, citations for *c.* 1380, *c.* 1460; cf. *enforse we ure silf*, p.92–5 above.

48 'Steps, degrees'; the plural should be 'grece' (*MED s.v.* **gre** n.(1)), but this seems to be a 'deliberate mistake' by the translator or scribe, perhaps by awkward analogy with **gre, greez** n.(2) 'favour, pleasure, good will'.

49 LL and AN end with 'pertinentis'.

50 The phrase 'þus ywryte' appears to mean 'this that is written' (= LL 'quod scriptum est'; *MED s.v.* **this** dem. pron.), but as the form 'þus' for 'this' does not occur elsewhere in the text, it is just possible that here it = 'thus' (as in the previous sentence and elsewhere in the text), in a substantival phrase meaning 'what is written thus'; cf. 'hit is wrete þus', just below in the same paragraph.

51 LL n.20.

52 The final 'e' is over erasure of a letter and 'e'; Hand B's 'e' is erased from the L.H. margin.

53 LL n.21.

54 The inserted 't' is in accordance with Hand B's 't' erased from the L.H. margin.

55 LL n.22.

56 'Restore the image of God in': *MED s.v.* **reformen** 1(c).

57 'Shame, humiliation': *MED s.v.* **meknesse** 2(b), citing an unpublished Wyclifite Concordance's version of this quotation: 'which schal refoorme the body of oure mekenesse, configurid ... to the body of his cleernesse'. The reference is to the body's fallen state.

58 LL n.23.

59 LL n.24.

60 The insertion is in greenish ink.

61 LL n.26.

62 Over erasure, in accordance with 'þe' erased from the R.H. margin.

63 LL n.27.

64 MS 'hevym'.

65 LL n.28.

66 'Beams, rays'.

67 'Eyelid' (LL 'palpebra'): *MED s.v.* **broue** 3.

68 LL 'obstaculum'; the form is not recorded in *MED s.v.* **obstacle.**

69 Followed by a light double stroke (touched in red) usually used as an end-of-line filler, though the word does not end a line.

70 'þa<u>n</u> þey schul' is in Hand C over erasure, in accordance with words erased from the R.H. margin, where only Hand B's 'schull' is still legible.

71 The clause 'than ... manere' has no equivalent in LL. The words 'succhе manere' are written as one, the two separated by a fine line.

72 The 'y' is obscured.

73 'Scattered' (LL 'dispersum'); the earliest example in *MED s.v.* **disparkelen, disparplen** 6 is *c.* 1384.

74 MS 'of of' (one before and one after the page break).

75 LL n.33; the word ('den') is evidence that the translator's exemplar had 'lacum' not, as LL, 'locum'.

76 The clause has no equivalent in LL.

77 Between 'o' and 'ȝ' is an erased caret, with 'w' erased from the L.H. margin.

78 LL ends with 'ipsorum' instead of 'eorum', which AN also has.

79 Preceded at the end of the previous line by 'Str' crossed out.

80 Followed by 'ne' erased from the R.H. margin: no corresponding correction is apparent in the text.

81 Followed by 'ne' erased from the R.H. margin: no corresponding correction is apparent in the text.

82 MS 'throwe' with 'r' and 'o' marked for transposition.

83 LL n.35.

84 David is not named in LL.

85 The following translation shows that the translator did not realize that 'etenim' ('truly') separated two quotations: '"Voluntatem" etenim "timencium se faciet Dominus"' (Ps. 144,19).

86 LL n.37.

87 LL n.38. The long 'i' in 'ischette' is inserted in a browner ink than that of the text, in accordance with long 'i' erased from the L.H. margin.

88 MS 'thy'.

89 The phrase 'grevaunce or hurtynge or eny manere dissese' = LL 'lesione'; 'dissese' means both 'distress' and 'disease'.

90 'Pools' (LL 'stagna').

91 LL 'Item illud vel consideracio eorundem locorum erit in arbitrio beatorum' ('In the same way, both that [travelling safely through hell] and the inspection of the same places will be by the choice of the blessed'); the translator expands, in an attempt to clarify.

92 LL n.40.

93 The 'g' ends a line, and has an untypical form possibly indicating Hand C.

94 The second 't' is added in a different ink between 'tha' and 'we'.

95 'Piercing' = LL 'lesio'.

96 The order differs from that in LL 'non ferrum, non ignis, non aqua'. This form of 'iron' (*MED s.v.* **iren**) occurs also at f.214^{r}.

97 'Loss' (LL 'incomodi'): *MED s.v.* **lost(e)** n.

98 'Retributive punishment'.

99 LL n.42.

100 The earliest example of the word in *MED* is dated before 1420 and probably not earlier than 1395.

101 LL 'vobis conveniant', AN 'a vous' – but of course the pronouns' minims are ambiguous in both.

102 'Delight'; MS 'sovoure'; however, the '-o-' form might be intentional, for *MED s.v.* **savourli** (b) records a fifteenth-century example of the error, and AN, though it has 'savour' here, has 'sovour' in the previous clause.

103 'savoure and gode velynge' = LL 'saporem' ('relish') (*MED s.v.* **felinge**) – cf. 'velyd', 'velid' f.223^{r}, 'vele' f.225^{v}.

104 'comp-' over erasure.

105 LL n.45.

106 LL n.46.

107 LL n.47.

108 LL n.48. ME omits the rest of the quotation, 'quoniam apud te est fons vite', although it is translated.

109 MS final 'd' erased.

110 'Adequate' = LL 'convenie<u>ns</u>'; the word is not attested before *c.* 1390 (*MED*).

111 'Pupil' (LL 'pupillam').

112 LL 'ferro'.

113 'Painful'.

114 The insertion is associated with an erasure of the word, in Hand D, from the R.H. margin.

115 'Insane'.

116 MS 'lemyns' with 'n' erased and 'y' joined, in the scribe's ink, to 's'.

117 The phrase means 'in addition'.

118 LL 'transitoria voluptas'.

119 MS 'peynnys', the second 'n' erased and the first joined to the penultimate letter.

120 The 'ys' is added at the end of the line, in accordance with a word in Hand B erased from the L.H. margin.

121 'Since' (*MED s.v.* **sitthe** conj.); this form occurs also at the beginning of §17: the scribe's spelling of this word includes 'sith(e, siththe, siþþe'.

122 The '-ys' is over erasure, with 'y' in Hand B erased from the R.H. margin.

123 The scribe's normal form is 'trewe(ly)', but cf. 'trwe', twice, on f.225r.

124 'Unless'.

125 Followed by 'that' crossed out.

126 'Continuous existence'; the word is not attested before *c.* 1390 (*MED s.v.* **continuaunce**).

127 LL 'sine defectu valeant habere' is expanded to a more positive statement of permanence: 'they myȝt have everemore abydyn<u>ge</u> and contynuaunce on hem'.

128 LL 'Accedat igitur', in full.

129 The phrase 'lauda d<u>eu</u>m' [or d<u>ominu</u>m]' over erasure, with erasure of 'lauda d<u>eu</u>m [or d<u>ominu</u>m]' from the R.H. margin.

130 MS 'they'.

131 The translator awkwardly explains the splitting of the quotation.

132 LL n.53.

133 The insertion is in accordance with 'be' in Hand B erased from the L.H. margin.

134 LL has 'pertinentis'. In ME, the rubric ends with a red *nota* (not used elsewhere in the text) resembling a division sign with two horizontal strokes, which occupies the end of the line below, where it thus separates the end of the paragraph's opening Latin phrase from the beginning of the translation.

135 Over erasure.

136 This is the only example of this form in this text, but cf. 'whas' ff.208r, 209r.

137 The form is not recorded in *MED s.v.* **feue**, but vocalic 'w' is found elsewhere in this text (cf. 'trwly' f.215r; 'trwe' f.225r).

138 MS ‘blessydnys’. The singular form where a plural is required is also used on f.222^{v}. The form adopted here occurs in full at the bottom of f.221^{r}.

139 Over erasure, in a different ink and hand (probably Hand B).

140 In Hand C over erasure, with erasure of ‘fro’ in Hand B from the L.H. margin.

141 Followed by erasure of ‘it’.

142 Over erasure, apparently in the scribe’s hand.

143 MS ‘we’.

144 LL n.57.

145 *MED s.v.* **mouen** v.(3) records the manuscript form under ‘errors’, and this is the only example of it in this text, the scribe’s usual form being ‘mygt’.

146 The insertion is in accordance with ‘y’ in Hand B erased from the L.H. margin.

147 MS ‘forȝynys’; the same error is made nine words further on.

148 MS ‘forȝynys’; the same error is made nine words back.

149 ‘Blame’ (*MED s.v.* **atwiten**).

150 See p.38 for the suggestion that this mistranslation may be due to corruption in the lost Latin exemplar.

151 LL n.63.

152 The phrase ‘ȝyt every seynt’ is over erasure; ‘ȝyt’ in Hand B is erased from the R.H. margin.

153 The second minim and ‘ge’ over erasure; ‘g’ in Hand B erased from the R.H. margin.

154 LL n.65.

155 The spelling has not been emended, although this form is not recorded in *MED s.v.* **compaignie**. The word does not occur elsewhere in the text. Perhaps we should read ‘companye’, but the nasalized vowel and glide combination produces some odd spellings of this word, and the form may originate in confusion about how to spell the sound cluster. Alternatively, the ‘-u’ might have been ‘-ii-’ in the exemplar, our scribe mistaking it for ‘-u’, and so adding ‘-y-’ to supply what he took to be the missing vowel. Misplacement of an ‘-n-’, marking some difficulty in determining just where the nasal belongs, seems less likely. We are most grateful to Professor Paul Schaffner (*MED*) for his advice on this form.

156 Over erasure in accordance with ‘schype’ in Hand B erased from the R.H. margin.

157 ‘oþer þengys’ is over erasure in Hand C, as is confirmed both by the spelling and the form of ‘y’; ‘þynges’ in Hand B is erased from the R.H. margin.

158 Initial ‘ȝ’ erased.

159 LL ‘patrem aut parentes’; this is apparently one of the translator’s many attempts to ensure that both genders are mentioned where the Latin mentions only the masculine: the use of ‘hir’ as well as ‘modir’ seems to be an unthinking feminization.

160 LL: 'videat apud se quid dicat, et quia non bene sentit veraciter intelligat'. The confused ME and corrupt AN may reflect corruption in an exemplar common to them alone. The inserted but unnecessary 'so', which is in greenish ink, and may be in Hand C, should perhaps be relegated to the apparatus.

161 Followed by 'thou' crossed out.

162 There is no equivalent in LL for 'thynke ... place'.

163 MS adds 'ryȝt as thou thynkest', which seems to be a form of dittography, the scribe's eye perhaps having leapt ahead to 'as thou thynkest' in a Middle English exemplar; see next note.

164 LL 'Idem ego de meo amico sencio, volo atque desiderio'.

165 LL 'necessarie'.

166 MS 'thys'.

167 The scribe often uses vocalic 'w', but the insertion appears to be in the scribal ink.

168 'Limbs, members': *MED s.v.* **membre**.

169 If not an error for 'another', this is a version of the form 'otir' (*MED s.v.* **other(e**).

170 There is no equivalent of 'dextra levaque velit intendere'; AN is also confused at this point.

171 The passage, perhaps omitted as a result of scribal eyeskip ('thedirward') is inserted in the R.H. margin in Hand C: it has no precise equivalent in LL. A long erasure at the bottom of the R.H. margin was no doubt once Hand B's version of the insertion: its details are now illegible even under ultra-violet light.

172 'By nature'.

173 A final 't' has been erased.

174 Followed by an erased letter, perhaps 'm', and with 'ne' in Hand B erased from the L.H. margin.

175 MS 'I louyd'.

176 'Assigned a permanent existence/dwelling-place [in heaven]' (*MED s.v.* **stablen** v.(1) 1, 2(c), 3(b)): LL 'constiterit'. The insertion is in accordance with an 'a' in Hand B erased from the R.H. margin.

177 LL 'De honore sanctorum qui'.

178 In Hand C, 'it ys' is over erasure, and a following caret was also erased; this is in accordance with 'ys' in Hand B erased from the R.H. margin.

179 LL n.69. An alternative emendation would be to 'worthy [be] worschipyd', with ellipsis of 'to' (*OED s.v.* **worthy** 7(b)).

180 Over erasure of a word ending in '-t', with 'e' in Hand B erased from the R.H. margin.

181 LL 'inter primates'.

182 LL 'amore ... flagraretur'.

183 LL shows that it is the wrath of the lord that was feared.

184 Followed by an erasure in the R.H. margin, with no apparent echo in the text.

185 MS 'Throwe' with 'r' and 'o' marked for transposition; there is an erasure in L.H. margin.

186 'Heirs'.

187 The whole word is over erasure in accordance with a word by Hand B erased from the L.H. margin. The scribe's usual form is 'trowist' or 'trowyst'.

188 'Pattern, model' (*MED s.v.* **forme** 3, 11(a); cf. the second citation in 2(a): God made souls 'to his fourme'). There is no equivalent in LL.

189 'comp' over erasure.

190 The form is used again on f.223r below.

191 *MED s.v.* **incredible, incredibil** does not record this form (LL 'incredibile').

192 Lat: 'superius'; strength is the subject of §5 above; see next note.

193 Lat: 'superius' again. Perhaps the failure to refer to the fifth chapter is evidence that the exemplar indicated these numbers in easily misread lower-case roman numerals.

194 'Power'; LL 'virtus'.

195 MS 'thyngkyth' with 'g' erased and 'n' and 'k' joined up.

196 LL n.71.

197 Followed by erasure of 'er'.

198 Over erasure, with 'there' in Hand B erased from the R.H. margin.

199 An inserted 'is' has been erased.

200 This could also be punctuated 'there ys, in Goddys wordys, "no transmutacioun ..."', signalling a biblical quotation, rather than applying the immutability of God to his words. The translator seems to have ignored 'nec vicissitudinis obumbracio'; as AN does not have an equivalent for 'vicissitudinis' either, but does have a redundant 'de' before the position in which one would expect the word for 'vicissitudinis', it is possible that a common Latin ancestor of both vernacular texts had a gap instead of 'vicissitudinis' (no doubt because his exemplar was illegible): in this case, AN copied literally, ignoring the gap, while the translator of ME (as is typical of his free handling of the source) noticed the deficiency, and avoided translating the whole phrase 'vicissitudinis obumbracio', with less confusing results.

201 MS 'mysvnquitynge' is unattested. The whole clause corresponding to LL 'quia Deus "apud quem non est transmutacio nec vicissitudinis obumbracio" eam non auferetpostquam semel dederit' is a crux. Unfortunately, 'inquitynge', an emendation which assumes scribal misreading of a flourished 'i' as 'v', is also unrecorded, but cf. *MED s.v.* **inquitablenesse** n. 'anxiety' and **inquiet(e** adj. 'disturbing'. The emendation gives the sense 'nor any unacceptable disturbance of man's reward' or '"no alteration", nor [is there] any uncomfortable anxiety about man's reward' – a free interpretation of 'eam non auferet postquam semel dederit' ('he will not take back that which he has once given

[i.e. the promise of the direct and perpetual vision of God]' – cf. AN 'ele non oustra puis q'il est une foiz doné'). This reading has the advantage of adhering to the overall sense of §15, which is about immutability. We could more violently emend to 'mys quitynge' or 'mysquitynge' ('incorrect payment in relation to man's deserving'). Lastly, we might simply emend to 'mys unquitynge' (following our transcription of 'v' as 'u' where appropriate), assuming a nonce-word 'unquitynge', giving 'mys unquitynge' the sense 'wrong witholding of reward for man's good behaviour' (cf. *OED s.v.* **unquit** adj., 'not repaid, left').

202 LL's error, 'quartadicima', is not echoed.

203 MS 'man mannys', divided by a line-ending.

204 The insertion, partly over erasure of a final 'e' on 'whan' and a caret, is in the L.H. margin, and marked in margin and text by a decorated cross; the hand may be C, but uses an untypical hooked hairstroke at the beginning of ascenders. The phrase, in Hand B, was also erased from the L.H. margin.

205 Opposite 'schip', which begins a line, there is a pencil cross in the L.H. margin.

206 In greenish ink, over erasure, in accordance with 'man' in Hand B erased from the L.H. margin.

207 The insertion, in Hand C, is in accordance with 'od' in Hand B erased from the L.H. margin. The scribe uses only the form 'gode' (19 times).

208 The '-ad-' is over erasure, in accordance with 'a' in Hand B erased from the L.H. margin.

209 The '-y\s/' is over erasure in Hand C, in accordance with 'ys' (possibly in Hand D) erased from the L.H. margin.

210 This is the only example of this form in the text: the scribe's usual form is 'woldist' (5 times), but he also uses 'woldys' and 'woldest' once.

211 'Rejoice' (*MED s.v.* **joissen**, where the form is not recorded). The word is one of several in the text showing the '-i' suffix on the infinitive: 'sy' over erasure, in accordance with Hand C's 'sy' erased from the R.H. margin.

212 The construction is either clumsy or elliptical ('as they that havyth [hit] ...').

213 First 'e' over erasure in accordance with a word erased from the R.H. margin.

214 MS 'seruuant' – a form recorded but not resolved to '-vu-' or '-uv-' by *MED s.v.* **servaunt**.

215 LL n.75.

216 The 'th-' over erasure; the spelling confirms Hand C – the scribe uses 'thynge'.

217 The insertion, at the foot of the page, in Hand C, was the result of scribal eyeskip ('blisse'). Hand B's version, not fully legible now even under ultraviolet light, is erased from the R.H. margin.

218 MS 'other is'; just possibly this may represent 'other his', in which case the separation should be retained – but the scribe does not use the form elsewhere.

219 'oþer men þat', over erasure of a caret, insertion and other words, is in accordance with Hand B's 'oþer me' erased from the L.H. margin.

220 MS ‘whan’ (LL ‘quem’).

221 The spelling suggests insertion by Hand C in accordance with Hand D’s ‘self’ in the L.H. margin (the scribe usually, though not always, uses ‘silf’). The caret is made over erasure of a now illegible punctuation mark.

221 So LL; MS ‘p<u>er</u>fectis’.

223 MS ‘blessidnys’; on f.215^{v} a singular form is also used where a plural is required; the form used here is found on f.221^{r}.

224 LL ‘quatuordecim partib<u>us</u> beatitudinis sive comoditatis’; the form ‘p<u>ar</u>fyȝtis’ is not recorded in *MED s.v.* **parfit** n.(2) ‘perfection, perfect fulfilment’, but is found *s.v.* **parfit** adj.

225 The translation is very free.

226 The ‘i<u>m</u>-’ ends a line; opposite in the R.H. margin is a cross in pencil.

227 Followed by ‘he wold’ crossed out.

228 Followed by ‘as he wold’ crossed out.

229 The ‘myȝ-’ ends a line; opposite in the R.H. margin is a cross in pencil.

230 ‘So ful’ is over erasure, in accordance with ‘so’, in Hand B, erased from the R.H. margin.

231 Followed by ‘or’ erased.

232 This is probably just an odd spelling of ‘un-’, other examples of which may appear when *MED* ‘U-’ is published. Professor Paul F. Schaffner kindly searched several hundred of the yet unpublished *MED* ‘un-’ words for us, but found no ‘unne-’ spelling; apart from those in Orm, there were even few ‘unn’s (e.g. *unnkinde* from the Fasciculus Morum). Forms in ‘-e-’, however, include *uneknowen* (*c.* 1396 *Book of London English* 234/16), *oneknowinge* (*c.* 1333 William of Shoreham, *Poems* 120/48), *oneiware* (*South English Legendary*, Corpus MS 452/110), which Professor Schaffner takes to represent ‘un-i-’, from ‘un-ge’, as suggested by forms in ‘-i-’ or ‘-ge-’. He finds no other evidence for a Middle English *unimighty*, but it is just possible that we have here a late and isolated Middle English example of OE *ungemihtig*, ‘-i-’ being not unknown as a productive infix in Middle English.

233 MS ‘seyth’, the ‘e’ erased and the ‘s’ and ‘y’ joined up. However, the scribe uses ‘seyth’ on f.215^{v} and f.222^{v}, so perhaps this correction is not scribal, and not of an error, in which case the original reading should be restored.

234 The insertion is in greenish ink, probably in Hand C, in accordance with a caret and ‘r’ erased from the R.H. margin.

235 LL n.76.

236 MS ‘fit’.

237 The major Anselm interpolation begins with this rubric and continues until the end of the rubric to §22.

238 ‘Abundance’ (*MED s.v.* **plenteth**) = LL ‘copia’. The ‘plen-’ ends a line; opposite in the R.H. margin is a cross in pencil.

239 This comma replaces a rare example of the scribe’s double *punctus*.

240 MS 'thynge'.

241 In the L.H. margin between the lines beginning 'ymade' and 'muche' is a cross in pencil.

242 LL 'Si enim bona est vita creata, quam bona est vita creatrix?' ('For if created life is good, how good is the life that brings forth life?'): the translator expands slightly, and makes the reference to God more specific.

243 Inserted by Hand C in L.H. margin, where a caret at the point of omission is under, and erased before, the rubrication, and Hand D's 'schal' and a corresponding double stroke are erased from the L.H. margin.

244 LL n.80. The insertion is in greenish ink, probably in Hand C, in accordance with a word erased from the R.H. margin.

245 This rubric and the rest within this paragraph are simply part of the text in LL.

246 LL n.83.

247 Over erasure, and preceded by erasure of two red letters, and followed by an erasure over which the red *punctus* is written.

248 Over erasure, with 'fortitudo' in Hand B erased from the R.H. margin.

249 The absence of initial capitals in the three words suggests that they may originally have followed the opening of a sentence; also, they are preceded by an erasure (perhaps of 'If') that might have been made by Hand C, who, preferring to see the text fully translated, as it is elsewhere, removed 'If' and inserted the English in the margin (see next note).

250 Insertion in R.H. margin in Hand C, with erasure of the same material under it, in Hand B; this material was written and erased again at the bottom of the margin.

251 LL n.86.

252 The word might, rather awkwardly, be an adverb (*MED s.v.* **bestly** adv.) modifying 'sowe' ('planted in the ground as one would an animal'). However, it seems to be contrasted with 'spirituale' and so to be an otherwise unattested adjective (= LL 'animale'): cf. *MED s.v.* **bestish** adj., 'unspiritual', where in the first citation 'bestych man' translates 'animalis ... homo'.

253 LL n.87. LL 'quorum seminatur corpus animale et surget corpus spirituale'.

254 See n.14 to Introduction.

255 MS 'lilf'; LL 'vita'.

256 The form confirms Hand C: the scribe uses 'schul'.

257 LL n.89.

258 MS 'in'; LL has '&', in the form which it is easy to misread as 'in'; see also Hand B's erased marginal correction, next note.

259 Insertion in L.H. margin in Hand C. Above, and again below it, Hand B's equivalent is erased: 'For rihtful men schullyþ lyve for evere & here'.

260 LL n.90.

261 See n.15 to Introduction for the conflation of these two.

262 LL n.92.

263 The equivalent of 'Si ebrietas, "inebriantur ab ubertate domus Dei"' is omitted. This may be the result of eyeskip from 'Dei' to 'Dei'; in view of the examples of scribal eyeskip in ME perhaps due to repeated Latin words (see p.32), it would appear that this omission was the translator's.

264 LL n.95.

265 LL n.98.

266 A further example of vocalic 'w'.

267 Over erasure in accordance with 'owne' erased from the R.H. margin.

268 The 'l' is inserted by Hand C in accordance with 'l' erased from the R.H. margin.

269 Over erasure.

270 LL n.105.

271 The passage was probably omitted by scribal eyeskip ('goddys'); the insertion is in the R.H. margin in Hand C; above it is Hand B's erased '& \þey/ schul be godys' (LL 'et dii vocabuntur et erunt').

272 LL n.107. LL '"heredes quidem Dei, coheredes autem Christi"'; the translator has apparently not recognized, and so has missed the sense of, the biblical quotation.

273 MS 'certey'; a final 'e' may have been erased in error (see next note).

274 Hand C wrote 'þat noþyng þere' over erasure, also erasing by mistake the final 'n' in the previous word. Hand B's barely legible 'nothing' was erased from the R.H. margin.

275 The word 'so' was added at the end of the line in accordance with Hand B's now erased caret and 'so' in the R.H. margin.

276 LL n.115.

277 Opposite in the L.H. margin is a cross in pencil.

278 Followed by 'thy' crossed out.

279 Opposite in the L.H. margin is a cross in pencil.

280 The modern foliator omitted number 226.

281 Both words in 'þan he' are over erasure, in accordance with 'he' erased from the R.H. margin.

282 MS '& none'. In LL the sentence reads 'Ergo in illa perfecta karitate innumerabilium beatorum angelorum et hominum, ubi nullus minus diliget alium quam se ipsum, non aliter gaudebit quisque pro singulis aliis quam pro se ipso.' Either the translator or the scribe may have misread an abbreviation mark as abbreviated 'et' or 'and'.

283 'Immeasurable' (LL 'absque estimacione'); the word is not recorded before 1375 (*MED*).

284 'Quality/rank of love' (LL 'dignitati dilectionis'); the '-te' is inserted in greenish ink in accordance with a correction erased from the R.H. margin.

285 Followed by erasure of a *punctus*.

286 LL 'An hoc sit gaudium'.

287 Added at the end of the line, in accordance with Hand B's 'to' erased from the L.H. margin, and caret inserted at the beginning of the next line, before 'seie'.

288 'Receive' (*MED s.v.* **underfong**).

289 LL n.113.

290 In the L.H. margin opposite is a cross in pencil.

291 The 'w' over erasure, in Hand C.

292 Opposite in the L.H. margin is a cross in pencil.

293 MS 'is thys', marked for transposition. This transposition and the next are no doubt in accordance with brief instructions (probably in Hand B) erased from the L.H. margin, and now illegible.

294 MS 'entre schul', marked for transposition.

295 LL n.114.

296 Opposite in the L.H. margin is a cross in pencil.

297 'nev<u>er</u>e asce<u>n</u>de' over erasure, in accordance with Hand B's 'nev<u>er</u>e' erased from the R.H. margin.

298 LL n.115.

299 Opposite in the R.H. margin is a cross in pencil.

300 MS 'love'.

301 Followed by 'nevere' crossed out.

302 'Oracio' does not appear a second time in LL's rubric.

303 LL 'Oro Deus, cognoscam te, amem te'; since ME omits the last two clauses from both rubric and translation, the error was the translator's.

304 The clause has no equivalent in LL.

305 The translator read or saw 'et tibi' for 'et ibi'; his exemplar presumably had 'et' unabbreviated.

306 'May your love for me grow' (LL 'crescat amor tuus').

307 The translator read or saw 'et tibi' for 'et ibi', as in the previous note.

308 There may be an associated erasure in the L.H. margin.

309 The insertion is in Hand C; the scribe uses only 'thy' (32 times).

310 Over erasure in the L.H. margin, in accordance with material erased from that margin.

311 Opposite in the L.H. margin is a cross in pencil.

312 The insertion is in Hand C.

313 Opposite the '-te' which begins a line is a cross in pencil in the R.H. margin.

314 Hand C wrote 'hyt' at the end of a line.

315 Lines of this kind representlong 'infills' composed of connected 'swung dashes' (hence 'tilde lines') which, like the names of contrasting pairs of qualities

written in the margins, are in red. The quality describing the blessed is in the margin above the level of the infill, that describing the damned is below it. Where they occur on the same page, the qualities in the margin are paired by brackets, each bracket drawn in red and blue. For the sake of clarity, the marginalia are given in footnotes to the infills to which they relate, rather than in footnotes to nearby words. Here **'Pulcri·** (MS **'Perulcri·'**) and **'Fedi·'** are in the R.H. margin. All such marginal annotations on ff.229^{v}–230^{v} echo those in LL. For the function of the 'tilde lines', see p.31 above.

316 Lines of this kind represent an 'infill', composed not of 'swung dashes' but of two long decorative strokes, the blue one below mirroring the red one above. For the function of the 'reflection lines', see p.31 above.

317 LL 'ipsi fuligine turpiores erunt'; ME offers an image extension rare in this translation.

318 The phrase 'evyn [in] the contrarie' = 'Just the opposite' (*MED s.v.* **even** adv. 16(b)).

319 **'Veloces·'** and **'Pigri·'** in the R.H. margin.

320 This is the exception to the rule that the scribe does not mark new paragraph subjects in the Recapitulation with paraphs.

321 The scribe has placed a 'tilde line' here instead of after 'have' following; perhaps his eye was confused by the close proximity of two occurrences of 'schul have' in the immediately following words: he identified the second 'schul have' as the place for a 'reflection line' (not a 'tilde line') and then momentarily mistook the first 'schul have' for the second. This is the only 'tilde line' – apart from that marking the distinction between 'Potentes' and 'Impotentes' on f.231^{v}/4, which is itself the subject of confusion – where there is no preceding *punctus elevatus*. **'Fortes·'** and **'Debiles·'** in the L.H. margin.

322 See previous note: the 'tilde line' was misplaced.

323 Followed by 'that they' crossed out in red.

324 This 'infill' is split between two lines, the first half consisting only of the upper, red, element.

325 'Freedom' (LL 'libertatem').

326 **'liberi'** and **'Clausi'** in the L.H. margin.

327 'Refreynyd of' = 'kept from' (LL 'prohibebuntur'): *MED s.v.* **refreinen** v.(2), 2(a).

328 **'Sani·'** in the L.H. margin, and **'Languidi·'** in the R.H. margin of the next page.

329 'Tormented': *OED s.v.* **torment**; cf. 'turmentyd' on f.231^{r}.

330 **'Voluptas·'** and **'Anxietas·'** in the R.H. margin.

331 An 'expansion' passage is skipped here, the equivalent of: '<Illi enim sicut ferrum ignitum quaque sui parte continet ignem sic in se voluptatem, mali vero sencient anxi[e]tatem.>' This creates the next two confusions in layout.

332 Followed by 'so' crossed out.

333 We begin a new paragraph with this clause, in accordance with our policy of following the Latin layout in §22 (see pp.39–40). This does not, however, represent the syntax actually presented in ME. Confused by the preceding omission of an 'expansion', the scribe now thinks that he is writing an 'expansion', and so he omits the 'tilde line' required here to mark the start of a new paragraph subject. The error has a 'knock-on' effect. '**Diuturnitas·**' and '**Brevitas·**' are in the R.H. margin.

334 The 'reflection line' required here is omitted as a result of the preceding 'tilde line' having been omitted. Perhaps it is eyeskip on 'but' that then leads the scribe to misplace his next 'tilde line', putting it 15 words later, after 'lyve', where it illogically interrupts a sentence on the damned.

335 In MS a 'tilde line' is wrongly placed here, as a result of eyeskip from 'but' above, just after the place where the infill should be, to 'but' here following.

336 '**Sapientes·**' and '**Insipientes·**' in the R.H. margin.

337 Preceded by 'they' crossed out.

338 'Deprived of': not recorded before *c.* 1350 (*MED s.v.* **depriven**).

339 'Insane'.

340 Followed by a light double stroke.

341 '**Amici·**' and '**Inimici·**' in the L.H. margin.

342 It is unusual for the beginning of a paragraph devoted to one of the states of the blessed soul and its opposite to be marked, as is nearly always the case in LL, with a paraph. This place is so marked both at the end of the preceding section and at the start of this one on a new line.

343 '**Concordes·**' and '**Discordes·**' in the L.H. margin.

344 LL 'Corpus enim et anima cuiusque sancti immo concordie tante omnes erunt electi.'

345 LL 'dissideant'.

346 Followed by a light double stroke.

347 '**Honorati·**' and '**Inhonorati·**' in the R.H. margin.

348 MS 'chothe'.

349 LL's 'inmortalite indutum' ('clothed with immortality') makes no mention of a stole. Perhaps this is evidence of the translator's being a religious.

350 'Just the opposite' (*MED s.v.* **even** adv. 16(b)).

351 *MED s.v.* **disput** n. gives only one doubtful citation (before 1400, not earlier than 1375) which may be an infinitive ('Despute, he sais, is na mistere be-twix þe wise in such a were'), and observes that the noun is 'not clearly attested until c1600'. The word is unambiguously a noun here. The phrase 'evyn contrarie ther aȝens yput at al dispute' – a considerable expansion of LL 'exhonorabitur' (AN 'en countrere sera honuree') – might mean 'just the opposite when placed in comparison with them – all in conflict' or 'just the opposite, being put all at enmity [with God]'.

352 Here MS has a 'tilde line' that should come after 'too' later in the line; it is hard

to see what misled the scribe. **‘Potentes·’** and **‘Impotentes’** in the L.H. margin.

353 This is the only example of this form in this text; the scribe’s usual form is ‘to’.

354 The ‘tilde line’ that should occur here is misplaced above (see previous note); however, the expected *punctus elevatus* that usually precedes such infills is correctly present: the scribe may have realized too late that he had misplaced the infill earlier in the text.

355 This is the only example of this form of ‘but’ (the scribe’s usual form) in this text.

356 **‘Securi·’** and **‘Invidi·’** in the L.H. margin.

357 Parts of the word, including ‘r’ and ‘y’, are overwritten in Hand C.

358 The translator misread ‘de malo in peius’ as ‘de malo in penis’ (AN has ‘de male en pys’).

359 The insertion is in accordance with a word erased from the L.H. margin.

360 Followed in MS by ‘h’’ roughly crossed out.

361 The ‘infill’ is followed by the mark used elsewhere to indicate transposition (or, as in the previous note, error); perhaps it relates to the fact that the pairing of the marginalized names of properties has broken down here, **‘Gaudentes·’** being in the L.H. margin of one page, and **‘Tristes·’** in the R.H. margin of the next.

362 This form of ‘nor’ is not used elsewhere in ME.

363 ‘Illusory, unreliable’ (*MED s.v.* **deceivable** 3(a)).

364 LL ‘In hac ergo vita nullus beatus esse querat nullus honores caducos adipisci contendat.>’

365 Followed by a light double stroke, and a now illegible phrase erased from the R.H. margin.

366 LL ‘Gaudium et exaltacio his qui Dominum Christum diligunt, meror et desolacio his qui illum contempnunt, cui gloria et imperium nunc et in perpetuum.’ ME shows a marked change of emphasis.

367 The scribe or the translator omitted an equivalent of LL: **‘Explicit libellus beati Anselmi Archiepiscopi Cantuarensis xiiii partibus beatitudinum.’** This omission, together with the above absence of the conventional closing phrase in praise of God, may indicate a curtailed exemplar. The last ME page is half empty, so the loss is not from our manuscript.

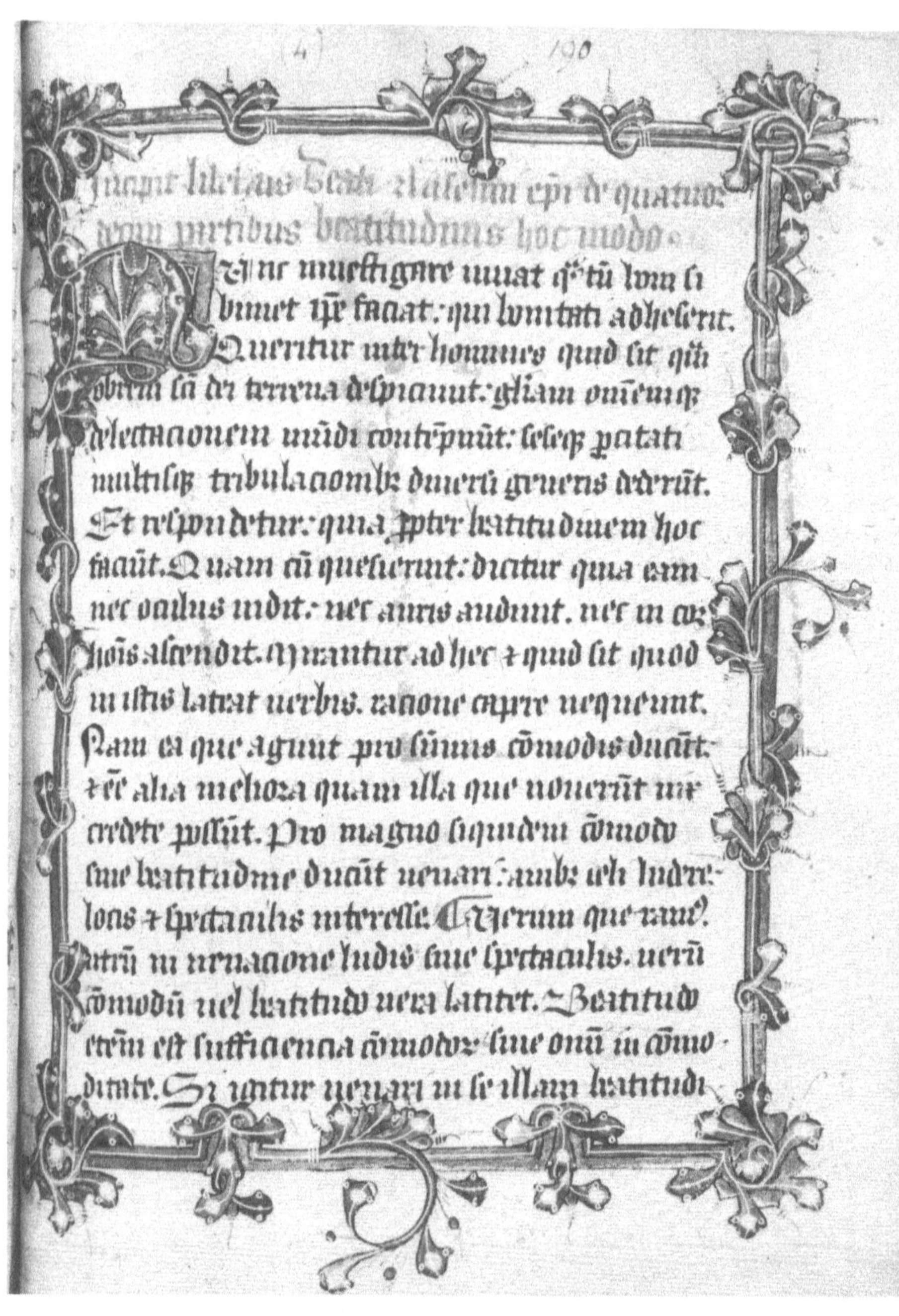

Incipit libellus beati Anselmi epi de quatuor
decim partibus beatitudinis hoc modo.
Dum ne investigare iuvat quantum bono si
bi veniet ipse faciat: qui bonitati adheserit.
Queritur inter homines quid sit quod
obitum sui dei terrena despiciunt: gloriam omnemque
delectacionem mundi contempnunt: seseque penati
multisque tribulacionibus diversis generis dederunt.
Et respondetur: quia propter beatitudinem hoc
faciunt. Quam cum quesierunt: dicitur quia eam
nec oculus vidit: nec auris audivit. nec in cor
hominis ascendit. Mirantur ad hec et quid sit quod
in istis latitat verbis. racione capere nequeunt.
Nam ea que agunt pro summis commodis ducunt.
et esse alia meliora quam illa que noverunt in
credere possunt. Pro magno siquidem commodo
sive beatitudine ducunt venari: aucupari vel ludicre
lorus et spectaculis interesse. Verum que ratio.
utrum in venacione ludis sive spectaculis. verum
commodum vel beatitudo vera latitet. Beatitudo
etenim est sufficiencia commodorum sine omni incommo
ditate. Si igitur venari in se illam beatitudi

Plate 3: The first page of the Latin text (f. 190r)
(Reduced)

DE QUATUORDECIM PARTIBUS BEATITUDINIS: THE LATIN[1]

[f.190r]

1 **<Incipit libellus Beati Anselmi episcopi de quatuordecim partibus beatitudinis hoc modo.>**

Nunc investigare iuvat quantum boni sibimet ipse faciat qui bonitati adheserit. Queritur inter homines, quid sit quamobrem sancti Dei terrena despiciunt, gloriam omnemque delectacionem mundi contempnunt, seseque parcitati multisque tribulacionibus diversi generis dederunt; et respondetur, quia propter beatitudinem hoc faciunt. Quam cum quesierint, dicitur quia eam 'nec oculus vidit nec auris audivit nec in cor hominis ascendit'.[2] Mirantur ad hec, et quid sit quod in istis lateat verbis, racione capere nequeunt. Nam ea que agunt pro summis commodis ducunt, et esse alia meliora quam illa que noverunt vix credere possunt. Pro magno siquidem commodo sive beatitudine ducunt venari, avibus celi ludere, iocis[3] et spectaculis interesse. ¶ Verum queramus, utrum in venacione, ludis, sive spectaculis, verum [p.128] commodum vel beatitudo latitet. Beatitudo etenim est sufficiencia commodorum sine omni incommoditate. Si igiturvenari in se illam beatitudi[f.190v]nem vel tale commodum habet, omni incommodo penitus caret. Sed non caret incommodo quia si careret sine intermissione quivis hominum venari valeret. Non igitur commodum istud ibi vel beatitudo. Simili modo in avium ludo[4] non reperitur[5] ista beatitudo, non in ioco, non in quolibet spectaculo. ¶ Ubi ergo est? Forsitan in magnis edificiis, in munitissimis castris, in auro et argento, in equis et magnis possessionibus. Sed si est in istis et qui hec habet beatus est, tunc ab omni sollicitudine, cura et labore liberatus est. At certe videmus quia hii qui hec habent maiori cura, sollicitudine atque labore gravantur. Non itaque in istis verum comodum vel beatitudo est. ¶ Ubi igitur queremus illam? Alias queramus si invenire volumus, quia in istis invenire non possumus. ¶ Notandum est duas esse beatitudines et duas miserias. Una beatitudo est quam Adam habuit in paradiso et perdidit, altera in celo quam habent angeli et sancti, quos Dominus assumpsit. ¶ Una miseria est in terra quam singulis horis patimur, altera in ergastulo inferorum [f.199r] quam perditi post mortem pacientur. Illa beatitudo, quam habuit Adam in paradiso, fuit temporalis. Illa vero celestis, propter quam factus est, eternalis. Illa miseria vel tribulacio, quam in presenti patimur, finem habet. Illa vero, que in inferno est, omni fine caret, que eciam 'mors' appellatur pro qua oratur, ne renatum 'mors secunda'[6] possideat.

2 <Quod beatitudo proposita gracius sapiat si per partes[7] lacius dividatur.>

Beatitudo igitur illa, que promittitur sanctis, tam magna est tamque mirabilis, ut eam 'nec oculus viderit nec auris audierit et in cor hominis non ascenderit'.[8] Cum itaque hanc pre magnitudine sui videre nequeamus, consideremus[9] quid nos in presenti vita naturaliter delectet, quid hoc sit quod bonum vel honestum videatur, si forte aliquid inveniri possit, unde illud admirabile quod dicitur 'oculum non vidisse et aurem non audisse'[10] lucidius appareat et saporem graciorem habeat. Nimis etenim paucis verbis comprehensum est totum illud quod electis promittitur. ¶ Et quoniam[11] hoc ita est occultum, ita inclu[f.199v]sum et multum ab infirmis mentibus separatum, conemur de tam excellenti gloria aliquid elicere, et [p.129] illud in plures partes ut lucidius clareat dividendo statuere. Profecto si grossum pomum datur infanti ad manducandum, pre nimia teneritudine sui parvuli oris illud mordere nequit.[12] Quod si particulatim inciditur, parvulus inde reficitur. Et quod prius intelligere cuius esset saporis non potuit, iam per frusta divisum cum sapore comedit. Servata igitur illa invisibili promissione Dei,[13] donec veniamus eum 'sicuti est',[14] intente rimemur quid corporibus, quid animabus nostris conveniat,[15] quid appetere, quove delectare libere ac sine offensa valeant, firmiter tenentes nichil honoris vel alicuius bonitatis deesse omnibus qui in illa felicitate[16] contigerit esse. Septem igitur michi videntur esse que possunt corporibus aptari, et sunt decentissima et ad beatitudinem sufficiencia. Hec itaque sunt: Pulcritudo, Velocitas, Fortitudo, Libertas, Sanitas, Voluptas, Diuturnitas. Anime quoque totidem numero convenire videntur, que hoc ordine computantur: [f.216r] Sapiencia, Amicicia, Concordia, Honor, Potestas, Securitas, Gaudium. Hec omnia electos Dei in illo beato regno habituros dubium non est,[17] cum illos inhabitet ac in illis[18] presideat de quo est quicquid usquam boni est et potens et gloriosus super omnia ineffabiliter est. ¶ Sed iam paulisper redeamus, et brevi raciuncula[19] hoc quod diximus ostendere conemur et a minoribus incipientes gradatim ascendamus.

3 <De pulchritudine sanctorum que est prima pars beatitudinis ad corpora eorum pertinentis.>

Queris de pulchritudine. Audi quod scriptum est: 'Iusti fulgebunt sicut sol.'[20] Tunc 'luna fulgebit sicut sol, et sol septempliciter sicut lux septem dierum'.[21] Si ergo corpora nostra 'fulgebunt sicut [p.130] sol',[22] qui multiplicatum lumen septem dierum habebit, magna et incomparabiliter magna illa pulchritudo erit. ¶ Accipe et illud: 'Salvatorem expectamus Dominum Ihesum Christum, qui reformabit corpus humilitatis nostre configuratum corpori claritatis sue'.[23] Certe quando Dominus in monte transfiguratus est coram dicipu[f.200v]lis suis 'resplenduit facies eius sicut sol'.[24] Cuius claritatis iocunditate Petrus delectatus 'Domine', inquit,[25] 'bonum est nos hic esse.'[26] ¶ 'Aspectus' quoque angeli qui sedit ad sepulchrum Domini apparuit 'sicut fulgor' celi.[27] Cum igitur tanta claritas hic fuerit unius angeli, quid putas quam gloriosa, quam magnifica pulchritudo erit, quando sanctorum milia numeroque carencia assimilata claro corpori Ihesu Christi Domini cum illo apparebunt? ¶ Hanc pulchram beatitudinem ac beatam pulchritudinem considerabat qui dicebat, 'Unam pecii a Domino, hanc requiram, ut inhabitem in domo Domini.'[28] De ista pulcritudine, que vere magna est beatitudo, multa in sacro eloquio inveniuntur. ¶ Huic beate pulchritudini subiunximus velocitatem.

4 <De velocitate sanctorum que est secunda pars beatitudinis ipsorum.>

Velocitatem tantam habebunt hii qui cum Deo erunt, quantam habet radius[29] solis, vel alicuius oculi clare videntis. Sol quippe ut in oriente super terram venit, mox in occidentem suum radium porrigit. Similiter radius oculi, dum palpebra aperitur, in celum aut [f.201r] in longum, si obstaculum non fuerit, vel quovis alio dirigitur. Sic utique corpora nostra, cum spiritualia fuerint et ad instar angelorum pondus aut gravitatem non senserint, facillime transmigrabunt quocumque voluerint. Nam in resurrectione corporum[30] singule partes uniuscuiusque hominis insimul coadunabuntur, ita ut, si manus vel pes alicuius aut aliud quolibet membrum in oriente sepultum aut a bestiis devoratum fuerit et reliquum corpus in occidente vel semptemtrione iacuerit aut in diversas[31] mundi partes dispersum sit, tam velociter totum corpus congregabitur quamcito oculus clauditur aut aperitur.[32] Babiloniam a Iudaea multa terrarum intercapedo dirimit et tamen in [p.131] momento angelus Abacuc de Iudea in Babiloniam sustulit, quem supra lacum[33] leonum posuit, qui Danieli prandium porrexit. Quo facto, Abacuc protinus restitutus est in locum suum. Mirari certe potuit ubi fuerit, quando se in loco proprio tam cito invenit. Talem itaque agilitatem quicumque[34] habebit, magnum munus, magnam proculdubio felicitatem habebit. Nec tamen felix iste sola ista felicitate contentus erit.

5 [f.201v] **<De fortitudine sanctorum que est tercia pars beatitudinis ipsorum.>**

Sequitur fortitudo, quam unusquisque beatorum tantam habebit, quantum centum milia hominum simul in presenti vita non habent. Nam mensura eiusdem valitudinis tanta erit, quantam is, qui eam habiturus est, elegerit. Si totam molem tocius terre uno digito movere voluerit, utique facillime poterit. Diabolus, Dei inimicus, ex fortitudine sue nature movet aerem, excitat ventos et tempestates, facit interdum terremotum multaque alia satis admiranda, unde et 'fortis armatus'[35] vocatur; et Deus electis suis non dabit vel parem fortitudinem vel certe multo maiorem et meliorem? Absit hoc ut aliquis senciat, ut sano capite quivis hominum sapiat. 'Voluntatem' etenim 'timencium se faciet'[36] Dominus, quibus eciam, ut alibi dicitur, 'nichil deerit'.[37] Si 'nichil deerit', nec fortitudo deerit. Aderit itaque, et non modica.

6 **<De libertate sanctorum que est quarta pars beatitudinis eorum.>**

Verum quia nec fortitudo nec velocitas nec pulchritudo aliquid appre[f.202r]ciatur illi qui liber non est, quod beata illa multitudo erit libera, dubium non est. Nam nulla materies, nullus ignis vel aqua sive alia quelibet materies eos poterit prepedire, ne intrent et exeant quocumque voluerint intrare vel exire. Libere Dominus clauso sepulchro exivit, libere infernum spoliavit, libere ad discipulos 'ianuis clausis'[38] intravit. Libere sancti Dei, si voluerint, infernum intrabunt, libere per ignem et ardentem picem transibunt, libere, quantum voluerint, ibi morabuntur absque lesione sui, quia in illa gehennali flamma nichil ardebit nisi tantum delicta. Et quoniam sancti Dei ab omni inquinamento peccati erunt purgati, per gelida et estuata, per diversa tormenta et stagna vaporancia transibunt illesi. Item illud vel consideracio eorundem locorum erit in arbitrio beatorum, et ad confusionem reproborum. Tanta erit eorum libertas, quanta fuerit habendi voluntas.

7 [p.132] <De sanitate sanctorum que est quinta pars beatitudinis eorum.>

Beate itaque libertati et tam libere beatitudini comitabitur gratissima sanitas. Sanitas igitur multa erit, quoniam [f.202v] 'absterget Deus omnem lacrimam ab oculis sanctorum, et mors non erit amplius neque luctus neque clamor nec ullus[39] dolor, quoniam priora transierunt'.[40] Qui bene considerare voluerit, nulla in nobis est in presenti seculo sanitas. Nam <ubicumque dolorem in corpore habemus, si quis partem illam paulisper duriter tetigerit pre dolore clamamus, sic quoque> in omnibus aliis membrorum nostrorum partibus, si aliquando durius tacti fuerimus, confestim lesi conqueremur. Et quare hoc, nisi quia ubique debiles et infirmi sumus? Electis autem Domini nulla lesio supervenire poterit, non ferrum, non ignis, non aqua eis nocebit. Nulla memoria alicuius incomodi, quod est hic passus quivis eorum qui ibi erit, poterit quicquam nocere, quoniam tanta habundancia iocunditatis ibi erit, ut de his que iam transierunt minime curet.[41] Quod si cura ei fuerit, ad libitum vindicandi se locum habebit. Sed necesse non erit, quia ipse Dominus dicit, 'Michi vindictam, ego retribuam.'[42] Hoc autem caveat qui Deo placere desiderat, ut vindictam sue iniurie Christo committat. Si autem semetipsum vindicare cepit, vindicem Deum [f.203r] eiusdem iniurie non habebit, quoniam quidem eam super se presumptuose accepit. Cui dicet Dominus, 'Quia maluisti te ipsum vindicare quam me expectare, non me amodo de vindicta debes interpellare.' Bene vobis conveniat. Si vero Domini consiliuum secutus vindictam suspenderit, felix erit, quia nulla offensa, nulla erit ei egestas, nulla imbecillitas, sed sana felicitas et felicissima sanitas. ¶ Hec omnia que dicta[43] sunt, valde bona sunt, sed si saporem non habent, quasi penitus infructuosa sunt. Si vero saporem haberent, proculdubio [p.133] incomparabiliter bona essent.

8 <De voluptate sanctorum que est sexta pars beatitudinis eorum.>

Necessario igitur adherit voluptas, que beatis illis[44] saporem tribuet, ut sapiant et intelligant 'quam sunt dilecta'[45] et iocunda 'tabernacula'[46] Domini, et quoniam 'melior est dies una in atriis' Ierusalem 'super milia'.[47] Voluptas ergo maxima erit et cunctos inmensitate iocunditatis inebriabit. Propheta clamat: 'Inebriabuntur ab ubertate domus tue, et torrente voluptatis tue potabis eos, quoniam apud te est fons vite.'[48] Vere mi[f.203v]rabilis ebrietas illa, mirabilis ubertas illa, mirabilis et domus illa! Utpote torrens precipitando defluit, sic admirabili dulcedine domus sue nos omnipotens Deus replebit. ¶ Et quoniam conveniens exemplum tante suavitatis, tante dulcedinis tanteque bonitatis invenire nequimus, consideremus amarissimum dolorem, quem habituri sunt reprobi, contra iocundissimam suavitatem, quam habebunt probi. Profecto si quis michi pupillam oculi ferro ignito transfoderet, magnum dolorem haberem. Et si aliam simili tormento transfigeret, multo maior dolor michi esset. Et si per omnia membra eadem pena michi fieret, idem dolor teneret, quid[49] putas esset? Nonne insanirem? Nonne penitus alterius mentis fierem? Cum me flamma undique circumveniret, undique combureret, undique pena coartaret, quid putas? cuius memoriae anima mea esset?[50] Sic itaque sed prorsus alio modo replebimur iocunditate a facie Dei, saturabimur ab ubertate domus Domini, inebriabimur a torrente voluptatis sive delectacionis ipsius Dei. Temporalis delectacio, transitoria voluptas, in qualibet corporis[51] parte solummodo sentitur, illa [f.204r] vero delectacio quemadmodum ignis per totum sentiretur, ita per omnes partes corporis et anime sencietur. Quasi totum corpus esset gula, sic delectabitur illa sancta iocunditate. Si enim male habent mali in omnibus sui corporis partibus quia bene agere noluerunt, multo iustius boni bene habebunt in omnibus suis membris quia bene fecerunt. Habebunt itaque sancti Dei hanc beatam voluptatem que veraciter est delectabilis, et beatitudo magna. ¶ Sed parum est hanc et alias supradictas habere, nisi eam cum ceteris sine defectu valeant habere.

9 **<De diuturnitate sanctorum que est septima pars[52] beatitudinis eorum.>**

Accedat igitur diuturnitas, que nullius finis novit metas. [p.134] Diuturnitas hec non novit finem quia sanctorum pulcritudo, velocitas, fortitudo, libertas, sanitas, voluptas non habent finem. Hec qui habuerit leto ore cantare poterit 'lauda Ierusalem Dominum, lauda Deum tuum Syon, quoniam confortavit seras portarum tuarum, benedixit filiis tuis in te',[53] quia vere benedicti erunt qui tali benedictione benedicentur.

10 **<De sapiencia sanctorum que est octava pars beatitudinis ad animas ipsorum pertinentis.>**

[f.204v] Igitur consideratis et breviter insinuatis partibus beatitudinis que corpori videntur competere partes quoque illas, quas supradiximus animabus convenire, adiuvante Domino perspiciamus. ¶ Partium igitur illarum prima est sapiencia, quam beati viri pleniter habebunt, ut nichil desit eis de omnibus que noscerevolent. Omnia quippe preterita, presencia et futura scient nec aliquid erit quod eorum noticie subtractum sit. Nec indigencia erit ut quis quem interroget, quis eius proavus fuerit, de cuius stirpe prodierit, quis ille vel illa[54] sit. Omnium li[n]guarum, omnium creaturarum, omnium artium habebunt scienciam, cogitatus eciam alter alterius aperte videbit. Quicquid feci vel facio in presenti vita omnes illi videbunt; quicquid eorum aliquis fecit et ego videbo si ibi fuero. Nec inde ruborem aliquis habebit, si in hac vita Deo per p[e]n[itent]iam[55] satisfacit. Omnes quippe s[c]imus[56] Petrum apostolum Dominum negavisse,[57] Mariam Magdalenam peccatricem fuisse, nec eos latet quia nos scimus.[58] Nam si lateret, tantum hoc legendo et concinendo pronunciamus ut latere non possit, et tamen inde nichil ruboris vel detrimenti habent. [f.197r] <Sed nec angeli sanctos despiciunt quia temptacionibus aliquando victi sunt, nec sancti angelos quia nullam quam vincerent temptacionem passi sunt. Si enim Michael diceret Petro, 'Tu Dominum negasti', posset Petrus respondere, 'Verum est quidem quod dicis; sed tu pro Domino numquam[59] vel unum colaphum sustinuisti.' Quod omnino non faciunt, sed ita existunt concordes, ac si omnes essent angeli vel homines.> Quare hoc? Certe quia facti sui penituerunt, et veniam consequuti sunt. Sed et nos si pro commissis veniam consequuti fuerimus, nichil de perpetratis[60] [p.135] culpis erubescemus. Nam qui nobis in hac etate[61] improp[er]aret[62] quod in infancia dum in cunis iaceremus faciebamus, nichil nobis constaret, eo quod tempus et etas illa iam pertransiret. 'Cum enim essem parvulus, sapiebam ut parvulus, cogitabam ut parvulus. Quando autem factus sum vir, evacuavi que erant parvuli.'[63] Sic itaque in illa beata vita nichil pudoris erit quod alter alterius facta videbit, si hinc per satisfactionem illuc Deo donante pervenerit. Quod enim Deus mundavit,[64] nemo inmundum iudicabit,[65] nemo [f.197v] improperandum fore putabit.

11 <De amicicia sanctorum que est nova pars beatitudinis eorum.>

Inter hec sanctorum agmina erit quoque indeficiens et perfecta amicicia. Nam unusquisque singulatim omnesque simul Deum ac Dominum suum plusquam semetipsos amabunt, et quisque quemlibet alium sicut semetipsum carum habebit. Nec se diliget plus quam alium, nec alium plus quam se; sed pari modo se et omnes alios diliget, Deum autem super se et omnes alios. ¶ Quod si dicat quis patrem aut parentes se amplius ceteris velle diligere, videat apud se quid dicat, et quia non bene sentit veraciter intelligat. Equidem tuum parentem quisquis es qui hoc dicis, que[m] tu veraci et ardenciori amore diligis, desideras ut omnes eundem diligant, et non minori amore quam tu eum diligis. Idem ego de meo amico sencio, volo atque desiderio; [p.136] idem omnes alii. Quapropter cum cupias, ut tuum amicum diligam, sicut me ipsum, et ego desidero ut meum amicum ames sicut te ipsum, necessarie amabis me et omnes alios sicut te, quatinus omnes alii diligant te veluti sese. Quod cum sit, erit magna et[66] [f.198r] perfecta amicicia, quia in singulis singulariter, et in omnibus communiter erit affectus perfecti amoris. Beata igitur amicicia que tantorum[67] beatorum spiritus copulat in eterna gloria.

12 <**De concordia sanctorum que est decima pars beatitudinis ipsorum.**>

Hinc nascitur amica concordia, que ad instar concordie que est in menbris nostris manebit iugiter inviolata. Membra siquidem nostra tantam habent inter se concordiam, utpote sunt oculi, ut nullo modo alter sine altero quicquam velit operari. Nam si unus oculus sursum vel deorsum, dextra levaque velit intendere, non indiget ut alterum moneat secum conspicere, quia nullo naturaliter vult aspicere absque alterius indissociabili conspectione. Tantam inter sese habent concordiam, ut quicquid unus voluerit hoc idem et alter desideret. ¶ Cetera quoque membra multa inter sese copulantur concordia. Nam pro pedibus et toto corpore[68] operatur manus, pro manibus et toto corpore prospicit oculus; pro oculo et toto corpore incedit pes, nudis intradum gressibus. Nec dicit pes, licet aliquando [f.198v] graviter cruentetur spinarum aculeis, se nolle amodo quoquam ire, nec manus quamvis vulneretur se nolle amplius operari; nec si contigerit ut manus securi pedem vulneret, aliqua adversus manum ira movetur. Tanta siquidem inter sese amoris adunantur concordia ut nulla racione inter se valeant dissentire occasione aliqua, immo quicquid alicui impenditur, omnibus sibimet impensum esse videtur. Omnia capiti serviunt, et se pro illo periculis opponunt. Ex quo manifeste perpenditur, quod capud plus quam se veraciter diligunt. Talis ergo erit concordia in illa beata beatorum patria, ubi nulla dissensionis invenitur [p.137] macula, ubi Deus in omnibus omnia erit, et super omnia omnibus carus erit. Ibi certe non minor inter omnes qui erunt membra Christi concordia firmabitur, quam modo in corpore corruptibili hominis corruptibilis invenitur, sed tanto maior atque preciosior illa erit, quanto constiterit, quia numquam finem habebit.

13 <**De honore sanctorum qui est undecima pars beatitudinis eorum.**>

[f.191r] [p.138] Honor quoque beatis illis magnus erit quia 'nimis honorati sunt amici tui, Deus'.[69] Honor iste tam magnus erit, ut ab humano ingenio comprehendi non possit. Ponamus tamen sub exemplo ut aliquis servus honoretur a domino. Certe si imperator aut rex aliquis servum suum honoraret ita ut illum a servitute liberaret, in ordine militum poneret, multum se debitorem domini sui servus ille esse putaret. Et si eum inter primates suos exaltaret? Quanto amore domini sui flagraretur? Causa domini[70] ab omnibus ei honor impenderetur, omnes illis servirent, ne indignacionem domini qui eum honoraret incurrerent. Si autem herus adhuc in tantum eundem diligeret ut illum sibi in filium adoptaret, heredem suum statueret, iam proculdubio servi exultacio pro honore illato modum nesciret. Qua ex re perpendi potest mirabilem esse illum honorem, qui alicui datur per Deum et omnium conditorem. Qui sibi servientes non solum in eterna pace perhenniter vivere faciet, nec solummodo amicos suos illos vocabit, sed filios et heredes regni celorum constituet. [f.191v] [p.139] Quid putandum est quantum honorem ab omni creatura habebit, fratrem vocabit, filium tenebit? Omnis ei creatura subdita erit, quod magnus et incomparabilis honor erit.

14 <**De potestate sanctorum que est duodecima pars beatitudinis ipsorum.**>

[p.137] Potestas eciam beatis illis tanta erit, quanta[m] quivis eorum voluerit. Nam quodcumque aliquis eorum in celo sive in terra, in mari vel profundo inferni fieri imperaverit, absque contradictione factum erit. Mirum videri potest quod dicimus, sed si bene consideratur ubi tunc [p.138] locati vel cuius corporis membra tunc erimus, et quia nichil deerit his qui Deum diligunt, nequaquam erit incredibile. ¶ Forte videbitur alicui potestas esse hoc, quod superius nominavimus fortitudinem, sed non est. Fortitudo siquidem superius prolata virtus est operandi, potestas autem hic enunciata virtus est precipiendi. Hanc potestatem veraciter habebunt sancti Dei, quoniam quidem omnia possidebunt cum filio Dei. Potestas hec erit potestas eterna, et idcirco his, qui eam habuerint, erit beatitudo non parva. [p.139] ¶ Satis magna et gloriosa sunt hec dona Dei, siquidem semper per[f.192r]durare poterint. Oportet itaque ut securitatem habeant, quatinus id quod habent semper servare valeant.

15 <De securitate sanctorum que est terciadecima pars beatitudinis eorum.>

Securitas ergo sufficiens erit, quoniam 'neque luctus neque dolor amplius ullus erit'.[71] Numquam perdere potero beatitudinem tam magnam, nisi voluero aut nisi Deus illam michi offerre voluerit, aut aliquis forcior illo qui eam auferat superveniat. Sed securus sum, quia si eam adeptus fuero, perdere nolo; securus quoque, quia Deus 'apud quem non est transmutacio nec vicissitudinis obumbracio'[72] eam non auferet postquam semel dederit; securus eciam quod nullus fortior illo supervenire poterit. Quare postquam ita est, ibi esse plenariam securitatem dubium non est.

16 <De gaudio sanctorum quod est quartadecima[73] pars beatitudinis ipsorum.>

Erit igitur pro his omnibus inestimabile gaudium, quod penitus supereminet sensus hominum. Nam quis cogitare potest gaudium, quod de seme[t]ipso unusquisque habebit, quando tantam pulchritudinem, velocitatem, fortitudinem, liberta[f.192v]tem, sanitatem, voluptatem, diuturnitatem, sapienciam, amiciciam, concordiam, honorem, potestatem, securitatemque habebit? Nullus sane hoc gaudium dicere potest quantum est, quia nullus in presenti vita illud expertus est. ¶ Verum si alicui amico tuo – tu quisquis es, qui ibi futurus es – idem gaudium Deus daret, qui[d] tibi videtur? Nonne multum gauderes? Et si duobus vel tribus aut certe pluribus et illis, quos non minus te amares, quid diceres? Vere magnum gaudium [p.140] haberes, et ultra quam dici potest exultares. Que quidem donacio nullo modo deerit, sed vere amicis et parentibus nostris karissimis, qui ibi per Dei mi[sericordi]am[74] erimus, illud idem gaudium dabit Dominus quatinus de illo qui supra nos erit gaudeamus, de nobis ipsis gaudeamus et de proximis nostris gaudeamus. Nempe gaudium illud tam magnum est, ut omnes capiat in se. Omnibus superabundabit, omnes circumdabit, omnibus ex omni parte erit. Sicut pisces undique circa se habent mare, sic sancti Dei illam magnificam suavitatem gaudii circa se undique habebunt, de quo dicitur, 'intra in gaudium Domini tui'.[75] <Gaudium perfectum solus ille potest habere, qui pre[f.193r]dictas omnes beatitudinis partes valet optinere. Quod ergo beacius isto, qui tanto replebitur gaudio? Adhuc tamen ad cumulum beatitudinis sue, aliud habebit unde magis possit gaudere. Quia enim quisquis sicut se alterum amabit, patet quia sic de illius felicitate ut de sua gaudebit. Quot ergo et quanta gaudia quisque

optinebit, qui de tot beatitudine sanctorum iubilabit? Quod si tantum de aliis quos ut se diliget, gaudebit; quantum de Deo quem super se diliget, exultabit? Tantam ergo beatitudinem possidebit, quantam mens humana estimare non sufficit.

17 **Quod Deum timentibus erit sufficiencia in omnibus.>**
Breviter perspectis quatuordecim partibus beatitudinis sive comoditatis, erit forsitan qui querit ad quid tanta pulchritudo, velocitas et alie nonulle partes debeant, cum solummodo beate vivere et ea habere, quibus vita non potest carere, satis possit sufficere. ¶ Sed sciendum est quia Deus in nullo indigens est, et sicut ille in omnibus est sufficiens, sic amici et ministri eius in omnibus erunt sufficenciam habentes. Si enim quisquam eorum in qualibet re sentiret se inpoten[f.193v]tem esse, non tantum gauderet, quantum faciet, cum se in omnibus veraciter sciat omnipotentem esse. Quare ut gaudium nostrum[76] sit plenum, nichil desit timentibus Deum.

18 <**Excitacio mentis ad contemplandum summum bonum et coniectacio quale et quantum sit hoc bonum.**[77]
Excita nunc anima mea, et erige totum intellectum tuum, et cogita quantum potes, quantum et quale[78] sit illud bonum, de quo tot ac tantorum manat copia bonorum. Si enim singula bona delectabilia sunt, cogita intente quam delectabile sit illud bonum quod continet iocunditatem omnium bonorum, et non qualem in rebus creatis sumus experti; sed tanto differentem, quanto differt creator a creatura. Si enim bona est vita creata, quam bona est vita creatrix? Si iocunda est salus facta, quam iocunda est salus que facit omnem salutem? Si amabilis est sapiencia que omnia condidit ex nichilo, denique si multe et magne delectaciones sunt in rebus delectabilibus, qualis et quanta est delectacio in illo qui fecit ipsa delectabilia?

19 **Que et quanta sint bona fruentibus Deo.**
O qui hoc bono fruetur, quid illi [f.194r] erit, et quid illi non erit? Certe quicquid volet erit et quod nolet non erit. Ibi quippe erunt bona corporis et anime, qualia 'nec oculus vidit, nec auris audivit, nec cor hominis[79] cogitavit'.[80] Cur ergo per multa vagaris, homuncio, querendo bona anime tue et corporis tui? Ama unum bonum, in quo sunt omnia bona, et sufficit; desidera simplex[81] bonum, quod est omne bonum, et satis est. Quid enim amas, caro mea, quid desideras, anima mea? Ibi est, ibi est quicquid amatis, quicquid desideratis. Si delectat

pulchritudo, 'fulgebunt[82] iusti sicut sol'.[83] Si velocitas aut fortitudo aut libertas[84] corporis, cui nichil obsistere possit, 'erunt similes angelis[85] Dei',[86] 'quorum seminatur corpus animale et surget corpus spirituale',[87] potestate utique, non natura. Si longa et salubris[88] vita, ibi est sana eternitas et eterna sanitas, quia 'iusti in perpetuum vivent',[89] et 'salus iustorum a Domino'.[90] Si sacietas,[91] 'saciabuntur cum apparuerit gloria Dei'.[92] Si ebrietas, 'inebriabuntur[93] ab ubertate domus Dei'.[94] Si melodia,[95] ibi angelorum chori concinunt[96] sine fine Deo. Si quelibet non immunda, erit munda[97] voluptas, 'torrente voluptatis sue potabit eos Deus'.[98] Si sapiencia, ipsa Dei sapiencia ostendet[99] eis se ipsam. Si[100] amicicia, diligent Deum plus quam se ipsos; et invicem tanquam[101] se ipsos et Deus illos plus quam illi se ipsos; quare illi [f.194v] illum[102] et se et invicem per illum, et ille se et illos per se ipsum. Si concordia,[103] omnibus illis erit una voluntas, quia nulla illis erit nisi sola Dei voluntas. Si potestas, omnipotentes erunt sue voluntatis ut Deus sue. Nam sicut poterit Deus quod volet per se ipsum, ita poterunt illi quod volent per illum, quia sicut illi non aliud volent quam quod ille, ita ille volet quicquid illi volent; et quod ille volet, non poterit non[104] esse. Si honor et divicie Deus suos servos bonos et fideles super multa constituet, immo filii Dei et dii 'vocabuntur'[105] et erunt; et ubi erit filius eius, ibi erunt, et illi 'heredes quidem Dei, coheredes[106] autem Christi'.[107] Si vera securitas e[s]t[108] certa,[109] ita certe[110] erunt numquam et nullatenus ista vel pocius illud bonum sic defuturum, sicut certi erunt se non sua sponte illud amissuros; nec dilectorem Deum illud dilectoribus suis invitis ablatur, nec aliquid Deo potencius invitos Deum et illos separaturum.[111] Gaudium vero quale aut quantum est; ubi tale ac tantum bonum est. Cor humanum, cor indigens, cor expertum erumpnis,[112] immo obrutum erumpnis quantum gauderes, si his omnibus abundares? Interroga intima tua, si capere possint gaudium suum de tanta beatitudine sua. Sed certe si quis alius quem omnino sicut te ipsum diligeres, eandem beatitudinem haberet; duplicaretur gaudium tuum, quare non minus gauderes pro eo [f.195r] quam pro te ipso. Si vero duo vel tres vel multo plures id ipsum haberent, tantundem pro singulis quantum pro te ipso gauderes si singulos sicut te ipsum amares. Ergo in illa perfecta karitate innumerabilium beatorum angelorum et hominum, ubi nullus minus diliget alium quam se ipsum, non aliter gaudebit quisque pro singulis aliis quam pro se ipso. Si ergo cor hominis de tanto suo bono vix capiet gaudium suum, quomodo capax erit tot et tantorum gaudiorum? Et utique quam quantum quisque diligit aliquem, tantum de bono eius gaudet; sicut in illa perfecta felicitate unusquisque plus amabit sine comparacione Deum, quam se et omnes alius secum. Ita plus gaudebit absque estimacione de felicitate Dei quam de sua et omnium alium secum. Sed si Deum sic diligent toto corde, tota mente, tota anima ut tam totum cor, tota mens, tota anima non sufficiat dignitati dilectionis: profecto sic gaudebunt toto corde, tota mente, tota anima, ut totum cor, tota mens, tota anima non sufficiat plenitudini gaudii.

20 **An hoc sit gaudium plenum quod promittit Dominus se servis suis daturum.**
Deus meus et Dominus meus, spes mea et gaudium cordis mei, dic anime mee si hoc est gaudium de quo nobis dicis per filium tuum: 'Petite et accipietis, ut gaudium vestrum sit plenum'.[113] Inveni namque gaudium quoddam plenum, et plus quam plenum. Pleno quippe [f.195v] corde, plena mente, plena anima, pleno toto homine gaudio illo: adhuc supra modum supererit gaudium. Non ergo totum illud gaudium intrabit in gaudentes, sed toti gaudentes intrabunt in gaudium. Dic, Domine, dic servo tuo intus in corde suo, si hoc est gaudium in quod intrabunt servi tui, qui intrabunt 'in gaudium Domini'[114] sui. Sed gaudium illud certe quo gaudebunt electi tui, 'nec oculus vidit, nec auris audivit, nec in cor hominis ascendit'.[115] Non dum ergo, Domine, dixi aut cogitavi quantum gaudebunt illi beati tui. Utique tantum gaudebunt, quantum amabunt; tantum amabunt, quantum cognoscent. Quantum cognoscent te, Domine, tunc et quantum te amabunt? Certe 'nec oculus vidit, nec auris audivit, nec in cor hominis ascendit'[116] in hac vita, quantum te cognoscent et amabunt in illa vita.

21 **Oratio pro hoc gaudio impetrando.**[117]
Oro, Deus, cognoscam te, amem te, ut gaudeam de te. Et si non possum in hac vita ad plenum, vel proficiam in dies, usque dum veniat illud ad plenum. Proficiat hic in me noticia tui, et ibi fiat plena; crescat amor tuus, et ibi sit plenus, ut hic gaudium meum sit in spe magnum, et ibi sit in re plenum. Domine per filium tuum iubes, immo consulis petere, et p[ro]mittis accipere, ut gaudium nostrum plenum sit. Peto, Domine, quod consulis per admirabilem consiliarium nostrum accipiam, quod promittis per [f.196r] veritatem tuam, ut gaudium meum plenum sit. Deus verax, peto accipiam ut gaudium meum sit plenum. Meditetur interim inde mens mea, loquatur inde lingua mea; amet illud cor meum, sermocinetur os meum; esuriat illud anima mea, siciat caro mea, desideret tota substancia mea, donec intrem in gaudium

Domini mei, qui est trinus et unus, Deus benedictus in secula. Amen.

22 Recapitulacio brevis de partibus predictarum beatitudinum bonorum, et de perfecta miseria malorum.>

[p.140] Cum itaque tanta sit beatitudo amicis Domini Jhesu, de inimicis eius quid erit? Certe non sic impii, non sic. Sed contra hoc quod sancti Dei erunt pulcherimi, erunt ipsi fedissimi. <Sancti ut sol rutilabunt, ipsi fuligine turpiores erunt.> Nec in resurrectione inmutabuntur in melius, sed sicut sancti Dei in die revelacionis Domini glorificabuntur, sic isti in perdicioni dampnabuntur.[118]

¶ Erunt felices ad omne quod voluerint velocissimi, erunt infelices pigirrimi. <Erunt illi veloces ut radius solis, qui in momento ab oriente in occidentem transibit,[119] isti vero tanto penarum primentur pondere, ut nec quidem pedem possint movere.>[120]

¶ Econtra validam beatorum fortitudinem habebunt miseri maximam debilitate[m]. <Erunt illi sic fortes ut eciam commovere terram possint, illi sic [f.196v] imbecilles, ut nec vermes ab oculis suis amovere possint.>[121]

¶ Iusti libertatem eundi quocumque voluerint habebunt, iniusti autem eterna clausura dampnati nusquam ire poterunt. <Illi nil pacientur quod nolint, sed agere permittentur quodcumque voluerint; isti vero ad omnia que noluerint cogentur, et ab omnibus que voluerint prohibebuntur.>[122]

¶ Electi Dei iugi sanitate pocientur, dampnati vero langore perpetuo cruciabuntur. <Illi sic sani erunt ut nequeant infirmari; isti ita infirmi ut non possint meditari.>[123]

¶ Boni saturabuntur voluptate domus Domini; mali replebuntur amarissimo poculo domus diaboli. <Illi enim sicut ferrum ignitum quaque sui parte continet ignem sic in se voluptatem, mali vero sencient anxi[e]tatem.>[124]

In bonis boni diuturnitatem [p.141] habebunt, in malis mali numquam fine carebunt. <Illi enim vivent quantum et Deus, isti vero non nisi moriendo vivere poterunt.>[125]

¶ Et[126] sicut probi maxima erunt prediti[127] sapiencia, sic improbi confundentur in sua insipiencia. <Illi enim perfecta, quo[128] Deus est, sapiencia replebuntur, eamque facie ad faciem intuebuntur; isti autem vera omnio sapiencia privati tantis urgebuntur doloribus ut non solum incipientes [f.205r] verum omnio et amentes.>[129]

Amici Dei summam habebunt amiciciam, inimici vero Dei maximam inter sese inimiciciam. <Bonum etenim queque sic Deus omnes qui

alii diligent boni, ut eum habere odio ultra non possint. Malum autem quemque sic Deus omnes qui boni habebunt odio, ut nec filius quidem pietatem habeat de patre in penis conspecto.>[130]

¶ Erunt beati pace perpetua concordes; erunt miseri iugi dissencione discordes. <Corpus enim et anima cuiusque sancti immo concordie tante omnes erunt electi, quante in presenti sunt oculi nostri. Mali vero in tanta discordia persistent, ut eorum corpus et anima semper dissideant. Nam et corpus animam odio habebit eo q[uo]d male unquam cogitaverit, et anima corpus quod male cogitata opere complevit, pro quibus omnibus torquebuntur in penis.>[131]

¶ Sancti[132] Dei honore magno sullimabuntur, dampnati vero multo dedecore primentur. <Sicut enim si quis imperator servulum habens languidum eum curari faceret, sanatum vestibus preciosis indueret, adornatum iuxta filium suum sedere faceret. Sicut in quantum[133] honoraret, sic unumquemque bonum ab omni corrupcione inundatum Deus pater honorab[i]t[134] cum enim inmortalite indutum assidere filium suum fecerit. Quisque vero malus sic econtra exhonora[f.205v]bitur, ut in omni fetore deiectus vermium eciam dominio subiciatur.>

¶ Iusti habebunt regiam potestatem precipiendi, iniusti carebunt potestate sese eciam quoque movendi. <Illi enim quicquid voluerint facere poterunt, isti vero nichil quod velint agere quibunt.>[135]

¶ Securi erunt boni[136] quod bonum illorum numquam peribit, timorem habebunt mali de malo in peius semper cadendi. <Illi enim et quicquid voluerint habebunt, et nichil ex eo se amissuros timebunt. Isti vero et semper tormenta que pacienter pavebunt, et numquam ex eis evadere poterunt.[137]

¶ Bonus quisque perfecte poterit gaudere, quia predictas omnes beatitudinis partes optinebit perfecte. Malus vero econtra tristicia summa replebitur, quia omnes miserie partes omnino dis pacietur. In hac ergo vita nullus beatus esse querat nullus honores caducos adipisci contendat.>[138] Gaudium et exaltacio his qui Dominum Christum diligunt, meror et desolacio his qui illum contempnunt, cui gloria et imperium nunc et in perpetuum. Amen.

<Explicit libellus beati Anselmi Archiepiscopi Cantuarensis [de] xiiij partibus beatitudinum.>

NOTES

1 Corresponding to p.127 of the edition of the *Dicta Anselmi* in R. W. Southern and F. S. Schmitt, *Memorials of St. Anselm*, Auctores Britannici Medii Aevi (London: Oxford UP, 1969). Page-references in square brackets are to this edition. Bold type is used for rubrics.

2 Cf. I Cor. 2,9.

3 MS 'locis'.

4 MS 'lodo', superscript 'u' added.

5 MS 'reppititur'. The correction is made in the L.H. margin by the annotator, who has been identified by Dr Malcolm Parkes as of the fifteenth century.

6 Cf. Apoc. 2,11; 21,8.

7 MS 'pater'.

8 Cf. I Cor. 2,9.

9 The word 'illud' is written in the R.H. margin opposite this word, with a number of faded ink crosses.

10 Cf. Is. 64,4.

11 Here as elsewhere, 'qm', with superscript bar.

12 MS 'nequid', with superscript correction to 'nequit'.

13 In the L.H. margin is written 'non de ani' with a final 9-like contraction, possibly to be expanded as 'non de animabus'. The sense should surely be 'The promise of the invisible God having been reserved, before we come to where we may see Him "as He is" let us diligently find out what sort of thing is proper to our bodies and what to our souls.' LL should perhaps read 'invisibili[s]', but the error seems to have existed in ALDQ, as it is found also in AN, and perhaps in ME (see ME n.40).

14 Cf. I Io. 3,2.

15 Since the Beatific Vision itself is beyond our earthbound intellect, and will only be enjoyed when God wills that we see Him directly, the nearest we can at present come to understanding the nature of God is to study the nature of the glorified human body and soul. *De quatuordecim partibus beatitudinis* is here presented as a kind of mystical exercise – an intellectual approach not only to the nature of man, but also to God. This passage is thus central to the purpose and dignity of the text.

16 There is a marginal curlicue opposite these words.

17 Near 'habituros dubium non est, cum' is written in the margin 'hoie vt sentire seu hu ...' (with a nasal bar over the 'i' in 'hoie') – for 'homine'?; the last word is cropped).

18 MS 'illos'; over 'ac in illos' is a superscripted 'abcissimus'.

19 Above this, in a later (?) hand, 'ramuculo', over an erasure, with superscript bar over first 'u'. There is a number of such additions to LL (see the notes): this one is perhaps significant, since the added word also occurs in the AN text (f.234^{v}; cf. AN n.47).

20 Cf. Mt. 13,43.

21 Cf. Is. 30,26.

22 Cf. Mt. 13,43.

23 Cf. Phil. 3,20.

24 Cf. Mt. 17,2–4.

25 MS 'inquid'.

26 Cf. Mt. 17,2–4.

27 Cf. Mt. 28,3.

28 Cf. Ps. 26,4.

29 In the L.H. margin before this word, 'aciës'.

30 MS 'corpor'', with stroke through descender of 'p'.

31 In the R.H. margin is 'siue in tumulo'; we are grateful to Dr Malcolm Parkes for confirming a reading first suggested by Dr Alan Fletcher after a conference paper on the work of this annotator, whose slipping pen renders deciphering difficult.

32 There is a marginal curlicue opposite these words.

33 MS 'locum'; cf. *DA* p.131, and Dan. 14,35. The error probably arises because of the word 'locum' in the next sentence. AN makes the same mistake at this point.

34 There is a marginal curlicue opposite these words.

35 Cf. Lc. 11,21.

36 Cf. Ps. 144,19.

37 Cf. Ps. 22,1.

38 Cf. Io. 20,26. The quotation operates on several levels. At the historical level it refers to Christ's passing through closed doors. It refers also to his escape from the tomb at the Resurrection, and to his Harrowing of Hell, the gates of which were broken at his entry – both occasions being traditionally prefigured by Samson removing the gates of Gaza – cf. *Biblia Pauperum: A Facsimile Edition*, ed. Avril Henry (Aldershot: Scolar, 1987) 104, 106; *The Eton Roundels: Eton College MS 177 'Figurae Bibliorum'*, ed. Avril Henry (Aldershot: Scolar–Gower, 1990) f.6^{r} and p.128, respectively, where the images are shown and the earlier patristic sources cited.

39 MS 'sed nec ullus'; 'sed' expuncted.

40 Cf. Apoc. 21,4.

41 MS 'curet', with superscript nasal bar (?) over the 'e'.

42 Cf. Rom. 12,19.

43 MS 'predicta'; 'pre' expuncted and crossed out.

44 Glossed in the R.H. margin: 'electis illis seu beatis'.

45 The words 'sunt dilecta' are marked for inversion; read 'dilecta sunt'?

46 Cf. Ps. 83,2.

47 Cf. Ps. 83,11.

48 Cf. Ps. 35,9ff.

49 MS 'quis'.

50 There is a marginal curlicue opposite these words.

51 Superscript 'r' added by the same or a similar hand.

52 Superscript 'r' added by the same or a similar hand.

53 Cf. Ps. 147,12ff.

54 MS 'ille'; a superscript 'a' appears to have been added (in a later hand?).

55 MS 'pniam', with superscript nasal bar over 'n'.

56 MS 'simus'. The correction is supplied in the L.H. margin; under it, in front of 'Magdalenam', is 'sub velura nota'.

57 Cf. Mt. 26,69–75; Mc. 14,66–72; Lc. 22,55–62; Io. 18,25.

58 MS 'scimus', with superscript 'c' added by the same or a similar hand. There is a marginal curlicue opposite these words.

59 MS 'numquiam'. There is a caret mark at the end of the word in the text, and in the R.H. margin an illegible comment ('no omne non' for 'nota omne non'?).

60 There is a marginal curlicue opposite these words.

61 There is a marginal curlicue opposite these words.

62 MS 'impparet', with stroke through descender of first 'p'.

63 Cf. I Cor. 13,11.

64 MS 'mandandavit'; read 'mandavit'?

65 Cf. Act. 10,15.

66 'Perfecta' as catchword at the bottom of f.197^{v}.

67 MS 'cantorum' (?).

68 MS 'corpere'.

69 Cf. Ps. 138,17.

70 There is a marginal curlicue opposite these words.

71 Cf. Apoc. 21,4.

72 Cf. Iac. 1,17.

73 MS 'quartadicima'.

74 MS 'miam', with no abbreviation mark.

75 Cf. Mt. 25, 21.

76 *Sic* MS, unabbreviated. Since this appears to be an echo of a biblical text (Io. 16,24), in which the Vulgate has 'vestrum' not 'nostrum', there might be a case for correcting to 'vestrum' here. The three other references to the same quotation, all in the long Anselmian interpolation from the *Proslogion* (f.195^{r}, twice on 195^{v}) have an ambiguous abbreviation which could be either 'vestrum' or 'nostrum', and which has been expanded to conform to the Vulgate reading

(in the case of the quotation) and to 'nostrum' elsewhere. This also conforms to the text in *S. Anselmi Cantuariensis Archiepiscopi opera omnia* I:120–121.

77 For the provenance of this interpolation, see Introduction, p.10.

78 MS 'male'. Cf. AN n.257.

79 There is a marginal curlicue opposite these words.

80 Cf. I Cor. 2,9.

81 Superscript 'x'.

82 'Pulchritudo' is written in the R.H. margin opposite this word, of which the last syllable is on the next line.

83 Cf. Mt. 13,43.

84 'Velocitas' is written in the R.H. margin opposite this word, of which the last two syllables are on the next line.

85 'Fortitudo' is written in the R.H. margin opposite this word, of which the last two syllables are on the next line.

86 Cf. Lc. 20,36.

87 Cf. I Cor. 15,44. 'Libertas' is written in the R.H. margin opposite this word, of which all but the first syllable is on the next line.

88 'Diuturnitas' is written in the R.H. margin opposite this word.

89 Cf. Sap. 5,16.

90 Cf. Ps. 36,39.

91 'Sacietas' is written in the R.H. margin opposite this word.

92 Cf. Ps. 16,15.

93 'Ebrietas' is written in the R.H. margin opposite this word.

94 Cf. Ps. 35,9.

95 Melodia is additional to the seven properties of the soul named earlier (f.207v in ME) and treated in the main paragraphs of the text: see Introduction, p.3–4.

96 'Melodia' is written in the R.H. margin opposite this word, of which only the first syllable is on this line.

97 'Voluptas' is written in the R.H. margin opposite this word.

98 Cf. Ps. 35,9.

99 MS 'ondet', with superscript bar over 'n'. *S. Anselmi Cantuariensis Archiepiscopi opera omnia* I: 119 has 'ostendet' in all manuscripts.

100 'Sapiencia' is written in the R.H. margin opposite this word.

101 'Amicicia' is written in the R.H. margin opposite this word, of which only the first syllable is on this line.

102 'Concordia' is written in the L.H. margin opposite this word, of which only the first syllable is on this line.

103 'Potestas' is written in the L.H. margin opposite this word, of which the first syllable is on the preceding line.

104 'Honor divitie' is written in the L.H. margin opposite this word.

105 Cf. Mt. 5,9.

106 'Securitas' is written in the L.H. margin opposite this word, of which the first syllable is on the preceding line.

107 Cf. Rom. 8,17.

108 The tironian abbreviation for 'et' is a superscript (later?) addition, following a caret after 'securitas'.

109 Superscript 'r', added by a (probably) later hand. A now illegible word, perhaps originally intended as an abbreviated form of *et cetera*, has been erased in the L.H. margin.

110 The word has a mark like a division sign over it; the sign is repeated in the R.H. margin, where it is followed by 'scilicet caro et anima'.

111 'Gaudium' is written in the L.H. margin opposite this word, of which the first three syllables are on the preceding line.

112 MS 'erumpnias', opposite which is written in the margin, against a cross, 'erupnas', with a nasal bar over the 'u'.

113 Cf. Io. 16,24.

114 Cf. Mt. 25, 21.

115 Cf. I Cor. 2,9.

116 Cf. I Cor. 2,9.

117 This rubric is apparently not in the manuscripts edited in *S. Anselmi Cantuariensis opera omnia* I:121.

118 'Pulchri' and 'Fedi' are written in the R.H. margin opposite this paragraph.

119 MS 'transilit'.

120 'Veloces' and 'Pigri' are written in the R.H. margin opposite this paragraph.

121 'Fortes' and 'Debiles' are written in the L.H. margin opposite this paragraph.

122 'Liberi' and 'Clausi' are written in the R.H. margin opposite this paragraph.

123 'Sani' and 'Languidi' are written in the L.H. margin opposite this paragraph.

124 'Voluptas' and 'Anxietas' are written in the L.H. margin opposite this paragraph.

125 'Diuturnitas' and 'Brevitas' are written in the L.H. margin opposite this paragraph.

126 'Sapientes' and 'Incipientes' are written in the L.H. margin opposite this paragraph.

127 MS 'predici' (?).

128 MS 'q^{o}', with superscript 'o'.

129 There is a marginal curlicue opposite these words.

130 'Amici' and 'Inimici' are written in the R.H. margin opposite this paragraph.

131 'Concordes' and 'Discordes' are written in the R.H. margin opposite this paragraph.

132 ‘Honorati’ and ‘Inhonorati’ are written in the R.H. margin opposite this paragraph.

13 MS ‘qua’, with superscript nasal bar.

134 MS ‘honorab^{t}’, with superscript ‘t’ (at end of line in MS).

135 ‘Potentes’ and ‘Impotentes’ are written in the L.H. margin opposite this paragraph.

136 There is a marginal curlicue opposite these words.

137 ‘Securi’ and ‘Invidi’ are written in the L.H. margin opposite this paragraph.

138 ‘Gaudentes’ and ‘Tristes’ are written in the L.H. margin opposite this paragraph.

BIBLIOGRAPHY

Allen, Hope Emily. *Writings Ascribed to Richard Rolle, Hermit of Hampole.* MLA Monograph ser., 3. New York: Oxford UP, 1927.

Anglo-Norman Dictionary. Ed. W. Rothwell *et al.* 7 fascs. London: MHRA, 1977–1992.

Der anglonormannische Boeve de Haumtone. Ed. A. Stimming. Bibliotheca Normannica, 7. Halle: M. Niemeyer, 1899.

The Anglo-Norman Lyric: An Anthology. Ed. David L. Jeffrey and Brian J. Levy. Toronto: Pontifical Institute of Mediaeval Studies, 1990.

Anonimalle Chronicle 1333–81. Ed. V. H. Galbraith. Publications of the U of Manchester, History Series, 45. Manchester: Manchester UP, 1927.

Anselm of Canterbury. Trans. J. Hopkins and H. Richardson. 4 vols. Toronto: Mellen Press, 1974–1976.

Anselm, St. *Anselm's Proslogion: With a Reply on Behalf of the Fool by Gaunilo, and the Author's Reply to Gaunilo.* Trans. M. J. Charlesworth. Oxford: Clarendon Press, 1965.

Baldwin, Mary. 'Some Difficult Words in the *Ancrene Riwle*'. *Mediaeval Studies* 38 (1976): 268–290.

Benedikz, B. S. *Lichfield Cathedral Library: A Catalogue of the Cathedral Library Manuscripts.* 3rd ed. Birmingham: Birmingham U Library, 1986.

Bestul, T. H. 'St Augustine and the *Orationes sive Meditationes* of St. Anselm'. *Anselm Studies* 2 (1988): 597–600.

'An Bispel'. *Old English Homilies and Homiletic Treatises (Sawles Warde, and Þe Wohunge of Ure Lauerd: Ureisuns of Ur Louerd and of Ure Lefdi, &c). of the Thirteenth and Fourteenth Centuries.* 1st Series, Parts 1–2. EETS os 29 and 34. London: Oxford UP for EETS, 1867–1868, repr. New York: Greenwood, 1969. 230–241.

Blake, N. F. 'Middle English Prose and its Audience'. *Anglia* 90 (1972): 437–455.

—— 'Varieties of Middle English Prose'. *Chaucer and Middle English Studies.* Ed. Beryl Rowland. London: Allen & Unwin, 1974. 348–356.

The Book of Showings to the Anchoress Julian of Norwich. Ed. Edmund Colledge and James Walsh. 2 parts. Studies and Texts, 35. Part II *The Long Text.* Toronto: Pontifical Institute of Mediaeval Studies, 1978.

Book Production and Publishing in Britain 1375–1475. Ed. Jeremy Griffiths and Derek Pearsall. Cambridge Studies in Publishing and Printing History. Cambridge: Cambridge UP, 1989.

Bourke, Vernon J. 'A Millennium of Christian Platonism: Augustine, Anselm and Ficino'. *Anselm Studies* 2 (1988): 527–557.

Brown, Carleton, and Rossell Hope Robbins. *Index of Middle English Verse.* New York: Columbia UP for the Index Society, 1943.

Brucker, Charles, 'La valeur du témoignage linguistique des traductions médiévales. Les constructions infinitives en moyen français'. *Linguistique et philologie (applications aux textes médiévaux). Actes du colloque des 29 et 30 avril 1977.* Ed. Danielle Buschinger. Amiens: U d'Amiens, Centre d'études médiévales, 1977. 325–344.

Bynum, C. W. *Jesus as Mother: Studies in the Spirituality of the High Middle Ages.* Publications of the Center for Medieval and Renaissance Studies UCLA, 16. Berkeley: U of California Press, 1982, repr. 1984.

A Catalogue of the Manuscripts Preserved in the U of Cambridge. 5 vols. Cambridge: Cambridge UP, 1856–1867, repr. Munich: Krause-Thomson, and Hildesheim: Georg Olms, 1980. Vol. 2 (1857).

A Catalogue of the Printed Books and Manuscripts in the Library of the Cathedral Church of Lichfield. London: H. Sotheran, 1888.

Colledge, Edmund. *The Medieval Mystics of England.* London: John Murray, 1962.

A Concordance to the Works of Saint Anselm. Ed. G. R. Evans. Millwood, NY: Kraus, 1984.

Constable, Giles. 'The Popularity of Twelfth-Century Spiritual Writers in the Late Middle Ages'. *Renaissance Studies in Honor of Hans Baron*, ed. A. Molho and J. A. Tedeschi. Florence: 1971. 3–28.

—— *Twelfth-Century Spirituality and the Late Middle Ages.* Medieval and Renaissance Studies, 5 (Chapel Hill, NC, 1971), repr. with the original pagination in his *Religious Life and Thought (11th–12th Centuries).* London: Variorum Reprint, 1979.

Le Cur Deus homo d'Anselme de Cantorbéry et le De arrha animae d'Hugues de Saint Victor traduits pour Philippe le Bon. Ed. R. Bultot and G. Hasenohr. Publications de l'Institut d'Etudes Médiévales, 2.6. Louvain-la-Neuve: U de Louvain-la-Neuve, 1984.

Cursor Mundi (The Cursur o the World): A Northumbrian Poem of the 14th Century in Four Versions, Two of Them Midland. Ed. Richard Morris. 7 parts. EETS os 57, 59, 62, 66, 68, 99, 101. London: Trübner for EETS, 1874–1893.

Doyle, A. I. 'A Survey of the Origins and Circulation of Theological Writings in England in the Fourteenth and Fifteenth Centuries'. Diss. U of Cambridge 1954.

Eadmer [Vita sancti Anselmi. English and Latin]: The life of St Anselm, Archbishop of Canterbury. Oxford Medieval Texts. Ed. R. W. Southern. London: Nelson, 1962; Oxford: Clarendon Press, 1972. [Parallel Latin text and English translation.]

Ellis, Roger. 'The Choices of the Translator in the Late Middle English Period'. *The Medieval Mystical Traditional in England: Papers Read at Dartington Hall, July 1982.* Ed. Marion Glasscoe. Exeter: Exeter UP, 1982. 18–46.

The Eton Roundels: Eton College MS 177 Figurae Bibliorum: *A Colour Facsimile with Transcription, Translation and Commentary*. Ed. Avril Henry. Aldershot: Scolar–Gower, 1990.

Evans, G. R. 'Sententia ad aedificationem: The *Dicta* of St Anselm and St Bernard'. *Revue Bénédictine* 92 (1982): 159–71.

Fouke le Fitz Waryn. Ed. E. J. Hathaway, P. T. Ricketts, C. A. Robson and A. D. Wilshere. ANTS, 26–28. Oxford: Anglo-Norman Text Society, 1975.

Gilbert, P. *Le Proslogion de S. Anselm: Silence de Dieu et joie de l'homme*. Analecta Gregoriana, 257, Ser. Facultatis Philosophiae, A.14. Rome: Editrice Pontificia Universitate Gregoriana, 1990.

Gillespie, Vincent. 'Vernacular Books of Religion'. *Book Production and Publishing in Britain 1375–1475*. Ed. Jeremy Griffiths and Derek Pearsall. Cambridge Studies in Publishing and Printing History. Cambridge: Cambridge UP, 1989. 317–344.

Glorieux, Palemon. *Pour revaloriser Migne: Tables rectificatives*. Mélanges de science réligieuse, 9me année. Lille: Facultés Catholiques, 1952.

Godefroy, F. *Dictionnaire de l'ancienne langue française*, 10 vols. Paris: F. Vieweg, 1880–1902. [Gdf]

The Golden Legend or Lives of the Saints as Englished by William Caxton. 7 vols. Temple Classics. London: Dent, 1900–1922.

Goldschmidt, E. Ph. *Medieval Texts and their First Appearance in Print*. Supplement to Bibliographical Society Transactions, 16. London: Oxford UP for the Bibliographical Society, 1943.

Grundriss der romanischen Literaturen des Mittelalters. Ed. E. Köhler and J. Frappier. Heidelberg: C. Winter, 1968– . [*GRLMA*]

Hauréau, B. *Initia operum scriptorum latinorum* [photographic reproduction of handwritten list in MS Paris, Bibliothèque Nationale, nouvelles acquisitions françaises 2400].

Heinrich Seuses Horologium Sapientiae. Erste kritische Ausgabe unter Benützung der Vorarbeiten von Dominikus Planzer OP. Ed. Pius Künzle. Spicilegium Friburgense, 23. Freiburg: Universitätsverlag, 1977.

Hodgson, Phyllis. '"A Ladder of Foure Ronges by the Whiche Men Mowe Wele Clyme to Heven": A Study of the Prose Style of a Middle English Translation'. *MLR* 44 (1949): 465–475.

Incipits of Latin Works on the Virtues and Vices, 1100–1500 A.D. Ed. Morton W. Bloomfield, Bertrand-Georges Guyot, Donald R. Howard and Thyra B. Kabealo. Cambridge, Mass.: Medieval Academy of America, 1979.

Jean de Vignay, Les Merveilles de la Terre d'Outremer. Traduction du XIVe siècle du récit de voyage d'Odoric de Pordenone. Ed. D. A. Trotter. Exeter: U of Exeter, 1990.

Jolliffe, P. *A Check-List of Middle English Prose Writings of Spiritual Guidance*.

Subsidia Mediaevalia, 2. Toronto: Pontifical Institute of Mediaeval Studies, 1974.

—— 'Middle English Translations of *De exterioris et interioris hominis compositione*'. *Mediaeval Studies* 36 (1974): 259–277.

Ker, N. *Mediaeval Manuscripts in British Libraries*. Vol. 3. Oxford: Clarendon Press, 1983.

Knowles, David. *The English Mystical Tradition*. London: Burns & Oates, 1961.

Lagorio, V., and R. Bradley. *The Fourteenth-Century English Mystics: A Comprehensive Annotated Bibliography*. New York: Garland, 1981.

Latham, R. E., *et al. Dictionary of Medieval Latin from British Sources*. London: Oxford UP for the British Academy, 1975– . [*DMLBS*]

—— *Revised Medieval Latin Word-List from British and Irish Sources*. London: Oxford UP for the British Academy, 1965. [*RMLWL*]

Lee, Arthur R. 'Anselm and Thomas of Buckingham: An Examination of the *Quaestiones super Sententias*'. *Anselm Studies* 1 (1983): 237–249.

Lewis, R. E., and A. McIntosh. *A Descriptive Guide to the Manuscripts of the Prick of Conscience*. Medium Ævum Monographs, n.s. 12. Oxford: Society for the Study of Mediæval Languages and Literature, 1982.

Le Livre de Sibile. Ed. Hugh Shields. ANTS, 37. London: Anglo-Norman Text Society, 1979.

Lovatt, Roger. 'Henry Suso and the Medieval Mystical Tradition in England'. *The Medieval Mystical Tradition in England: Papers Read at Dartington Hall, July 1982*. Ed. Marion Glasscoe. Exeter: Exeter UP, 1982. 47–62.

A Manual of the Writings in Middle English 1050–1400. Ed. John Edwin Wells. (with 9 supplements). New Haven, Conn.: Yale UP, 1916–1951. [*Manual*(1)]

A Manual of the Writings in Middle English 1050–1500. Gen. ed. A. E. Hartung. New Haven, Conn.: Connecticut Academy of Arts and Sciences, 1986–. 9 vols. to date. [*Manual*(2)].

Medieval Translators and Their Craft. Ed. Jeanette Beer. Studies in Medieval Culture, 25. Kalamazoo: Western Michigan U, 1989.

The Medieval Translator: The Theory and Practice of Translation in the Middle Ages. Ed. Roger Ellis *et al.*, Cambridge: Cambridge UP, 1989.

The Medieval Translator II. Ed. Roger Ellis. Westfield Publications in Medieval Studies, 5. London: Centre for Medieval Studies, Queen Mary and Westfield College, 1991.

Memorials of St Anselm. Ed. R. W. Southern and F. S. Schmitt. Auctores Britannici Medii Aevi, 1. London: Oxford UP, 1969.

Middle English Prose: A Critical Guide to Major Authors and Genres. Ed. A. S. G. Edwards. New Brunswick, NJ: Rutgers UP, 1984.

The Middle English Weye of Paradys *& the Middle French* Voie de Paradis*: A Parallel-text Edition*. Ed. F. N. M. Diekstra. Leiden: E. J. Brill, 1991.

Mirk's Festial: A Collection of Homilies by Johannes Mirkus (John Mirk). Ed. Theodore Erbe. EETS ES 96. London: Oxford UP for EETS, 1905.

Mirour de Seinte Eglyse. Ed. A. D. Wilshere. ANTS, 40. Oxford: Anglo-Norman Text Society, 1982.

Morgan, Margery M. '*A Talking of the Love of God* and the Continuity of Stylistic Tradition in Middle English Prose Meditations'. *RES*, n.s. 3 (1952): 97–116.

Mynors, R. A. B., and R. M. Thomson. *Catalogue of the Manuscripts in Hereford Cathedral Library.* Woodbridge: Boydell & Brewer, 1993.

The Pilgrimage of the Lyfe of the Manhode. 2 vols. Ed. Avril Henry. EETS OS 288, 292. London: Oxford UP for EETS, 1985, 1988.

Pope, Mildred K. *From Latin to Modern French, with Especial Consideration of Anglo-Norman.* Manchester: Manchester UP, 1934.

The Prayers and Meditations of Anselm. Trans. Benedicta Ward. Harmondsworth: Penguin, 1973.

The Pricke of Conscience (Stimulus Conscientiae): A Northumbrian Poem by Richard Rolle de Hampole. Ed. R. Morris. Berlin: Philological Society, 1863.

Les Proverbes de Salemon. Ed. C. Claire Isoz. ANTS, 44–45. London: Anglo-Norman Text Society, 1988.

Pseudo-Anselm. '*Meditatio* 21'. *PL* CLVIII 817–820.

—— '*Miraculum de conceptione Beatae Mariae*'. *PL* CLIX 323.

The Register of Walter de Stapeldon, Bishop of Exeter (A.D. 1307–1326). Ed. F. C. Hingeston-Randolph. London, 1892.

Richardson, H. G. 'Letters of the Oxford Dictatores'. *Oxford History Society*, n.s. 5 (1942): 360–416.

Riehle, Wolfgang. *The Middle English Mystics.* Trans. Bernard Standring. London: Routledge & Kegan Paul, 1981. First published 1977 as *Studien zur englischen Mystik des Mittelalters unter besonderer Berücksichtigung ihrer Metaphorik.*

Robbins, Rossell Hope, and John L. Cutler. *Supplement to the Index of Middle English Verse.* Lexington: U of Kentucky Press, 1965.

S. Anselmi Cantuarensis Archiepiscopi opera omnia. Ed. F. S. Schmitt. 6 vols. Seckau: [n.p.], 1938; Edinburgh: Nelson, 1946–1961.

Sawles Warde. The Katherine Group: Edited from MS Bodley 34. Ed. S. T. R. O. d'Ardenne. Bibliothèque de la Faculté de Philosophie et Lettres, 215. Paris: Société d'Edition 'Les Belles Lettres', 1977. 165–85.

Schleich, G. 'Zur Textgestaltung der mittelenglischen Bearbeitung von Susos Orologium Sapientiae'. *Archiv für das Studium der neueren Sprachen und Literaturen*, Neue Folge 52 (1927): 36–50, 178–192.

Scott, Kathleen. 'Design, Decoration and Illustration'. *Book Production and Publishing in Britain 1375–1475.* Ed. Jeremy Griffiths and Derek Pearsall. Cambridge Studies in Publishing and Printing History. Cambridge: Cambridge UP, 1989. 31–64.

Seymour Papers 1532–1686. Ed. Marjorie Blatcher. Historical Manuscripts Commission. Vol. 4 of Calendar of the Manuscripts of the Marquis of Bath [here called *Report of the Manuscripts of the Most Honourable the Marquess of Bath, Preserved at Longleat*]. London: HMSO, 1968. 5 vols. 1904–1980.

The South English Legendary. Ed. Charlotte D'Evelyn and Anna J. Mill. 3 vols. EETS os 235, 236, 244. London: Oxford UP for EETS, 1956–1959.

Southern, R. W. *Saint Anselm and His Biographer: A Study of Monastic Life and Thought 1059–c.1130*. Cambridge: Cambridge UP, 1963.

Speculum Sacerdotale, Edited from British Museum Add. MS 36791. Ed. Edward H. Weatherley. EETS os 200. London: Oxford UP for EETS, 1936.

A Talkyng of the Loue of God: Edited from MS Vernon (Bodleian. 3938) and Collated with MS Simeon (Brit. Mus. Add. 22283). Ed. M. Salvine Westra. The Hague: M. Nijhoff, 1950.

Tobler, A., and E. Lommatzsch, *Altfranzösisches Wörterbuch*. 10 vols. Berlin: Weidmann, 1925–1936; Wiesbaden: Steiner, 1954– . [TL]

The Vernon Manuscript: A Facsimile of Bodleian Library, Oxford, MS Eng.Poet.a.1. Intro. A. I. Doyle. Cambridge: D. S. Brewer, 1987.

La Vie de Seint Auban: An Anglo-Norman Poem of the Thirteenth Century. Ed. A. R. Harden. ANTS, 19. Oxford: Anglo-Norman Text Society, 1968.

Ward, Benedicta. 'Faith Seeking Understanding: Anselm of Canterbury and Julian of Norwich'. *Julian of Norwich*. Oxford: SLG Press 1973. 26–38.

—— 'Inward Feeling and Deep Thinking: The Prayers and Meditations of St Anselm Revisited'. *Anselm Studies* 1 (1983): 177–183.

Wartburg, W. von. *Französisches etymologisches Wörterbuch*, 25 vols. Bonn: Schroeder *et al.*, 1922– . [*FEW*]

Waters, Stacy. '*The Pricke of Conscience*: The Southern Recension, Book V'. Diss. U of Edinburgh, 1976.

—— 'A History of *Pricke of Conscience* Studies'. *Studia Neophilologica* 55 (1983): 147–151.

Westlake, Elizabeth. 'Learn to Live and Learn to Die: Heinrich Suso's *Scire mori* in Fifteenth-Century England', Diss. U of Birmingham, UK, 1993.

Wichgraf, W. 'Susos Horologium Sapientiae in England nach Handschriften des 15. Jahrhunderts (Fortsetzung)'. *Anglia*, Neue Folge 41 (1929): 269–287.

Williams, T. W. *Somerset Medieval Libraries*. Bristol: Somerset Archaeological and Natural History Society, 1897.

—— 'Gloucestershire Medieval Libraries.' *Transactions of the Bristol and Gloucester Archaeological Society* 32–33 (1908–1909): 78–195.

Wilmart, A. *Auteurs spirituels et textes dévots du moyen âge: Études d' histoire littéraire*. Paris: Bloud & Gay, 1932.

—— *Bibliothecae Vaticanae Codices Reginenses Latini*. 3 vols. Rome: Vatican, 1945. Vol. 2.

—— Introduction. *Méditations et prières de saint Anselme.* By A. Castel. Maredsous: Abbaye de Maredsous, 1923.

'Þe Wohunge of Ure Lauerd' edited from British Museum MS Cotton Titus D. XVIII together with 'On Ureisun of Ure Louerde,' 'On Wel Swuðe God Ureisun of God Almihti,' 'On Lofsong of Ure Louerde,' 'On Lofsong of Ure Lefdi,' 'Þe Oreisun of Seinte Marie' from the Manuscripts in which they occur. Ed. W. Meredith Thompson. EETS os 241. London: Oxford UP for EETS, 1958.

Yorkshire Writers: Richard Rolle of Hampole and his Followers. Ed. Carl Horstmann. 2 vols. London, 1895–1896. Vol. 2: 443–445.

www.ingramcontent.com/pod-product-compliance
Ingram Content Group UK Ltd.
Pitfield, Milton Keynes, MK11 3LW, UK
UKHW042008190726
13854UKWH00005B/2208

9 780907 570103